OFFICER'S
MANUAL
of
PERSONAL
FINANCE
and
INSURANCE

*Principles
and Techniques
for the
Armed Forces
Officer*

*a complete revision of
Managing Insurance and Personal Finance*

OFFICER'S
MANUAL
of
PERSONAL
FINANCE
and
INSURANCE

ASSOCIATES
IN THE
SOCIAL SCIENCES,
U.S. MILITARY ACADEMY,
WEST POINT

STACKPOLE BOOKS

OFFICER'S MANUAL OF PERSONAL FINANCE AND INSURANCE

Copyright © 1971 by
THE STACKPOLE COMPANY
Published by
STACKPOLE BOOKS
Cameron and Kelker Streets
Harrisburg, Pa.   17105

ISBN 0-8117-1154-4
Library of Congress Catalog Card Number 79-140746
Printed in U.S.A.

O money, money, money, I am not necessarily
one of those who think thee holy,
But I often stop to wonder how
thou canst go out so fast
when thou comest in so slowly.

–Ogden Nash

CONTENTS

4. TAXES

5. CONSUMER CREDIT

PART TWO: GOVERNMENT SURVIVOR AND RETIRED BENEFITS

PART THREE: LIFE INSURANCE

PART FOUR: APPENDICES

APPENDICES

PREFACE

ALL OFFICERS are managers of resources. The outstanding officer is the one who gets the greatest from the men and material assigned to him. A good military manager should, in the first instance, be a good manager of his own affairs. The purpose of this text is to help the Armed Forces officer assess and manage the financial problems he will face during his career. It is designed to assist him in sharpening his abilities in general financial management as well as in his role as family financial manager.

The technique advocated in this text is the development of a financial plan based on sound economic principles. In essence, we focus on helping the officer develop a balanced financial plan that makes the last dollar spent on either current consumption or savings equally satisfying. A balanced plan will be achieved when the planner no longer thinks he can improve his plan by shifting a dollar from savings to current consumption or vice versa. In effect, with such a balance, he has determined that his future needs are provided for satisfactorily without excessively cutting down on his current standard of living. He is also satisfied that he is achieving the highest current standard of living without subjecting himself or his family to the risk of financial disaster.

The balanced position can, we maintain, be accomplished within an officer's income. There is an old saying that you will never get rich on officer's pay. But there is no doubt that an above-average standard of living can be obtained on an officer's income if it is utilized with reasonable efficiency.

The financial matters with which this book is concerned are those involved in (1) allocation of resources to the satisfaction of current needs, (2) planning for living while in retirement from active duty, (3) planning for the contingency of dying while on active duty, and (4) planning for the contingency of dying while retired from active duty.

Major changes in emphasis have been incorporated in this text which differentiate it from the previous publication. Areas of increasing concern to the officer have been added or expanded. Some of these areas involve the recent "Truth In Lending Law", rising automobile costs, and the changed tax and state bonus situation resulting from the Southeast Asia conflict. Major sections have also been added to the chapters concerning house rental, sources of credit, and media for savings and investment.

No text, of course, can hope to solve each individual's specific financial problems. This text acquaints the officer with the general information and techniques useful in handling financial management problems successfully. For the officer who requires more sophisticated sources of information, bibliographies have been included in the text. Before making any decisions requiring up-to-date information, the officer should consult some of the original sources referred to throughout the text.

This book derives from a long series of publications on the subject matter by Associates in the Social Sciences. This group includes BG Herman Beukema, G.A. Lincoln (BG, USA, Ret.), LTG William S. Stone, USAF, Robert F. McDermott (BG, USAF, Ret.), Robert E. Carignan (LTC, AUS, Ret.) and MAJ Robert L. Grete, USAF. This particular publication is primarily the product of the efforts of MAJ Norbert W. Frische, USAF, Assistant Professor of Insurance and Personal Finance who has sole responsibility for the opinions and judgments expressed herein. In such a detailed, changing, and complex subject there may be some errors of fact. The current author claims responsibility for these and asks forgiveness. Significant contributions were made by many other current Associates in the Social Sciences, especially LTC Lee D. Olvey, Professor of Social Sciences, as well as by individuals in various governmental and private agencies, such as the Social Security Administration, the Veterans Administration, the Institute of Life Insurance, the Insurance Information Institute, the Finance and Accounting Office, USMA, and other experts to whom we owe a debt of gratitude.

The text is sold to the Service Academies at a discount. Any royalties that may accrue are assigned to a private, non-profit foundation for furthering military educational activities.

AMOS A. JORDAN, JR.
Professor of Social Sciences
United States Military Academy

West Point, New York

Part **ONE**

MANAGING
PERSONAL FINANCE

Which I have earned with
the sweat of my brows.
—Cervantes

CHAPTER 1

THE OFFICER'S INCOME

THE PROBLEMS of financial management are economic in nature because they involve allocation of limited resources to the satisfaction of competing human wants. One scarce resource that the Armed Forces officer has to allocate is his income. Normally, textbooks on personal finance consider the problem of maximizing income, since the larger the income, the more adequately human wants can be satisfied. Because officers must devote their full attention to military duties, only a few find themselves in a position to add income from employment outside of the Service. Thus the income of the typical officer's family will be composed of his Service pay and allowances, income derived from savings and investments, and the earnings of other members of the family. Outside income, as such, may be limited, yet we believe it is possible for the Armed Forces officer to live as well as his civilian contemporaries.

The purpose of this chapter is to introduce the officer to his pay and allowances. We will consider each of these in detail; but, first, let us compare the military income of Armed Forces officers with that of the civilian population.

COMPARISON WITH CIVILIAN PAY

While the defense of our country demands an officer force motivated by more than monetary remuneration it is interesting to compare the pay and allowances of the Armed Forces officer with the income earned in other occupations. Chart 1-1 projects the annual pay of Armed Forces officers based upon a 30-year career with promotions at reasonable progression intervals. The chart data is taken from the pay and allowance table in effect on 1 December 1970. The basic data on which the chart is based can be found in the Appendix Tables C-2, C-4 and C-5. However, the monthly subsistence allowance of $47.88 for all officers is explained later in this chapter.

Now we shall compare the income data on the Armed Forces officer's annual pay chart with that earned in civilian occupations. An escalation in pay has occurred in some civilian occupations since the latest available data was tabulated. However, in this comparison we will ignore the time difference. Table 1-1 shows the median annual money income of persons who earned income in various occupations. These figures compared with those in Chart 1-1 enable us to draw some meaningful comparisons. As an example, we can see that the pay of an officer will exceed that of 50% of those working (employed civilians) when he is an 0-1 with less than two years service drawing basic pay plus subsistence and quarters allowances. Also, the figures in Table 1-1 allow us to assess when the pay of an officer will exceed the median of those working in a particular occupation. For example, if the median income of professional and technical workers is $9370 per year, then Chart 1-1 shows that the base pay plus subsistence allowance received by an 0-3 will exceed that of such workers when the 0-3 completes 4 years service. If quarters allowance is included the $9370 income is exceeded by an 0-2 with 3 years service. Even the highest median occupational income of $14,135 earned by self-employed professional and technical workers is exceeded by the basic pay, subsistence and quarters allowance of an 0-4 with 12 years service. If the officer draws hazardous duty pay, then he exceeds the professional median as an 0-3 with 6 years service. These examples help illustrate that the money earnings of Armed Forces officers soon exceeds that earned by most people in the various occupations.

A second comparative analysis can be made using Table 1-2. This table assesses the percentage of families in various income levels and shows that only 12% of all households earn $15,000 or over. Yet an officer reaches this category as an 0-4 with 14 years service considering basic pay plus subsistence and quarters allowances. As a rated or flying officer he reaches the top 12% or $15,000 classification as an 0-4 with 10 years service. As Table 1-2 shows, even a newly commissioned officer earns more income than approximately 40% of the families in the U.S. if only his base pay plus subsistence and quarters allowances are included. By the time he is

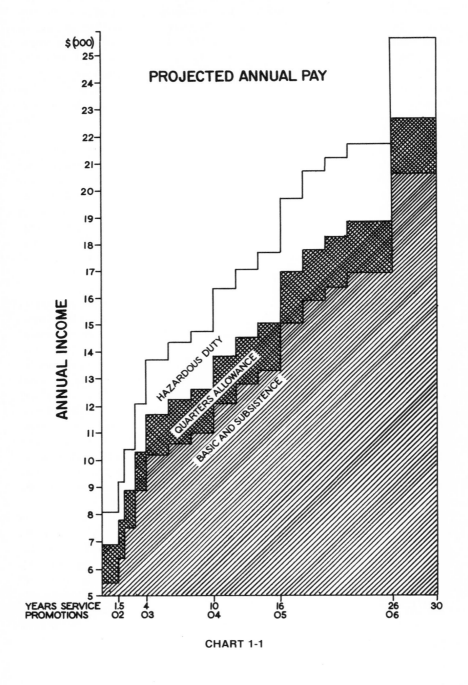

CHART 1-1

Median Annual Money Income of Persons with Income
1967

OCCUPATION	MALE	FEMALE
Professional, technical and kindred workers	$ 9,370	5,210
Self-employed	14,135	2,068
Salaried	9,150	5,337
Farmers and Farm Managers	3,439	1,330
Farm Laborers and Foremen	1,696	586
Managers, Officials, Proprietors, except farm	9,267	4,474
Self-employed	7,239	2,796
Salaried	9,922	5,055
Clerical workers	6,380	3,844
Salesworkers	6,814	2,116
Craftsmen, foremen and kindred workers	7,224	3,826
Operatives and kindred workers	5,858	3,218
Service Workers, except private household	4,532	2,076
Laborers, except farm and mine	3,979	2,628
Employed civilians*	6,610	3,157

*Includes persons in other occupations, not shown separately.

Source: Statistical Abstract of the United States, 1969, p. 327.

TABLE 1-1

PERCENT DISTRIBUTION OF FAMILIES IN HOUSEHOLDS
BY MONEY INCOME LEVEL: 1967

Income Class	% in Class	% in this Class and Lower Ones
$15,000 and over	12.0	100.0
10,000 to 14,999	22.3	88.0
7,000 to 9,999	24.3	65.7
5,000 to 6,999	16.1	41.4
3,000 to 4,999	12.8	25.3
Under $3,000	12.5	12.5

Source: Statistical Abstract of the United States, 1969, p. 323.

TABLE 1-2

ESTIMATED AVERAGE LIFETIME EARNINGS
OF PROFESSIONAL MEN

| | LIFETIME EARNINGS FROM AGE 18 TO 64 | | |
	Average	4 Years High School	4 or more years-college
Doctors	$717,000	--	$721,000
Dentists	589,000	--	594,000
Lawyers	621,000	--	642,000
Engineers:			
Aeronautical	395,000	$378,000	418,000
Electrical	372,000	327,000	406,000
Mechanical	360,000	339,000	399,000
Civil	335,000	285,000	380,000
Natural Scientists:			
Geologists	446,000	--	470,000
Physicists	415,000	--	431,000
Chemists	327,000	274,000	351,000
Biologists	310,000	--	322,000
Social Scientists:			
Economists	413,000	--	432,000
Psychologists	335,000	--	345,000
Statisticians	335,000	--	387,000
Teachers:			
Elementary School	232,000	--	241,000
High School	261,000	--	265,000
College	324,000	--	328,000
Accountants	313,000	286,000	362,000
Clergymen	175,000	156,000	184,000

Source: Occupational Outlook Handbook (1966-67 edition), p. 20.

TABLE 1-3

an 0-3 with 4 years service his basic pay plus subsistence and quarters allowance exceed the earnings of 65.7% of the families in the U.S. Numerous other comparisons show that the pay of the Armed Forces officer is favorable to that earned by those in other occupations.

A third comparison can be made using Table 1-3, which shows the average estimated lifetime earnings of various professional men, according to their educational level. The estimates include the total 46-year earnings of various professional men from age 18 to 64. Obviously, it is very difficult to calculate the total 46-year earnings of the average officer. Few officers serve for over 30 years, and many retire after 20 years of service. Many officers supplement their incomes with civilian employment after military retirement. Thus the military pay of officers is normally only a portion of the money they earn between ages 18 and 64.

Nevertheless, useful comparisons can be made. Chart 1-1 indicates that an officer serving 30 years might earn in basic pay plus subsistence and quarters allowance a total income of over $465,600; if he is rated, the total income would exceed $540,400. Thus, especially since these latter numbers are based on 30-year instead of 46-year earnings, we again see that an officer can expect an income that compares favorably with the averages earned in other professions. If we add to these earnings the retirement income of an officer the figures compare even more favorably.

Let us assume that the officer retires as a Colonel with 30 years service. His retirement income would then be 75% of the basic pay of a Colonel with 30 years service. From Appendix Table C-2 we see that the basic pay of an 0-6 with over 26 years service is $1671.30 per month or $20,055.60 per year. For 30 years service he would draw 75% of this amount or $15,041.70 as an annual retirement income. If we assume that he is age 53 at retirement and lives to age 64 then he would collect during these 11 retirement years prior an additional income of $165,458.70 during the 46 year period compared in Table 1-3. In addition to this income he may be able to supplement his income from civilian employment during his retirement years. And, as later chapters will point out, the officer who establishes a systematic investment program early in his career can accumulate large amounts of capital which will enable him to take advantage of exceptionally broad economic opportunities. While the officer does not have the opportunity to become very wealthy on his Service pay alone, he certainly does well compared to all other income earners in the country he is dedicated to defend.

It must be admitted that the above comparisons should be qualified. First, there are aspects of a military career that are not commonly found in alternative civilian occupations. The military officer is subject to duty 24 hours a day, 7 days a week, under the Uniform Code of Military Justice. He can be ordered into combat and lacks the option of quitting before his commitment is completed. He can be moved frequently and is asked to endure family separations of various lengths. These moves and separations may entail additional living expenses. Another expense may be his membership dues in the officer's open mess.

Secondly, however, there are financial benefits which are not explicit in an officer's gross income. For example, he is entitled to medical and dental care at Government expense, and much of the medical care for his dependents is also cost-free. If he serves long enough to retire from active duty or becomes disabled, he is entitled to retirement or disability pay. His family is also entitled to substantial survivor benefits should he die while on active duty. Later chapters discuss these "fringe benefits." In this chapter, only direct monetary compensation is considered. And finally, he enjoys certain tax advantages and normally can reduce the cost of many of his family's expenditures by purchasing in a Commissary or Exchange Store.

One might note that one of the continuing problems facing groups studying the structure of military pay is that of determining a method of computing the dollar value of such fringe benefits. Obviously, their precise value will vary from individual to individual. The importance of their value, however, will become apparent when we see that the military officer can provide for the economic well-being of his family without as much out-of-pocket expense as most of his civilian counterparts.

THE OFFICER'S PAY AND ALLOWANCES

The 1965 Pay Act (Public Law 89-132) required the President to direct an annual review of military pay and allowances to determine their adequacy. In addition, the President was required to direct a complete review of the principles and concepts of military compensation at least every four years, beginning 1 January 1967. In accordance with such direction, a Military Compensation Policy Board was convened in December 1966 to conduct the first Quadrennial Review of Military Compensation. This interservice Task Force study, headed by Rear Admiral L.E. Hubbell, recommended sweeping changes in the military compensation system. While few of its recommendations have resulted in legislation as of the time of this writing, the study is expected to influence future planning and legislative proposals, especially if the movement toward an all-volunteer military force gains momentum.

Understanding your income is the first step in successful financial management. Income is the resource available for satisfying the financial needs of the officer and his family. Once you know what your gross income is, you can then devote your attention to its efficient allocation. Your gross income is the sum of numerous pays and allowances that vary in accordance with your grade, length of service, and type of duty. The Service ranks and titles corresponding to various pay grades are listed in Table 1-4. Let us now consider the major components of an officer's monthly gross pay.

Basic Pay. All members of the Uniformed Services on active duty and in pay status are entitled to basic pay. Tables C-2 and C-3, Appendix C, show the several monthly basic pay tables that have been in use from 1 July 1969. As new pay schedules are enacted by Congress, they may be obtained from your Finance Officer and inserted as Appendix Table C-1.

Since basic pay varies with years of service, it is essential to know what service is creditable in the computation of your basic pay. Without going into all the special cases set forth in the Career Compensation Act of 1949, as amended, in general the service to be counted in computing cumulative years creditable for pay purposes:

1. Includes full time for all periods of active and inactive service (to include service prior to the attainment of eighteen years of age) as a commissioned officer, commissioned warrant officer, warrant officer, Army field clerk, flight officer, and enlisted person in any Regular or Reserve (to include National Guard) component of any of the Uniformed Services.

2. Does not include service as a cadet, midshipman, or ROTC student.

TABLE OF EQUIVALENT GRADES

Commissioned Officers

Title

Grade	Army, Air Force, Marine Corps	Navy
	General of the Army; General of the Air Force	Fleet admiral
O-10	General	Admiral
O-9	Lieutenant general	Vice admiral
O-8	Major general	Rear admiral
O-7	Brigadier general	Commodore
O-6	Colonel	Captain
O-5	Lieutenant colonel	Commander
O-4	Major	Lieutenant commander
O-3	Captain	Lieutenant
O-2	First lieutenant	Lieutenant (junior grade)
O-1	Second lieutenant	Ensign

Warrant Officers

Grade	Army	Navy	Air Force	Marine Corps
W-4	Chief warrant officer	Chief warrant officer	Chief warrant officer	Chief warrant officer
W-3	Chief warrant officer	Warrant officer	Chief warrant officer	Chief warrant officer
W-2	Chief warrant officer	Warrant officer	Chief warrant officer	Chief warrant officer
W-1	Warrant officer	Warrant officer	Warrant officer	Warrant officer

Enlisted Persons

Grade	Army	Navy	Air Force	Marine Corps
E-9	Sergeant Major of the Army, Command Sergeant-Major, Staff Sergeant Major	Master Chief Petty Officer/Navy, Master chief petty officer	Chief Master Sergeant/Air Force, Chief master sergeant	Sergeant Major/Marine Corps, Sergeant major, Master Gunnery sergeant
E-8	First sergeant, Master sergeant	Senior chief petty officer	Senior master sergeant	First sergeant, Master sergeant
E-7	Sergeant first class, Platoon sergeant	Chief petty officer	Master sergeant	Gunnery sergeant
E-6	Staff sergeant	Petty officer, first class	Technical sergeant	Staff sergeant
E-5	Sergeant	Petty officer, second class	Staff sergeant	Sergeant
E-4	Corporal	Petty officer, third class	Sergeant	Corporal
E-3	Private first class	Seaman	Airman first class	Lance corporal
E-2	Private E-2	Seaman apprentice	Airman	Private first class
E-1	Private E-1	Seaman recruit	Airman basic	Private

Note: The enlisted grades in the Army also include the following specialists: E-7 Specialist 7, E-6 Specialist 6, E-5 Specialist 5, E-4 Specialist 4

TABLE 1-4

Cadets and midshipmen of the four Service academies and aviation cadets of the Navy and Marine Corps are entitled to monthly pay at the rate of 50% of the basic pay of an 0-1 with two or less years of service.

Subsistence Allowance. All officers are entitled to a monthly subsistence allowance of $47.88 regardless of their pay grade and whether or not they have dependents.

Quarters Allowance. When government quarters are not available, an officer is authorized an allowance according to his pay grade and whether or not he has dependents (see Appendix Table C-4).

Under certain conditions an officer may be permitted to occupy government quarters which have been declared "substandard." In this event, he continues to receive his quarters allowance and reimburses to the government a fair rental for the substandard quarters.

An officer without dependents in a pay grade above 0-3 may elect not to occupy government quarters assigned to him and instead receive basic allowance for quarters at his authorized rate unless the Service Secretary determines that military operational conditions require otherwise or while the officer is on sea duty or field duty.

Payment of basic allowance for quarters to members of the Uniformed Services *without dependents* is authorized while the member is in travel or leave status (including delay enroute) between permanent or temporary duty stations. For example, quarters allowance is authorized to newly commissioned graduates of the Service Academies, *without dependents,* while they are in travel or leave status between the Academies and their first duty stations. A member getting married will start drawing quarters allowance with dependents from the date the dependent is acquired regardless of whether he is in travel or leave status. He will continue to draw it except when government quarters are provided for his family.

Hazardous Duty Incentive Pay. Special pay additives are awarded to officers as an incentive to voluntarily specialize in certain hazardous duties. An officer serving as a crew member involving frequent and regular participation in aerial flight, or assigned to a submarine or other submersible vehicle is entitled to incentive pay according to his grade and length of service. The incentive pay for these duties ranges from $100 per month for an 0-1 with less than two years service to $245 for an 0-6 (see Table C-5).

An incentive pay of $110 per month is payable to officers while they are:

1. Assigned to duties requiring frequent parachute jumps.

2. Required to participate in frequent and regular aerial or glider flights as other than a crew member.

3. Involved in the demolition of explosives as a primary duty, including training for such duty.

4. Assigned to duty inside a high- or low-pressure chamber.

5. Assigned to duty as a human test subject in experiments of thermal stress, acceleration, deceleration, etc.

6. Involved in intimate contact with persons afflicted with leprosy.

7. Involved in frequent and regular participation in flight operations on the flight deck of an aircraft carrier.

Officers meeting the performance requirements for more than one of the above hazardous duties during the same time period are entitled to a maximum of two types of incentive pay provided they are assigned to a unit whose mission requires the performance of both types of hazardous duty.

Special Pay. In addition to any other pay or allowances to which he is authorized, certain officers are entitled to special pay while serving as medical or dental interns.

1. *Medical and Dental* officers are entitled to special pay according to their years of active medical or dental service, as indicated in Table C-6. Officers are not entitled to the special pay while serving as medical or dental interns.

2. *Veterinary* officers are entitled to $100 per month.

3. *Diving Duty Pay.* Officers who are qualified and designated as divers by proper authority and are assigned to and performing diving duty are authorized diving pay of $110 per month.

4. *Hostile Fire Pay.* Except in time of war declared by Congress, and under regulations prescribed by the Secretary of Defense, a Serviceman may be paid special pay at the rate of $65 per month for any month in which he was present in a designated "hostile fire area." An officer who is injured by hostile fire, explosion of a hostile mine or any other hostile action is entitled to hostile fire pay for a period of up to three months while hospitalized. The Comptroller General has ruled that this includes persons wounded mistakenly or accidentally by friendly fire in the presence of a hostile force or while in action in the face of a hostile force. Injuries or illnesses due to the elements, exhaustion or self-inflicted wounds are not considered battle casualties and therefore are not included in the eligibility for hostile fire pay while hospitalized.

5. *Responsibility Pay.* A Service Secretary may designate positions of unusual responsibility which are of a critical nature to an Armed Force under his jurisdiction, and may pay special pay to an officer who is entitled to the basic pay of grade 0-3, 0-4, 0-5 or 0-6 and who is performing the duties of such a position. The monthly amounts for such officers are $50, $50, $100 and $150 respectively. This pay was first made effective on 1 June 1970 when the Secretary of the Army was authorized to designate the district senior advisor jobs in Vietnam as positions of unusual responsibility. As a result officers in pay grades 0-3 and 0-4 who serve in DSA positions in Vietnam are authorized special responsibility pay. Men promoted to a higher pay grade while serving as DSA's may receive the special pay authorized for that grade.

6. *Continuation Pay For Nuclear Submarine Officers.* Navy officers in the submarine service commissioned after 30 June 1960 and having less than 10 years of commissioned service on or before 30 June 1973 who meet the specific other requirements in SECNAV Instruction 7220.65 may execute a written agreement to remain in active submarine service for one period of 4 years beyond any other period of obligated active service. The amount payable is determined semiannually by the Secretary of the Navy. When an officer's agreement is accepted, the total amount payable becomes fixed at that time, but may not exceed $3,750 for each year of the active service agreement.

Overseas Station Allowances. In addition to the allowances discussed above, there are three types of station allowances currently authorized for payment to Servicemen on permanent duty in certain overseas areas.

A Housing and Cost-of-Living Allowance may be authorized to defray the average excess costs experienced in certain specified areas outside of the United States. Representative payments range from $0.20 to $12.40 per day for housing and from $0.20 to $13.05 per day for living costs.

A Temporary Lodging Allowance may be authorized to reimburse a Serviceman for more than normal expenses incurred at hotels or hotel-like accommodations and public eating places outside the United States. Payments are generally authorized for certain periods, when reporting in, not to exceed 60 days, during which the Serviceman and/or his dependents must occupy commercial facilities while awaiting permanent quarters. Payment is also authorized for the last 10 days preceding the date of departure of the Serviceman when departing from his permanent duty station with permanent change-of-station (PCS) orders. Payments are authorized only when the Serviceman actually utilizes the specified commercial facilities.

An Interim Housing Allowance is payable to a Serviceman who is required and does procure non-Government family-type housing prior to the arrival of his dependents in the area of assignment outside the United States. The allowance is payable for 60 days or to the date prior to the arrival of dependents, whichever occurs first. The daily rate is equal to the housing allowance authorized for that area (as described above).

Family Separation Allowances. These allowances compensate Servicemen for extra expenses incurred as a result of separation of the Serviceman from his family. There are two types, both of which are payable in addition to any allowance or per diem to which the Serviceman is entitled:

Type I. This FSA is to compensate a member with dependents for added expenses incurred by the member when he must maintain two homes. A Serviceman with dependents who is on permanent duty outside of the U.S. or in Alaska, is entitled to a monthly allowance equal to the quarters allowance payable to a Serviceman without dependents in the same pay grade if:

a. The movement of his dependents to his permanent station or a place near that station is not authorized at the expense of the United States and his dependents do not reside at or near that station; and

b. Government quarters, or a housing facility under the jurisdiction of a Uniformed Service, are not available to him.

Type II. This FSA is to compensate the member for the added expenses incurred by the member's family when he is separated from it by PCS or TDY for long periods of time. Except in time of war or of national emergency declared by Congress, and in addition to any allowance received under 1. above, an officer with dependents who is entitled to a quarters allowance is entitled to a monthly allowance equal to $30 if:

a. Transportation of his dependents to his permanent duty station is not authorized at government expense and his dependents do not live at or near his permanent duty station.

b. He is on duty aboard a ship, away from the home port of the ship continuously for more than 30 days.

c. He is on temporary duty away from his permanent station continuously for more than 30 days, and his dependents do not reside at or near his temporary duty station. This includes members required to perform a period of TDY before reporting to their initial station of assignment.

To receive Family Separation Allowance No. 2 the Service member must maintain a home subject to his management, control and supervision. If his dependents reside as guests or visitors in the home of relatives of friends and the Service member maintains no other dependent residence subject to his management and control, Family Separation Allowance No. 2 is not authorized. FSA 2 is not authorized while the Service member's dependents are living in government quarters.

Uniform Allowance. A cash allowance for uniform purchase is awarded to some, but not all, newly commissioned officers. Individuals commissioned as Regular officers (except ROTC officers) receive no allowance. Newly commissioned Reserve officers generally receive a total of $300. If commissioned from the enlisted ranks, the allowance varies from $100 to $300 depending on the Service and circumstances.

RECEIVING PAY AND ALLOWANCES

An officer may elect to receive his pay and allowances, in whole or in part, by allotment, by collecting funds at his Finance Office, by check sent to him, or by check sent to a bank where he has an account. Each of these methods has its advantages under different circumstances. Generally, there is nothing to prevent changing from one method to another or in using a combination of methods as circumstances change. However, a check in payment for TDY cannot normally be sent to a bank, but only to the member's home or office.

One important factor should be pointed out. If an officer is reported missing, besieged, beleaguered, interned, or captured, the advantage is decidedly in favor of the bank allotment method because then all allotments in force continue to be paid unless his status changes to deceased. Moreover, an allotment to a joint checking account is preferable to an allotment direct to a named dependent.

To illustrate, let us take an example of three members, each reported missing in action, each with a wife and children, and each drawing pay of $300 per month after tax and insurance deductions. If member A is drawing his $300 overseas and sending $200 to his dependents each month by money order, then their income ceases when he is reported missing. If member B makes out a $200 allotment to his wife and retains $100 for personal expenses, then the $100 per month is not available to her when he is reported missing. If member C makes out an allotment to a joint bank account for the entire $300, then he can draw checks on this account for personal expenses before he becomes a casualty, and his wife has the entire $300 available to draw checks on when he is reported missing.

Actually, some relief is provided by regulations for the dependents of member A. Every Serviceman is required to complete a form, Record of Emergency Data, or authorized substitute, on which he designates the amount of pay he wishes to be allotted to his dependents in the event he is reported missing. Even if he designates 100 percent, however, his wishes may not be granted unless his dependents can show dire need and emergency.

Bureau of the Census. *Statistical Abstract of the United States.* Washington: U.S. Government Printing Office, Published annually.

Department of Defense. *Modernizing Military Pay, Report of the First Quadrennial Review of Military Compensation.* Vol. I. Washington: U.S. Government Printing Office, 1 November 1967. (The Hubbell Plan)

Department of Labor, Bureau of Labor Statistics. *National Survey of Professional, Administrative, Technical and Clerical Pay.* Bulletin No. 1654. Washington: U.S. Government Printing Office, 1969.

Sharff, Lee S., ed. *Uniformed Services Almanac.* Washington: Uniformed Services Almanac, Published annually.

Traveling may be one of two things—
an experience we shall always remember,
or an experience which, alas, we shall
never forget.
                    —Rabbi Julius Gordon

CHAPTER **2**

TRAVEL AND
OTHER ALLOWANCES

THE ARMED FORCES officer and his family can expect to be among the more mobile members of society. Indeed, many Service members consider the opportunities for travel for themselves and their dependents one of the most desirable facets of a Service career. The government, of course, tries to lessen some of the difficulty and expense involved in moving and travel by either moving the personnel and their possessions or reimbursing them for some of the expenses incurred. A knowledge of which expenses can be claimed may very well keep the Armed Forces officer from incurring expenses which are not reimbursable by the government.

TRAVEL ALLOWANCES

Permanent Change Of Station. An officer traveling on permanent change of station (PCS) orders will receive allowances, usually elective with the traveler, as follows:

    1. Mileage at the rate of 6 cents per mile—no per diem.

    2. Transportation in kind (Government vehicle or aircraft) plus a per diem in lieu of subsistence or meal tickets.

    3. Transportation request plus a per diem in lieu of subsistence or meal tickets.

    4. Reimbursement for the actual cost of transportation authorized

and used where transportation requests are not available at the time and place required, plus per diem.

5. When a traveler procures transportation at his own expense on a common carrier in an amount of $15 (plus tax) or less, he may elect to receive actual cost of transportation without regard to transportation requests being available.

Per diem at a rate of up to $25 is allowed for the time necessary to perform travel by the transportation employed or for constructive travel over the official route, whichever is less. However, when travel is directed (as distinguished from authorized) and performed by a particular mode of transportation other than by privately-owned conveyance, reimbursement is at the prescribed rate for the time necessary to perform the travel by the mode of transportation directed. The per diem rate for the day of departure from the old permanent station and for the day of arrival at the new permanent station is prorated in 6-hour quarters.

Reimbursable expenses, as indicated for temporary duty (see below), are also authorized while traveling on a PCS per diem basis (see sub-pars. (2), (3) and (4) above). An officer is reimbursed only for the travel performed between the locations indicated in the orders or from the location where the orders were received to final destination, provided the latter distance is shorter.

Allowances for travel performed under cancelled, revoked or modified orders are payable under a variety of conditions and circumstances. In general, the payment of transportation and travel allowances is authorized for travel performed by the member or his dependents under orders which are later revoked, modified or cancelled after departure from the old station and while in a delay enroute or leave status prior to reporting in to the new station.

An officer traveling under PCS orders which are cancelled, or modified enroute is entitled to allowances as follows:

1. If the orders are cancelled, round-trip allowances for the distance from the old duty station to the point where the cancellation was received, not to exceed the distance from the old station to the contemplated new station and return.

2. If the orders are modified to name a new station, allowances for the distance from the old station to the point where notification of the change was received, and then to the last-named station, not to exceed the distance from the old station to the last-named station, via the first-named station.

3. An officer on PCS orders who takes a leave of absence before arriving at the new station is not deprived of the allowances to which he would be entitled had he not taken leave. If the orders are cancelled or modified while he is on leave, he will be entitled to allowances as prescribed in 1. and 2. above.

It is suggested that you contact a Finance Office for guidance in the particular case.

PCS Travel Time. You can compute how many days travel time you are authorized not chargeable as leave based upon the examples listed below.

1. If you travel the entire distance by POV—you are allowed one day for each 300 miles of the official distance plus one additional day for the remaining distance if 150 miles or more.

2. If you travel the entire distance by common carrier—you are allowed one day for each 720 miles of the official distance.

3. If you travel partly by POV and partly by common carrier—you would first consider the distance traveled by POV and apply the formula in 1. above; and then consider the distance traveled by common carrier and apply the formula in 2.

Overseas travel and travel performed by government-furnished transportation is based on the elapsed time.

TDY Transportation Allowances. An officer traveling on temporary duty (TDY) orders is entitled to receive allowances (unless otherwise directed), elective with the traveler, as follows:

1. Mileage at the rate of 5 cents per mile for the distance.

2. Mileage at the rate of 7 cents per mile for travel performed by privately owned conveyance under orders authorizing such travel as more advantageous to the government.

3. Transportation in kind.

4. Transportation request.

5. Reimbursement for the cost to the traveler of the transportation authorized if transportation requests are not available at the time and place required.

When common carrier transportation over $15 is obtained at the member's expense, and transportation requests are available, reimbursement must be limited to five cents per mile. In many instances the cost of common carrier transportation substantially exceeds the authorized reimbursement at five cents per mile, so the use of TR's is generally recommended for this type of travel. Examples of representative distances are shown below.

Payment of Mileage at 5¢ versus Actual Cost of Air Travel

	Total Miles		Reimbursement at 5¢		Round Trip
		Common		Common	Air Jet-
New York NY to:	Highway	Carrier	Highway	Carrier	Tourist
Washington, D.C.	534	568	26.70	28.40	38.00
Chicago, Ill.	1656	1794	82.80	89.70	90.00
Kansas City, Mo.	2454	2662	122.70	133.10	134.00
El Paso, Tex.	4320	4538	216.00	226.90	220.00

NOTE: Common carrier distance is used only when the travel is performed entirely by common carrier.

TDY Per Diem Allowance. In addition to one of the above allowances a member is entitled to receive a per diem allowance. The per diem rates for travel within the United States are indicated in Table 2-1. A member in pay grade 0-6 or below on TDY at a military installation must secure a certificate of non-availability of government quarters and/or government mess (including Officer's Open Mess) for submission with a travel voucher. In the absence of such certificates, government quarters and mess are deemed available even though not occupied or used, and settlement of per diem must be made at the lower rate. For travel outside the United States the per diem rates vary for different countries. These rates are published in the Joint Travel Regulations (JTR) which should be consulted before traveling outside the United States.

Officers graduated from any of the Service Academies when traveling under orders to the first station to which they are permanently assigned are entitled to the permanent change-of-station allowances for the distance actually traveled under such orders, not to exceed the official distance from their home or from the Service Academy, as may be designated in their orders, to such first duty station via any temporary duty station as may be directed en route, including the Service Academy in cases involving authorized travel from home. When travel to first duty station involves a period of temporary duty at the Academy from which graduated before reporting to first duty station, no per diem is payable for such period of temporary duty.

TDY Reimbursable Expenses. Over and above the transportation and per diem allowances indicated above, members on TDY orders may be reimbursed for certain expenses incident to their travel. These include:

1. Expenses incident to taxi fares between places of abode or business and stations, wharves, airports or other common carrier terminals.* Fares or fees in excess of $15.00 will be supported by a receipt.

Any time mileage is paid for any portion of a leg of a journey, taxi fares cannot be paid on that leg of a journey. For example, on an authorized trip to the Pentagon you decide to drive a POV from West Point, N.Y. to JFK International Airport and then use a transportation request for an airline flight to Washington, D.C. You then cannot claim a taxi fare from Washington National Airport to the Pentagon because you are being paid POV mileage for a portion of the leg of the journey. The payments for the taxi portion of the leg are affected by the POV mileage claim portion. In this case the use of a government vehicle or TR from West Point to JFK would make the taxi fare in Washington, D.C. reimbursable.

2. Tips to Pullman porters, not to exceed $1.00 per calendar day.*

3. Tips to baggage porters, Red Caps, etc., at customary local rates, but not including tips for baggage handling at hotels; the number of pieces of baggage handled will be shown on the claim.*

TABLE OF PER DIEM RATES WITHIN THE UNITED STATES[t,v,z]

	Officers	Enlisted
a. For travel by all modes of transportation (except as provided in items (1), (2), and (3))	\$25.00[o]	\$25.00[w]
(1) For travel by surface common carrier on days other than the day of departure from, the day of return to, or the day of arrival at, the permanent duty station	11.80[o]	11.80[w]
(2) For travel by inland or coastal vessels, see par. M 4210.		
(3) When meal tickets are issued or reimbursement for meals and quarters is required, see subpar. 3.		
*b. For the day of arrival at point of temporary duty or delay (except as provided in items 1 and 2 and subpar. 6)	11.80[n,o]	11.80[n,w]
*c. For the day of arrival at or return to permanent station	11.80[o]	11.80[w]
d. For delays incident to travel and for temporary duty:[x]		
(1) Government quarters not available or not utilized, as applicable, and Government mess not available	25.00[o]	25.00[w]
(2) Government quarters available or utilized, as applicable--Government mess not available:		
(a) Open mess not available	11.80[o]	11.80[w]
(b) Open mess available	8.00[o]	7.00[w]
(3) Government mess available--Government quarters not available or not utilized, as applicable	18.20	15.70
(4) Government quarters available or utilized, as applicable, and Government mess available (except as provided in item f of this table)	4.50[p]	2.00
e. For periods of temporary duty performed by a member with his unit, or a detachment thereof, when that unit or detachment is ordered by name or number away from its permanent station under conditions when Government quarters are available without charge and Government mess is available.[x]	2.00[q]	2.00
f. For periods of temporary duty under instruction at the Defense Management Systems Course, Naval Post Graduate School, Monterey, Calif., when Government mess and Government quarters are available	5.00	NA
g. For periods of temporary duty under instruction at the Civil Service Commission Executive Seminar Centers, Kings Point, N.Y., and Berkeley, Calif.	2.50	2.50

[n]This per diem allowance will be increased by a flat amount of \$13.20 (not subject to proration under subpar. 2) if other than Government quarters are used.

[o]For each meal available to officer members in a Government mess a deduction of \$2.25 will be made in all cases except that when the officer member is entitled to per diem under item a(1) or b for periods of less than a full day the deduction will be \$1.50 per meal and that when the officer member is entitled to per diem under item d(2)(b) the deduction will be \$1.15 per meal. In no case will the total deduction for any day exceed the amount of per diem applicable for that day.

[p]When subsistence is furnished by the Government without charge to officer, this amount will be reduced to \$2.00 per day.

[q]This per diem allowance will be increased by the excess, if any, of the daily cost of food in the Government mess over one-thirtieth of the monthly basic allowance for subsistence.

[t]Open mess will be disregarded in all situations except that indicated in item d(2) of this table.

[v]In no case will the net amount of per diem paid exceed \$25. For officers in pay grades 0-7. 0-8, 0-9, and 0-10, Government quarters and messing facilities will not be considered as available unless actually utilized (see par. M 4451).

[w]Enlisted members in a travel status entitling them to per diem will not be required to pay for meals furnished from a Government mess (including box lunches), except that enlisted members who are authorized a basic allowance for subsistence while on temporary duty and who take meals in a Government mess may be required to pay the charge established for such meals by the appropriate regulations of the Service concerned. For each Government meal available to enlisted members, a deduction of \$3.10 will be made in all cases except that when the enlisted member is entitled to per diem under item a(1) or b for periods of less than a full day the deduction will be \$2.35 per meal and that when the enlisted member is entitled to per diem under item d(2)(b) the deduction will be \$1.67 per meal.

[x]The per diem rates contained in terms d and e will be applicable from 0001 on the day after the day of arrival at place of temporary duty or delay and will terminate at 2400 on the day prior to the day of departure therefrom. The applicable rate will not be affected by round-trip temporary duty travel away from such place when departure and return are in the same calendar day.

[z]These per diem allowances will be increased by the daily cost incurred for use of Government quarters, as substantiated by a statement of the member concerned; provided that reimbursement for such charges for use of quarters under jurisdiction of any Uniformed Service in the Department of Defense will not exceed \$2. When such charges are levied over weekly or monthly periods, the cost will be prorated over the period the Government quarters were actually utilized. When, during a period of temporary duty, a member is required by virtue of his temporary duty assignment to procure Government quarters under the jurisdiction of the Department of Defense at two different locations in the same calendar day, per diem allowances will be increased by the daily cost incurred for each set of quarters, not to exceed a total of \$4 each day. When, under the same circumstances, a member is required to procure additional Government quarters not under the jurisdiction of the Department of Defense, per diem allowances will be increased by the daily cost incurred. In no case will these additions result in a total per diem of more than \$25.

NOTE: portions of the footnotes are omitted here.

TABLE 2-1

4. Expenses incident to checking and transfer of baggage. The number of pieces checked will be shown on the claim.*

5. Reimbursement of registration fees incident to attendance at meetings of technical, professional, scientific, or other non-Federal organizations is authorized. This authorization must be included in the orders authorizing the TDY.

6. The costs of shipping excess baggage (such as exceeding the airline baggage weight limitation) will be reimbursed only when authorized in orders.

7. Expenses of operation of government conveyances such as cost of gasoline, oil, repairs, non-personal services, guards, and storage are reimbursable when such expenses are necessary and government facilities are not available.

8. Cost of storage of government automobiles when government storage facilities are not available.

9. Cost of official telephone or telegraph messages.

10. Ferry fares, bridge, road and tunnel tolls are reimbursable when travel is performed by government highway transportation.

The items above that are followed by an asterisk are not reimbursable when mileage allowance is authorized TDY.

Overseas Duty. Travel overseas, on either TDY or PCS orders is a subject too lengthy to be covered here. You are advised to consult the appropriate section of the Joint Travel Regulations, particularly if the transportation of dependents and household goods is authorized to your overseas station. Also, you will generally receive special instructions pertaining to such travel from the headquarters issuing your orders.

TRAVEL ALLOWANCES FOR DEPENDENTS

PCS Orders. All officers are entitled (with exceptions, some of which are noted below) to transportation of dependents at government expense upon a permanent change of station. Within the United States the entitlement is, in general, for travel performed from the old station to the new station. If the member is transferred overseas to a location where for military reasons his dependents are not permitted to accompany him, he is entitled to transportation of dependents at government expense from the place at which the dependents are located on the date he received such orders to any place in the Continental United States which he may designate. In this case special authorization is required for the transportation of the dependents to Hawaii, Alaska, the Panama Canal Zone, or Puerto Rico.

Dependents Acquired On Or Before The Effective Date Of Orders. Except upon graduation from a Service Academy, a member who acquires a dependent after the date of his departure (detachment) from his old permanent duty station incident to permanent change of station orders but on or before the effective date of those orders will be entitled to transportation of such dependent from the place where the dependent is acquired to the new permanent duty station. Such entitlement is without regard to whether temporary duty is directed or performed en route or whether either the old or new station is within or outside the United States.

Travel From Other Than Old Permanent Station To Other Than The New Permanent Station. Transportation of dependents at government expense is authorized for travel performed from other than the old permanent station to the new permanent station not to exceed the entitlement from the old to the new station. The Service Secretary concerned may authorize or approve transportation of dependents at government expense from a location other than the old permanent station to a location other than the new permanent station, provided that entitlement will not exceed that from the old permanent station to the new permanent station. Places at which dependents reside and from which the member commutes daily to his permanent station will not be considered as places other than the old or the new permanent station.

Graduates Of Service Academies. When commissioned and ordered to active duty, a graduate of a Service Academy is entitled to transportation of dependents at government expense for travel performed by dependents incident to such orders, not to exceed entitlement from the farther point, home of record or Service Academy, to his permanent station, irrespective of the point designated in the orders (Service Academy or home of record) from which the officer's travel is directed to be performed. When dependents are acquired after the date of an officer's departure (detachment) from a Service Academy incident to his active duty orders but on or before the effective date of the orders, the officer will be entitled to transportation of dependents at government expense for travel performed by such dependents to the member's new duty station from one of the following:

1. The home of record.
2. The Service Academy.
3. The place where the dependents are acquired, not to exceed entitlement from the farther point, home of record, or Service Academy, to the member's new permanent station, provided that in the event the dependents travel from the place acquired to the home of record or Service Academy prior to the effective date of active duty orders, the place named in item 1 or 2, as appropriate, will apply. Such entitlement is without regard to whether temporary duty is directed or performed en route.

Monetary Allowance. Transportation in kind may be furnished to dependents or a monetary allowance may be paid in lieu of transportation. A member who elects to transport his dependents at his own expense is entitled to a monetary allowance, not to exceed 18 cents per mile, for all dependents, as follows:

Six cents per mile for each dependent 12 years of age or over, not to exceed two such dependents; and 3 cents per mile for each additional dependent 12 years of age or over. Dependents under 12 years of age but over 5 years are entitled to 3 cents per mile. As an example, a wife and two children over 12 years old would be computed as follows: wife, 6 cents per mile; 1st child, 6 cents per mile; second child, 3 cents per mile; or a total of 15 cents per mile for dependent travel.

Do not file a dependent travel claim:

1. Until travel has actually been performed. Advance payment of this allowance is not authorized.

2. When travel is not for the purpose of establishing a bona fide residence at a destination.

3. For travel for which the government furnishes transportation.

4. For travel performed before receipt of your PCS orders or before receipt of official notice that PCS orders will be issued.

5. For a child under 5 years of age.

6. For dependent parents unless they actually reside in your household.

7. Except for those dependents who actually perform the travel. Dependents not moving should not be included in your claim.

8. For travel if dependency did not exist on the effective date of your orders directing PCS.

SHIPMENT OF HOUSEHOLD GOODS

Weight Allowances. Members of the graduating classes of Service Academies who are commissioned as officers, are authorized shipment of household goods from the Academy from which they graduate to their first permanent duty station. In addition, they may ship household goods from their Academy to their home or from their home to their first permanent duty station.

Officers ordered on a permanent or temporary change of station are authorized an allowance usually sufficient to cover the cost of packing, crating, and shipping their household belongings. This allowance is based upon the rank of the individual member as indicated in Table C-7, Appendix C. In general, the weights indicated in the permanent change of station column are authorized whenever travel of dependents is authorized.

The allowances in Table C-7 represent the actual net weights authorized to be shipped at Government expense. When shipment is forwarded by commercial van, the allowance is increased by 5 percent. The shipping allowance is not given to the member in money nor are the savings resulting from his shipping a lesser weight than authorized collectible by him. The cost of packing, crating, and unpacking any unauthorized articles or weight in excess of prescribed weight allowance will be borne by the owner.

Regardless of rank or grade, an officer is entitled to transportation of professional books, papers, and equipment when certified by him as necessary in the performance of his official duties. Shipment of these items is in the same manner and under the same conditions as the other household goods except that the weight is without charge against the weight allowance prescribed.

Ordinarily the transportation officer designates the method of shipment; however, if the owner desires a method other than the one designated by the Transportation Officer and the cost is greater, the owner is required to pay the excess. In many cases, particularly on short moves, it is advisable to be moved by van in order to obviate the necessity for packing and crating. Consultation with the Transportation Officer is recommended before requesting shipment of household goods.

Oversea Area Moves. The personal property and equipment you or your dependents will need for wear, use, comfort and/or convenience when traveling to your new oversea duty station is described as personal baggage.

Unaccompanied baggage is the portion of your prescribed household goods weight allowance which is shipped, separately from the bulk of household goods, direct to your new duty station in connection with your travel to and from oversea areas. This weight is a part of your total permanent change of station or temporary duty allowance. You may ship such baggage in the weight corresponding with your rank as indicated below.

1. Military personnel on permanent change of
   station (PCS):
   General Officers (0-8, 0-9 and 0-10) . . . . 1,000 pounds
   General Officers (0-7) and Colonels (0-6) . . . . 800 pounds
   All other officers . . . . 600 pounds
2. Military personnel on temporary change of
   station (TDY:
   General officers . . . . 800 pounds
   All other officers . . . . 350 pounds
3. Dependents of military personnel:
   Each adult . . . . 350 pounds
   Each child under 12 years old . . . . 175 pounds

You may take 66 pounds of baggage for yourself aboard the plane on which you travel, 66 pounds for each child under 12 years old, and 100 pounds for each adult dependent. This is considered accompanied baggage.

Storage Of Household Goods. Joint Travel Regulations explain the conditions under which transportation and temporary storage of household goods are authorized at government expense. The facilities to be used are determined by the Transportation Officer, based on the requirement and what is considered to be more advantageous to the government. There are two types of storage—nontemporary and temporary.

1. Property is placed in nontemporary storage when items will not

be needed by you or your dependents at your new duty station or during your oversea tour of duty. Property designated for this type storage will normally be placed in the nearest approved commercial facility to the location of your household goods. You should plan very carefully in advance just which items you want placed in this type storage, because they will not usually be available to you for an extended period of time.

2. When all, or a part, of your property is to be shipped but will arrive at destination before you will require it, storage is authorized for a period of 90 days. This is called temporary storage. If you have more than one lot of property to be moved, it is recommended that you schedule the pickup times for different days. Plan early to separate the items to be put in storage.

If commercial facilities are utilized, each individual should see that his possessions are adequately insured. The maximum liability of the government is limited to $10,000. There are also limitations on the maximum allowance claimable on certain categories or types of property. For example, the maximum amount allowable per claim on books is $1000. When the household goods are received, the owner should realize that by signing the transportation receipt he not only acknowledges delivery but usually indicates receipt in good condition, unless exceptions are noted in the signed receipt. In all instances a prompt check should be made for damage and, if appropriate, a claim made against the carrier immediately. The time limitation for claims against commercial carriers in most instances is 9 months; 2 years in the case of claims against the government.

When damage occurs, whether during transporation or storage, claim may be made against the government. However, a demand should be made against the carrier before the claim is filed. If the individual packs the items himself, whether transportation and storage are under commercial or government control, his chances of collecting for concealed damages are minimized.

ADVANCE PAYMENTS

The financial hazards of a permanent change of station, particularly for the married member, must be considered both from the standpoint of expenses and expenditures. A rule of thumb is that any change of station will cost a member one month's base pay after all travel allowances are received. This is the expense or financial loss. To make matters worse, the expenditures involved must be made over a short period of time. A Serviceman may draw an advance payment of up to 3 months' base pay and travel allowances in connection with a permanent change of station and an advance payment of up to 30 days' travel allowances in connection with temporary duty. (Advance payments of transportation allowances for dependents and for movement of household goods are not authorized.)

Advance Of Pay. Upon permanent change of station an officer may be paid an advance in pay. The amount advanced may be up to 3 month's base pay less all tax withholdings, less FICA, less any indebtedness due the Government. The fact that there may be temporary duty enroute on PCS will not preclude the payment of an advance of pay. The advance of pay may be made at any time after receipt of orders, but not later than 30 days after reporting to the new permanent station. It may be made in one, two, or three payments.

The approval of the Commanding Officers is not required on advances of pay to commissioned officers or warrant officers. Normally, the amount of the advance will be fully liquidated within a period of six months. When assigned to MAAG or Military Missions in foreign countries, which involve unusually large expenditures of funds, the Deputy Chief of Staff for Personnel, or the Major Commander, may authorize liquidation of the advance of pay over a period of not to exceed 12 months. Each advance payment must be liquidated in full before any subsequent advance payment may be made.

Advance Payment Of Travel Allowances—PCS. A member in receipt of orders directing a permanent change of station who desires an advance payment of travel allowances must elect to receive only one of the following types of allowances:

1. A mileage allowance not to exceed the product of the mileage rate and the official distance between the points named in the travel orders.

2. In the event government transportation requests are issued, per diem not to exceed the estimated or expected number of days necessary to complete the travel directed.

3. If temporary duty is involved on orders directing PCS, mileage allowance plus per diem for the period of TDY not to exceed 30 days.

Advance Payment Of Travel Allowances—TDY. A member under orders directing temporary duty travel other than in connection with a PCS, who desires an advance payment of travel allowances must elect to receive only one of the following allowances:

1. Per diem not to exceed 30 days.

2. Monetary allowance in lieu of transportation plus per diem not to exceed 30 days.

In addition to one of the above types of allowances, Commanding Officers may authorize an advance to cover unusual expenses expected to be incident to the travel. Such unusual expenses may be, but are not limited to, telegraph and telephone toll calls required in the conduct of official business. Where a period is in excess of 30 days, advance payment of travel allowances may be made for each 30-day period. However, before any additional advance is made all preceding travel advances must be settled in full for the accrued per diem advances at the end of each 30-day period.

DISLOCATION ALLOWANCE

A dislocation allowance (DLA) equivalent to one month's Quarters Allowance (BAQ) is also payable when your dependents have actually made their move. (Dislocation allowance is not payable if trailer movement is elected.) Payment is made at your next permanent duty station except when you are moving to a restricted area. Then you may present to any Finance Officer two copies of your PCS orders for payment.

This dislocation allowance is taxable and a Form W-2, Wage and Tax Statement, will be furnished you upon payment. You are required to attach this Form W-2 and include the DLA with your taxable income on your tax return at the end of the year. (Tax is not deducted if you are in a "Combat Exclusion Month." This means that you and your dependents must have completed the move in the same month you are in a combat zone.) The DLA is payable for one PCS move per fiscal year, with certain exceptions—Service School assignments and on special ruling by a Service Secretary. The one allowance per fiscal year limitation does not apply in case of a declared national emergency or war. A dislocation allowance is not payable on orders from home to first duty station, or from last duty station to home.

TRAILER ALLOWANCE

Trailer allowance is for the transportation of a house trailer, which is used as a residence, within the United States, within Alaska, and between the United States and Alaska. Transportation of a house trailer outside the United States is at the personal expense of the member.

If you own a house trailer and receive permanent change of station orders, the Transportation Officer will provide government transportation or hire a commercial carrier to move the trailer. Any cost over the usual 74¢ a mile must be borne by you. Or you may move the trailer yourself and receive an allowance of 11¢ a mile. The Joint Travel Regulations do not state that a trailer should be a certain size or type, only that it must be used as a residence by you and/or your dependents. No advance payment for travel allowance is authorized.

Your application for government transportation of a house trailer or claim for reimbursement must be supported by a statement that:

1. You understand that you cannot receive dislocation allowance (DLA) for the move.

2. You have not and will not make a claim for DLA.

3. You have not and will not request shipment of household goods or baggage at government expense.

Headquarters, Department of the Army. *Personal Property Shipping Information.* DA Pamphlet 55-2. Washington: U.S. Government Printing Office, December 1968.

He will always be a slave, who
does not know how to live upon
a little.

—Horace

CHAPTER **3**

FINANCIAL MANAGEMENT

IN ONE RESPECT, the officer and his family can be thought of as an economic unit. If we assume that the officer is the only breadwinner in the family, then we can consider it his duty to provide a satisfactory income for the members of his family as long as they are dependent upon him. This, we can say, is his financial goal. To determine what income would be considered satisfactory, we would first have to consider the economic needs of the family and determine whether or not they could be satisfied with the amount of income available.

Need determination is a matter of individual family decision based upon realistic appraisals and individual value judgments. One family might think that sending their children through college is a basic necessity, while another family might decide that if the boy doesn't get an appointment to a Service Academy, then he can work his way through college the best way he can. Such decisions are not susceptible of precise economic analysis; they depend upon the individual family's own value judgments. The techniques outlined in this book will be helpful to the officer once he has made such basic decisions.

As a practical matter, however, goals must be realistically set in accordance with the projected amount of income available. If your needs are much greater than your income will pay for, you may have to decide that your wife must become an income earner also. As a matter of fact, many junior officers marry women who are highly skilled teachers, medical workers, etc., who want to continue their work after marriage. Again, such decisions are an individual family matter.

BASIC PROBLEM OF FINANCIAL MANAGEMENT

The basic problem in financial management is how to allocate income between current needs and savings for future contingencies. Both current expenditures and savings must be provided for out of current income. If the officer knew that he would be the last surviving member of his family, and that he would be gainfully employed until his death, he would not need to save any income. His only motive for saving then would be so he could buy most efficiently some consumption good, such as a car or refrigerator, in the future. All he would have to do would be to support his children until they became 18-21 years of age, and support self and wife until death.

The problem is, however, that we must live with uncertainty. Income could be interrupted by premature death, disability, retirement, or involuntary unemployment. Needs could be greatly increased if a substantial portion of one's personal assets, such as a home, car, or other personal property were destroyed. Thus the officer must somehow decide how to allocate his income to satisfy both his current economic needs and protect his family against such personal hazards.

APPLICATION OF MARGINAL ANALYSIS
TO FINANCIAL PLANNING

Financial management is a matter of applied economics. The task facing the financial manager is to allocate his income so as to maximize the satisfaction of his family's short-run and long-run economic needs. The economic techniques used to accomplish this are derived from the principles of marginal analysis.

Marginal analysis seeks to balance conflicting forces or pressures until there is no incentive for further change. It concerns itself with matters of choice or decision-making. Whenever one decides to do one thing, it is at the cost or sacrifice of all other alternatives. For example, if I decide to go to a movie, it means that I cannot go bowling or go to church, etc. Such other alternatives are the opportunity cost of the activity I actually decide to carry out.

Obviously, if all of the alternative activities were to involve the same cost or sacrifice, it would be foolish for me to select an activity that was less satisfying to me than one of my alternatives. This should amount to common sense. We slightly complicate the problem when we make the costs or sacrifices of the alternative courses of action different in amount. Now we must attempt to compare the amount of benefit per unit of sacrifice that we derive from each alternative.

In the problems of personal financial management, we would usually be talking about the amount of benefit per dollar. For example, we might enjoy eating steak more than hamburger. But if we go to the store and find that the price of steak is twice that of hamburger, we might buy hamburger because, for our one dollar of expenditure, we get more enjoyment out of the larger quantity of hamburger that we can buy. Or, we might find that we would buy some combination of the two. This combination would reflect the balance of the conflicting forces involved in our alternative choices. Now, it must be quickly admitted that applying the techniques of marginal analysis to our financial problems has some very serious limitations.

We cannot precisely quantify the amount of benefit we derive from certain activities or goods. We cannot sit down and compile a chart that would quantitatively compare all the benefits that we would derive from all possible alternative expenditures. But these practical limitations do not render the marginal theory useless.

It is the pattern of thought that is important. It is the realization that we are making financial decisions which have opportunity costs. It means acceptance of the principle that if you allocate income to one item of expenditure knowing that you would derive greater satisfaction from an alternative use of that money, then you are not acting in the most rational way.

The foregoing is by no means a complete exposition of the theory of marginal analysis. If a more complete explanation is desired, the reader can consult any good text in the field of microeconomics. The above discussion, however, should adequately demonstrate the guiding philosophy of decision-making in the field of financial management as it is treated in this book. The steps, or evaluations that you should perform to accomplish your goal (the optimum allocation of income among competing needs) are outlined next.

STEPS TOWARD A BALANCED FINANCIAL PLAN

STEP 1 is to program your income. In Chapter 1 of this text you were introduced to the Service pay system. A statement of your pay and withholdings can be obtained from your finance officer. To program your income, you merely construct a Family Income Chart as in Chart 3-1 for the time period that you would like to consider.

In the present instance, let us consider a monthly gross income of $1,000. This amount is useful because it makes percentage relationships obvious. It might be pointed out, however, that this also approximates the

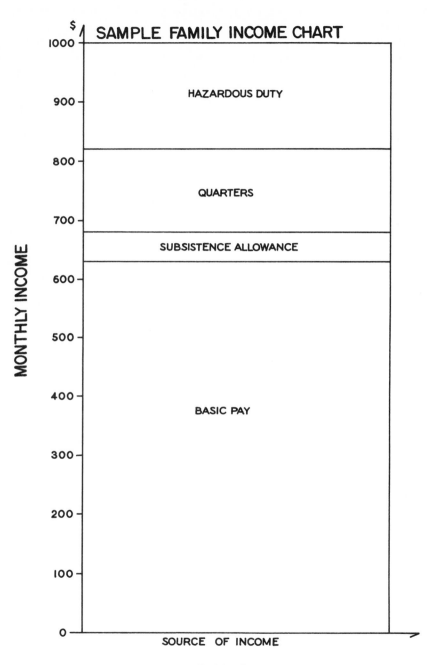

CHART 3-1

actual gross pay of an 0-2 (over 3 years service) drawing quarters allowance and hazardous duty pay.

It is useful to construct a graphical display of your pay and allowances. Such displays are indicated in Charts 1-1 and 3-1. Funds to which you are entitled during any selected period of time can be graphically added together to indicate the money resources to be allocated for various expenditures. Using the month as the selected time period is usually most useful, especially when it is used as a tool of financial management. If we plot this dollar figure on the vertical axis of a graph, we can proceed to Step 2, or the programming of your current expenditures and savings. The Family Income and Expenditure Chart (Chart 3-2) combines the information portrayed on Chart 3-1 with expected expenditures, and thus is a graphical aid to managing your income in the short run. Only after you understand your income can you allocate income rationally.

STEP 2 is to program your current expenditures and savings on your income chart. For officers already on active duty, this requires nothing more than examining their various kinds of expenditures. This tells how income is presently being allocated. It should be readily apparent that this second step involves nothing more than a budget. You will probably be surprised to learn how much you have actually been spending on certain items when you total up your cancelled checks, department store bills, etc.

SAMPLE FAMILY INCOME AND EXPENDITURE CHART

INCOME ALLOCATION	BUDGETED AMOUNT	AMOUNT REMAINING
FEDERAL INCOME TAX	$60	$940
FICA	28	912
LIFE INSURANCE PREMIUMS	60	852
SAVINGS AND INVESTMENTS	52	800
HOUSING	210	590
FOOD * HOUSEHOLD * PERSONAL	200	390
CHURCH AND CHARITABLE GIFTS	100	290
TRANSPORTATION	65	225
CLOTHING AND CLOTHING SERVICES	77	148
TELEPHONE	21	127
RECREATION	57	70
OTHER	11	59
SET-ASIDES	59	0

DOLLARS OF MONTHLY INCOME

CHART 3-2

For the young man about to become commissioned, one who is without experience in allocating a family income, this means drawing up a tentative budget based on the experience of another family or the averages. These expenditures are then programmed on your Family Income Chart thereupon revealing what your income is and how it is being used.

As you gather up the data on your expenditures, certain categories will become apparent. Some expenditures may be difficult to classify. You should try to develop a classification system which most readily meets your family's needs. There are many personal finance texts and other budgeting aids which might help you listed in the bibliography. The following list of categories may be a helpful tentative grouping.

1. Federal, State and Local Income Tax—Normally you are dealing with the amount withheld from your pay. Your experience might indicate that the withholding is typically more or less than your tax liability. Any discrepancy will have to be taken into consideration in your budget.

2. Social Security Tax (FICA)—This is also withheld from your pay.

3. Life Insurance Premiums—Premiums can usually be paid by government allotment. Thus, as with withholdings, the amounts allotted will not show up in your "take-home" pay.

4. Savings and Investments—Include here money which is definitely being placed beyond the reach of current consumption. This would be your planned program upon which your retirement and survivorship programs are based. Allotments may also be useful for budgetary control in this category.

5. Housing—If you rent, include utilities. If you own a house, include mortgage, tax and fire insurance escrow payments, utilities, allowance for maintenance and repair, and insurance of personal property and personal liability. The last item is placed in this category since such insurance is normally part of a Homeowner's package or is billed as if it were one policy with the fire insurance on the home.

6. Food, Household and Personal—These items are lumped together here for convenience of calculation. Normally this will be your spending in the Commissary and Exchange Store. If you seek greater accuracy, you can break this into three categories.

7. Church and Charitable Gifts—Whether this is considered a fixed or flexible expense depends upon your system of giving.

8. Transportation—Include here auto expenses such as gasoline, oil, insurance, registration, maintenance and tire allowance, and car loan payments if you are making them. Whether or not you include depreciation will depend on your method of family accounting. Note, however, that although depreciation is certainly a cost of owning an automobile, it is not an out-of-pocket expense. It doesn't show up until you buy another car.

Therefore, it makes more sense to provide for the purchase of your next automobile by setting aside sufficient funds every month. Such set-asides would compensate for depreciation. If you cannot avoid car loan payments, however, such out-of-pocket expense should be included in this category.

9. Clothing and Clothing Services—Include expense for laundry and dry cleaning sent out.

10. Telephone Service.

11. Recreation—Include club bills, baby-sitting fees spent to release you for recreation, etc.

12. Other Consumption Expenditures—List any categories that are useful to you in your planning. Categories for tobacco and alcoholic beverages might be applicable. If so, the amounts spent in these categories might surprise you. If you anticipate medical outlays, they also should be budgeted.

13. Set-asides for Future Expenditures—Include amounts being set aside for specific purchases such as durable goods (refrigerator, television set, chair, table, etc.), automobile, education, etc. Also include installment payments and interest payments which must be met out of your income.

After computing and classifying your current expenditures, graph them on your Family Income and Expenditure Chart. A simple piece of graph paper will suffice. When you are finished, the chart should look something like Chart 3-2, which is a fictitious rather than typical allocation. Some average allocations of income are presented in Table 3-1 and Chart 3-3.

STEP 3 is to perform your first reallocation of income by "balancing at the margin." This is nothing more than spotting the obvious faults in your present way of spending money that have been exposed on your Family Income Chart. You may find that your club bill is way out of line or that supporting two cars just isn't worthwhile.

The question to ask yourself (and the other members of your family) is simply this: "Is there any way that I can shift dollars from one category of expenditures to another to increase the total satisfaction or benefit my family can derive from my income?"

Note that "satisfaction" in the economic sense does not mean materialistic pleasure. Satisfaction is defined in terms of your family's goals as determined by your family. Money is a resource that can be used to achieve certain ends. Your family must set priorities on the various wants that money can provide. For example, one might place a high priority on charitable giving for spiritual reasons.

This quite obviously is not allocated income to satisfy a material need. Yet, such an allocation might yield a great deal of satisfaction to the family because of the way in which that family has defined its goals. You must examine your family's goals and determine whether or not you can reallocate your income to better achieve them.

DISTRIBUTION OF PERSONAL CONSUMPTION EXPENDITURES

(BY MAJOR GROUPS OF GOODS AND SERVICES)

	1968	1969	1970**
Total goods and services* - - - - - - - - - - -	536.6	576.0	600.4
Durable goods - - - - - - - - - - - - - - -	83.3	89.8	89.4
Automobile and parts - - - - - - - - - -	37.0	40.4	38.3
Furniture and household equipment - - -	34.2	36.0	37.3
Other - - - - - - - - - - - - - - - - -	12.1	13.5	13.9
Nondurable goods - - - - - - - - - - - - -	230.6	243.6	255.4
Food and beverages - - - - - - - - - - -	115.0	119.8	125.9
Clothing and shoes - - - - - - - - - - -	46.3	49.9	51.0
Gasoline and oil - - - - - - - - - - - -	19.1	21.3	22.8
Other - - - - - - - - - - - - - - - - -	50.1	52.7	55.7
Services - - - - - - - - - - - - - - - - -	222.8	242.6	255.6
Housing - - - - - - - - - - - - - - - -	77.4	83.7	88.3
Household operation - - - - - - - - - -	31.2	33.5	35.0
Transportation - - - - - - - - - - - - -	16.1	17.5	18.4
Other - - - - - - - - - - - - - - - - -	98.1	107.9	113.9

* In billions of dollars
** First quarter of 1970

SOURCE: _Survey of Current Business_, May 1970.

TABLE 3-1

Knowing that money spent on one thing means that you cannot spend it on something else (opportunity cost) can bring some sobering thoughts into an analysis of your financial affairs. If you spot any obvious deficiencies in your present income allocation, pull in on your belt, draw up a budget incorporating the necessary changes, and carry through on your change in family spending habits. You should note at this point that the bulk of Part I of this text discusses several major problems associated with your management of money in daily living. These should give you some basic insights into how you might more efficiently manage your budget.

STEP 4 in your attempt to establish a plan for the optimum allocation of your income, is to program your new allocation on a revised (but still tentative) Family Income and Expenditure Chart. If no revisions were required as a result of your hard look at the status quo in Step Three, you should merely proceed to the next evaluation with your original plan.

STEP 5 is to draw up three financial plans to test the adequacy with

THE PERSONAL INCOME AND CONSUMER EXPENDITURE DOLLAR IN 1970*

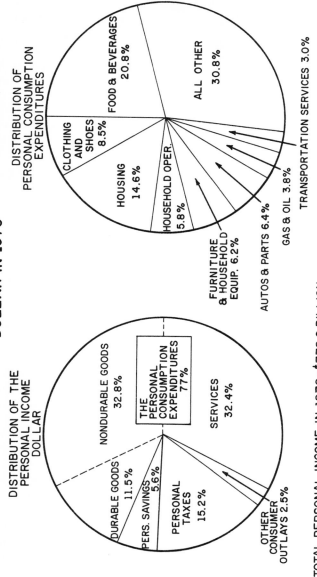

DISTRIBUTION OF PERSONAL CONSUMPTION EXPENDITURES

FOOD & BEVERAGES 20.8%

ALL OTHER 30.8%

CLOTHING AND SHOES 8.5%

HOUSING 14.6%

HOUSEHOLD OPER. 5.8%

FURNITURE & HOUSEHOLD EQUIP. 6.2%

AUTOS & PARTS 6.4%

GAS & OIL 3.8%

TRANSPORTATION SERVICES 3.0%

DISTRIBUTION OF THE PERSONAL INCOME DOLLAR

NONDURABLE GOODS 32.8%

THE PERSONAL CONSUMPTION EXPENDITURES 77%

SERVICES 32.4%

DURABLE GOODS 11.5%

PERS. SAVINGS 5.6%

PERSONAL TAXES 15.2%

OTHER CONSUMER OUTLAYS 2.5%

TOTAL PERSONAL INCOME IN 1970-$778.6 BILLION

*END OF 1st QUARTER 1970

Source: U.S. Department of Commerce, Office of Business Economics

CHART 3-3

which your present allocation of income is meeting future economic needs. These three plans are:

1. a retirement plan;
2. an active duty survivorship plan; and
3. a retirement survivorship plan.

Chapters 11, 12, and 13 discuss how to construct these plans.

STEP 6 is to reallocate income based on your evaluation of the above three plans. Your evaluation will give you a ready picture of how well your existing allocation of income is providing for future contingencies. You may find that your future needs are not adequately provided for, and that balancing at the margin would clearly require the shifting of some dollars from current expenditures to insurance, savings, or investments. This would be true because the additional benefit your family derives from added future security is greater than the cost or sacrifice caused by the reduction in current consumption expenditures.

You may, however, find that reallocation should go the other way. You may find that an ambitious insurance salesman has saddled you with a tremendous amount of endowment insurance which does not suit your needs. By reconstructing your insurance and savings-investment program, you might be better able to provide for future needs and shift some dollars into current consumption where they will bring greater rewards.

STEP 7 is to reprogram the four graphical devices we have been using, based on the changes resulting from our analysis in Step 6. Your financial plan should now be constructed so that you cannot shift dollars from one category of use to another and say that you would derive greater benefit from the new allocation. Once this situation has been reached, you are ready to move on to the next step.

STEP 8 is: CARRY OUT YOUR PLAN! All your planning is to no avail if you refuse to carry it out. All you would accomplish would be to demonstrate systematically that you were acting in an irrational way. The importance of Step 8 cannot be overemphasized. If you base your financial plan on a systematic savings program and then, in one of life's weaker moments, blow your entire savings account on an around-the-world vacation, you may have a great time for a few days at the expense of a great deal of hardship in retirement years.

Finally, as STEP 9, you must periodically review your financial plan. It is wise to perform this re-evaluation once a year—perhaps after you calculate your income tax. At a minimum, your financial plan should be re-evaluated each time your family experiences a major change affecting family finances. Such changes include the addition of new members to the family, the death of members of the family, receipt of significant inheritances, a change in station which forces a significant change in income or expenditures, and so on.

If you ignore the responsibility for periodic re-evaluation, the price will be some amount of foolishness in your spending, or if a major change has occurred, the possibility that a major peril to family financial security is not being properly provided for. It should be pointed out that, in general, Servicemen are notorious mismanagers of their personal finances. Even high-ranking officers have managed to leave their widows destitute. A little time spent in planning, coupled with the discipline to stick to the plan, can prevent such a tragedy. We believe that adequately providing for the economic needs of the family is the duty of the Armed Forces officer.

What you must attempt to do is to make decisions as rationally as the uncertainties of life will permit. To be rational, you must have some idea of how much uncertainty is associated with each of your decisions, and determine how to best protect your family against the risks prevailing. For example, you do not know when you will die. Yet you know that there is a risk of dying within the next five years. If you were to die within the next five years, the loss of your income to your family might mean economic disaster. You might thus decide to protect your family against this risk by purchasing life insurance. In so doing, economic uncertainty is converted to economic certainty. For a known premium, you can eliminate the risk of financial disaster.

Note that if you survive the five-year period, you should not complain that you had made a bad decision because you could have put the amount spent on premiums into a savings-investment program. Since the future could not be predicted, you could not allocate income in the way hindsight indicates to be optimum.

Decisions must be made in an environment of uncertainty and you must allow for the risks you face as rationally as you can, using the experience of the past as a guide.

FAMILY FINANCIAL STATEMENTS

Individuals, like business firms, can use two primary financial statements to assist them in evaluating their financial condition: the Income Statement (otherwise known as a Profit and Loss Statement or an Earnings Report) and the Balance Sheet. The Family Income and Expenditure Chart (Chart 3-2) corresponds to the Income Statement. It shows the flow of income and expenditures (costs) over a selected period of time. For the business firm, an excess of income over costs during the statement period is called profit. For the family, an excess of income over operating or consumption expenditures is called savings. Note that the Income Statement is a record of financial operating activities over a period of time.

Suppose that a family were to spend more than its income during any given period of time. Would this mean that the unit would be bankrupt? Not usually. Solvency would depend upon the effect the deficit had on the net worth. For example, if a family has no debts and a $10,000 savings account, a small deficit in the monthly budget would not have serious consequences. The deficit could easily be financed by reducing the size of an asset, such as the savings account.

In the terms of an accountant, because its assets exceed liabilities this family has a positive net worth. Assets are the things of value possessed by the family. Liabilities are the claims creditors have on those assets. Net worth is the residual claim the family has on the assets. Thus, Net Worth = Assets - Liabilities. If liabilities were to exceed assets, thus making net worth a negative figure, the family would then be considered insolvent or bankrupt. The Balance Sheet is the financial statement used to evaluate solvency.

The Balance Sheet is a financial statement showing the financial condition of a family or firm at any given instant. You can construct your own Family Balance Sheet by filling in Chart 3-4. In calculating this, you must take care to use the market value of furniture and the car, the cash surrender value of insurance policies, the cash value of savings and the like. If the total net worth of the family does not increase, you are neglecting major purchases, savings and provisions for security. Note that the transactions that are recorded on an Income Statement have a definite effect upon successive balance sheets. Thus, money saved out of monthly income and accumulated in a savings account would show up on the next Balance Sheet as an increase in assets (savings account) and, all else remaining equal, a corresponding increase in net worth.

The mark of a successful savings and investment program is successive increases in net worth. This is the means by which you can satisfy financial goals established by the family.

BUDGETARY CONTROL

What devices are available for budgetary control? Some families have used an envelope system. The paycheck is converted to cash and placed into envelopes for the various budgeted items. Other families use a strict bookkeeping system. The budgeted figures are written out and may not be exceeded during the income period. Other families use a checkbook or a combination savings account-checkbook system to keep tabs on how well the budget is being followed. For the officer, the government allotment system introduces another device which can be useful in budget management. The system which appears as one of the most useful to the officer is a government allotment-savings account-checkbook system.

THE GOVERNMENT ALLOTMENT SYSTEM

The Serviceman is authorized to have specified sums automatically deducted from his pay for certain purposes. These deductions, called allot-

Family Balance Sheet

DATE: _____

Assets		Liabilities	
Cash		Charge Accounts	_____
a. on Hand	_____	Other Bills Due	_____
b. in Checking Accounts	_____	Notes Payable	_____
c. in Savings Accounts	_____	Life Insurance Loans	_____
U. S. Govt. Bonds	_____	Accrued Interest Payable	_____
Corporate Bonds	_____	Accrued Taxes Payable	_____
Common Stocks	_____	Real Estate Mortgage	_____
Other Corporate Securities	_____	Chattel Mortgages	_____
Cash Value - Life Insurance	_____	Installment Debts	_____
Money Owed Me	_____	(Automobile, furniture, etc.)	
Real Estate Owned	_____		
Household Furnishings	_____		
Automobile	_____		
Other Personal Property	_____		
Other Assets (itemize)	_____		
Total Assets (Owned)	_____	Total Liabilities (Owed)	_____

Total Owned _____

- Total Owed _____

= Net Worth _____

CHART 3-4

ments, are classified differently by the Army and Air Force on the one hand, and the Navy and Marine Corps on the other. But allotments of pay by all Services are authorized for the same purposes and are subject to the same prohibitions.

Allotments are classified according to the purposes for which authorized. The Army and Air Force classify these as follows:

1. Class Q to provide support for the dependents of enlisted members in pay grades E-4 (4 years or less service), E-3 and below.

2. Class E for support of dependents, savings, payment of premiums on commercial life insurance, etc. Class E allotments may be made generally to:

a. An individual or a banking institution for the support of the Service member's dependents or to provide limited financial assistance to relatives not legally designated as dependents.

b. A banking institution or association for credit to a savings, checking, or trust account. Only one such allotment may be made by an individual.

c. The Internal Revenue Service for payment of delinquent Federal income taxes.

d. Lending agencies for repayment of loans obtained for the purchase of a home, including a mobile home or house trailer used as a residence.

e. A commercial life insurer for the payment of premiums for insurance on the life of the allotter, or for repayment of loans or interests thereon.

f. The U.S. Government for payment of indebtedness incurred by reason of defaulted notes guaranteed by the Federal Housing Administration or the Veterans Administration.

g. The U.S. Government for repayment of indebtedness incurred by overpayment of pay and allowances.

h. Army Emergency Relief, Navy Relief Society, or Air Force Aid Society for repayment of loans.

i. The American Red Cross for a loan repayment.

3. Class N for the payment of premiums of National Service Life Insurance and U.S. Government Life Insurance.

4. Class S to provide for depositing amounts to a member's savings deposit account (Class "E" in Air Force, "J" in Navy and Marine Corps).

5. Class B and B-1 for the purchase of U.S. Savings Bonds.

6. Class X to provide support of dependents under emergency conditions.

7. Class L to permit an enlisted member to authorize the finance officer to pay his net pay and allowances to the member's designated dependent(s) or to a bank or savings institution for credit to the member's account.

It is recommended that you consider using allotments to pay life insurance premiums and to allocate funds to your savings-investment program. If this is done, your "take-home" pay will be net of your income tax and Social Security taxes withheld, life insurance premiums, and systematic savings. You may encounter one difficulty in this regard. At the present time, one cannot send more than one allotment to a bank or savings institution. You cannot allot to a savings association and to the bank in which you maintain a checking account unless one allotment is sent to the bank in the name of your wife for "support" reasons. However, you may have one allotment sent to a checking or savings account and have the remainder or unallotted portion of your pay (your local payment) sent to another banking institution rather than directly to you.

This can be accomplished through an allotment and by instructing your Finance Office to send the remainder of your paycheck directly to your bank for deposit into your account (or your joint account or wife's account).

If you find that restrictions on allotments make certain uses impossible, you can automatically write checks when your pay is deposited, or you might be able to use automatic transfer services provided by your bank. In this latter case the bank will agree to automatically transfer a portion of your checking account allotment to a savings account. In any event, make it difficult to withdraw funds from your savings program unless such a withdrawal is in accordance with your financial plan.

We may conclude that by using allotments and automatically written checks in conjunction with a savings account which can maintain cash reserves for emergencies and set-aside payments, one can maintain rather tight budgetary control without the necessity of keeping cumbersome records of each expenditure. At the end of each quarter or other convenient interval, a few minutes spent looking through your bank account books will quickly reveal how well you are meeting your budget. If you find that you are spending more than your income, a new appraisal is in order. If you find that you are able to stay consistently under a budget figure, try to transfer the unused funds into your savings account until your next periodic review. At that time, you might want to draw up a new budget which better reflects an optimum allocation of income for your family.

American Bankers Association. *Personal Money Management.* New York: American Bankers Association, 1967.

*Cohen, Jerome B. and Arthur W. Hanson. *Personal Finance.* 3d ed. Homewood, Illinois: Richard D. Irwin, Inc., 1969.

*Donaldson, Elvin F. and John K. Pfahl. *Personal Finance.* 4th ed. New York: The Ronald Press Company, 1969.

First National City Bank of N.Y. *Spending Guide.* New York: First National City Bank (n.d.)

Kinney, Jean and Cle Kinney. *How to Get 20 to 90% Off On Everything You Buy.* New York: Parker Publishing Company, Inc., 1968.

*Phillips, Elmo Bryant and Sylvia Lane. *Personal Finance.* 2nd ed. New York: John Wiley and Sons, Inc., 1969.

*Rodda, William H. and Edward A. Nelson. *Managing Personal Finances.*Englewood Cliffs, N.J.: Prentice-Hall, Inc., 1969.

*Troelstrup, Arch W. *Consumer Problems and Personal Finance.* 3rd ed. New York: McGraw-Hill Book Company, 1969.

*Unger, Maurice A. and Harold A. Wolf. *Personal Finance.* 2nd ed. Boston: Allyn and Bacon, Inc., 1969.

Excellent monthly consumer information magazines are:

Changing Times. The Kiplinger Washington Editors, Inc., Editors Park, Md., 20782.

Consumer Reports. Consumers Union of U.S., Inc., Mount Vernon, N.Y. 10550.

*Standard personal finance texts referred to in succeeding bibliographies.

*The best tax is the one the
other fellow pays.*

CHAPTER **4**

TAXES

ONE ITEM of income allocation which unfortunately cannot be subjected to critical review through the process of marginal analysis is that which goes to Federal, State, and local governments in taxes. Servicemen are subject to Federal income and Social Security taxes, certain taxes levied by the State and local areas in which they reside, and certain taxes levied by the State of their domicile. The purpose of this chapter is to point out some of the major obligations and exemptions applicable to officers.

PERSONAL RESPONSIBILITIES

Many individuals have special tax problems and general rules do not apply uniformly in every case. Thus it is wise to consult your Legal Assistance Officer or other competent tax authority on matters that may be peculiar to your individual tax problem. From a personal finance point of view, you should make sure that you pay in taxes everything that the law requires of you, but nothing more.

In other words, the taxpayer should attempt to avoid incurring tax liabilities, but should be sure not to evade them. Tax avoidance is proper and is expected by tax officials. It is accomplished through careful planning and knowledge of how tax laws should be applied. Tax evasion, such as making false claims to tax authorities in order to reduce taxes paid, is illegal. To meet your responsibilities in this area, you should learn how the tax laws apply to you, keep adequate records for tax authorities, plan to avoid all unnecessary tax liabilities, and submit accurately completed tax forms as required.

FEDERAL INCOME TAX

The Federal income tax structure is extremely complicated. It is based upon the Internal Revenue Code, official rulings, and the decisions of the tax and other Federal courts. For the typical officer, however, the calculation of Federal income tax liability is not too difficult. All members of the Armed Forces are subject to the monthly withholding tax. You may get a current income tax withholding table from the local Internal Revenue Service Office. An example of such a table is included as Table C-8 in the Appendix.

You are required to file a statement (Form W-4) with your Finance Office recording the number of dependents you wish to claim for withholding purposes. You cannot declare more dependents than you actually have, but if you wish to compensate for investment income, etc., on which no tax is withheld, you are permitted to declare fewer dependents than you actually have.

Most officers prefer to have their withheld taxes equal their actual tax liability so as to avoid additional tax payments and the necessity of filing a Form 1040-ES used by the Internal Revenue Service for periodically collecting any tax due in excess of the taxes being withheld from you. Since no income taxes are automatically withheld while serving in a combat zone, it is often advisable that officers, who are limited to a $500 exemption, request withholding in order to avoid the hardship of having to meet their tax liability with a lump sum payment.

Tax-Forgiveness. The Internal Revenue Code provides a tax-forgiveness provision for members whose death results from service in a combat zone. This tax-forgiveness applies not only to income for the taxable year in which the member dies, but also for any prior year ending on or after the first day he served in a combat zone after 24 June 1950. Furthermore, any tax liability outstanding against such a member at the time of his death shall be cancelled or abated.

Filing A Tax Return. All officers must file a tax return with either the nearest District Office of the Internal Revenue Service or with the one nearest the officer's permanent home (domicile). Income tax returns and final payments become due on 15 April.

Military personnel and government employees returning from Vietnam are allowed to file income tax returns after the normal April 15 deadline provided they do so within 180 days after departing that country. Also, these personnel are exempt from paying interest on the tax as long as the return is filed within the extension period. However, not all computers of the Internal Revenue Service know of this interest exemption, and send out penalty bills anyway. If you receive a bill for penalty interest and don't think you should pay it, see your Legal Assistance Officer.

During January of each year, you should receive a Withholding Statement (Form W-2) from your Finance office. This form will state your taxable income, income tax withheld, and Social Security tax (FICA) withheld. By using the applicable pay tables, you should verify that your Form W-2 is correct. To verify your taxable income (wages paid subject to withholding), you must calculate the pay you received in the following categories:

1. Basic pay to include longevity pay. (Note: Enlisted men and warrant officers are not taxed on any Service pay received while in a combat zone. Officers may exclude $500 a month during any part of which they served in the combat zone.)

2. Special pay (Medical, Dental, Veterinary, Foreign and Sea Duty, Proficiency, Diving, Responsibility, and Hostile Fire).

3. Incentive pay for hazardous duty (Flight, Parachute, Demolition, Leprosarium, Thermal Stress, Human Acceleration or Deceleration Tests).

4. Interest on Soldiers', Sailors', or Airmens' deposits.

5. Readjustment pay.

6. Severance pay (except for disability).

7. Dislocation allowances.

8. Lump-sum payments for unused accrued leave.

9. Enlistment allowances and reenlistment bonuses.

10. Specialists' rating pay.

11. Mileage allowances for yourself and your dependents and allowances for temporary duty travel which are deemed to be "expenses that are accounted for by your employer" and need not be reported unless the amount of reimbursement exceeds the actual expenses, in which case you must report the excess as income. However, there may be situations (TDY over 30 days at an installation) where the expenses incurred exceed the reimbursement, in which case it would be to your advantage to report the income and expense.

The figure you arrive at should agree with that figure on your Form W-2 (except for the amount in item 11).

The following items are excluded from taxable income and should not be reported on the Form W-2:

1. Basic allowance for quarters.

2. Subsistence allowances.

3. Value of quarters and subsistence received in kind.

4. Oversea station allowances.
5. Allowances received for uniforms.
6. State bonuses paid for military service.
7. Mustering out pay.
8. Dividends on Government insurance.
9. Personal money allowances.
10. Travel allowances (other than dislocation allowance).
11. Family separation allowances.
12. Combat zone pay (when combat zone exclusion applies).
13. Sick pay (after the first 30 days if not combat-connected).
14. Forfeiture of pay (to be deducted from basic pay).
15. Detention of pay (taxable when actually paid).
16. Death gratuity.

It should be pointed out that this is also an excellent time to verify that the pay you received during the year was the pay that you should have received. In the process of verifying this, you can check the amounts of income tax and FICA withheld against the current tables to verify that these are the amounts that should have been withheld. A FICA table is included as Appendix Table C-10.

Once you have verified that the information on your Form W-2 is correct, you may complete your Form 1040 tax return.

The Form 1040 is a single sheet upon which you may report your income, withholdings, deductions, and exemptions. Supporting schedules may be attached according to the needs of the individual taxpayer. Each year you will receive an instruction booklet accompanying your tax return forms. If this does not supply the detail you need to complete your tax return, refer to the income tax aids listed in the bibliography. If you still have questions, your Legal Assistance Officer and officials of the Internal Revenue Service stand ready to help you.

STATE AND LOCAL TAXING AUTHORITIES

Members of the Armed Forces, like all citizens of the United States, are subject to state taxes unless state laws specifically exempt them from all or part of their tax liabilities while they are in the Service. The problem each Serviceman faces is knowing to which state he is obligated and for what taxes.

Domicile and Residence. Before setting down a few rules to guide you in determining your liabilities, there are definitions you must know. There are two legal words which define your relationship with a state or territory or the District of Columbia—domicile and residence. There is a third term—legal residence—that fits somewhere between these two.

1. *Residence* is established in a state by residing in that state. About all you have to do is pack up some or all of your belongings and

move there. Residence involves your physical presence, or the presence of your living quarters from which you may be briefly absent. If you are living in government quarters on a Service installation you are usually a resident of the state in which that installation is located.

2. *Domicile* is a broader term that includes residence and other factors. Actual or physical residence, however, is not essential to retain domicile after domicile is once acquired. Domicile involves residence plus intent to remain. By being born a citizen of the United States, you acquire a domicile in a state or territory, and keep that domicile until you move to another state and deliberately choose to move your domicile there. No court action is involved in the change—just your intent to abandon one domicile and assume another. A naturalized citizen chooses the state of his domicile.

3. *Legal Residence* is a term often used to mean domicile or to differentiate from temporary residence. It comes up frequently in the case of dependents. Generally speaking, your wife becomes the legal resident of your state of domicile when she marries you. Similarly, your children are legal residents of your state of domicile. It is not necessary that your wife or children ever reside in your state of domicile for them to become legal residents. For example, if you are born and brought up in Connecticut and enter the Service from that state you might marry a girl from Nebraska and have children born in four other states or overseas and never be stationed in or even visit the State of Connecticut. Nevertheless, your dependents are all legal residents of the State of Connecticut. It is their state of domicile until you establish a new domicile or until they independently establish domiciles.

Everyone has a legal residence somewhere and only one at any given time. This legal residence may be in the state where a person was born, i.e., domicile of origin, or it may be at a place he has chosen, i.e., domicile of choice. Once established, legal residence continues until legally changed. One legal residence is not legally abandoned until a new one is established.

The legal residence of your father at the time you were born is your domicile of origin. If your father moved before you attained the age of 21 years, your legal residence changed coincident with that of your father, unless you left your home at an earlier time. The legal residence of the mother is irrelevant, since the mother acquires the father's legal residence at the time of the marriage. Legal residence changes only by a voluntary and positive action. A mere attempt or desire to make a change is not sufficient. As a general rule, the acquisition of the domicile of choice is accomplished by being physically present at the place where legal residence is sought with the intention of both abandoning the former domicile and remaining in the new indefinitely (or with no present intention of moving therefrom).

The three elements of physical presence, abandonment of the old domicile, and intent to remain indefinitely in the new domicile must be entertained concurrently. Actual physical presence is required to acquire a domicile of choice. Once a person has established a legal residence in a particular place by being physically present there with the required intent, temporary absence does not cause legal residence to change. Also, a person whose presence at a place is not through free choice is not required to have a legal residence there merely because of his presence. Thus, Servicemen assigned to a particular post in a particular state do not ordinarily acquire legal residence at that post or even in that state. However, if the physical presence of a Serviceman at a place is accompanied also by a bonafide intent to remain there indefinitely, that place may become his legal residence.

In answering the question, "What is my legal residence?" each person must consider the facts of his own case. There is no hard and fast rule that applies to all cases. Certain factors should be considered. Some are more important than others, but each can be used as evidence of the intent of the Serviceman:

1. Place of birth.
2. Permanent place of abode.
3. Payment of state income taxes or payment of taxes on intangible personal property—this is excellent evidence of legal residence.
4. Voting by absentee ballot—one of the best tests.
5. State from which the Serviceman entered the military Service.
6. Consistent statement of legal or "permanent" address on Federal income tax returns and continuous filing in the same Internal Revenue district.
7. Filing with state authorities an approved certificate or other statement indicating legal residence.
8. Collecting veterans' benefits available:
    a. Bonus payments.
    b. Burial allowance.
    c. Domiciliary care.
    d. Educational benefits.
    e. Hospital care.
    f. Land settlement benefits.
    g. Loans.
    h. State civil service preference.
    i. State job preference.
    j. State unemployment benefits.
    k. Veterans' homes.

Thus it is possible for you to have a domicile in one state and a temporary residence in another or even two residences at once. Most of us in the Armed Forces are in this position while we are serving inside the United States.

Some Rules On State Tax Liabilities. The basic rule to remember is this: for taxation purposes, you lose neither residence nor domicile "solely by reason of being absent therefrom in compliance with military or naval orders;" nor shall a new residence or domicile be acquired solely by being physically present. Other rules which apply to you and your dependents are as follows:

1. Your state of domicile or legal residence may tax your Service income and any other income (such as dividends and interest) no matter how or where it is earned.

2. Your state of temporary residence (by virtue of military orders) may tax any income you or your dependents derive from services performed or sources within that state. Military pay may not be so taxed by the state of temporary residence.

3. Your state of temporary residence (by virtue of military orders) cannot tax your personal property located in the state. By the same token, your state of legal residence could tax you for this personal property. As a rule, however, a state does not attempt to tax your personal property that is not physically located within the state.

4. You are required to procure state automobile license tags from the state in which your real property is situated, without regard to your residence or domicile.

5. You are not required to procure state automobile license tags from the state in which you are temporarily residing (by virtue of military orders) provided your vehicle bears valid license plates issued by the state, territory or the District of Columbia of which you are a legal resident or in which you are domiciled.

6. If you procure your state automobile license tags from the state in which you are temporarily residing, you are required to pay only the registration fee. You are not required to pay any additional tax which is levied solely to raise income for the state.

State Taxes. Chart 4-1 indicates those states having income and sales taxes effective on 31 December 1969. Many of the states which levy income taxes exempt all or part of active-duty Service pay, or exempt such pay under certain conditions (e.g., during wartime). Retail sales taxes levied by many states must be paid by all purchasers, regardless of Service affiliation. Similar taxes may be levied by local taxing authorities. However, such taxes and other state and municipal taxes are deductible in computing Federal income tax.

In the past many persons were able to avoid payment of taxes due the states because the courts of one state refused to entertain suits for the collection of taxes due another state. However, the concept of "reciprocity" has evolved whereby more than half of the states now have laws requiring their courts to recognize and enforce the tax liabilities imposed by the other states.

As the states have become increasingly hard pressed for funds, they

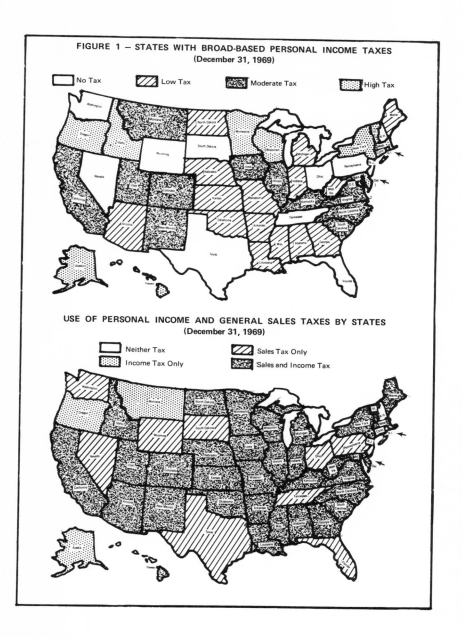

FIGURE 1 – STATES WITH BROAD-BASED PERSONAL INCOME TAXES
(December 31, 1969)

No Tax   Low Tax   Moderate Tax   High Tax

USE OF PERSONAL INCOME AND GENERAL SALES TAXES BY STATES
(December 31, 1969)

Neither Tax   Sales Tax Only
Income Tax Only   Sales and Income Tax

SOURCE: Advisory Commission on Intergovernmental Relations.

CHART 4-1

have increased their aggressiveness in the collection of taxes owed. All members of the Armed Forces have been required to state their "legal residence" so that the matching of individual W-2's and state of "legal residence" is now possible. Copies of the Federal W-2 forms, showing annual earnings by Servicemen and issued to every member of the Armed Forces are now being furnished to the following taxing authorities that have requested them: Alabama, Alaska, Arizona, Arkansas, California, Colorado, Delaware, District of Columbia, Georgia, Hawaii, Idaho, Indiana, Iowa, Kansas, Kentucky, Louisiana, Maryland, Massachusetts, Michigan, Minnesota, Mississippi, Missouri, Montana, Nebraska, New Mexico, New York, North Carolina, North Dakota, Oklahoma, Oregon, South Carolina, Utah, Vermont, Virginia, West Virginia, and Wisconsin.

Although state laws vary, pay earned in a combat zone and disability retired pay is generally tax-free. Many states follow the Federal government's combat zone exclusion, allowing $500 per month tax-free pay for all other officers. Also, many states defer the filing and payment of income taxes for those in Southeast Asia until 180 days after their return to the U.S. Some states that do have state income taxes also exempt all active duty pay and many others have individual exemptions varying from $1000 to $3000.

Absentee Servicemen (those somewhere overseas) in addition to those in combat zones come in for tax breaks in some states. For example, Louisiana exempts all Service pay outside the U.S. for the duration of the Vietnam conflict.

Many states have adopted the New York provision exempting income outside the state if the Serviceman (1) does not maintain an abode within the state, (2) does maintain one in some other place, and (3) does not spend more than 30 days in N.Y. Two catches in the New York provision are that income earned within New York is still taxable and living in government quarters outside the state does not count as an "abode."

Generally speaking, a Serviceman in a state other than his home state is liable to the state in which he's stationed for any income from non-military employment.

State laws often contain numerous provisions and exemptions. Servicemen should check with their state revenue department for details.

Local Taxes. The following local taxing authorities have also requested Federal W-2 Form information:

1. Alabama: Gadsden and Opelika.

2. Kentucky: Covington, Frankfort, Lexington, Louisville and Paducah.

3. Michigan: Battle Creek, Detroit, Flint, Grand Rapids, Highland Park, Lansing, Lapeer and Saginaw.

4. Missouri: Kansas City and St. Louis.

5. New York City.

6. Pennsylvania: Bradford, Chester, Lancaster, Lancaster County, Philadelphia, Pittsburgh and Wilkinsburg.

While Pennsylvania and Ohio have no state income taxes, over 1600 of their municipalities have local income taxes. However, both states exempt all Service pay from these local income taxes.

Retired Pay. Retired Servicemen pay no income tax on retired pay in Alaska, Arkansas, Hawaii, Michigan and Minnesota. Some states give partial tax exemptions for various reasons. These include: California, Colorado, Delaware, Maryland, Oklahoma, Oregon, South Carolina and Virginia. Disability pay is exempt in Alabama, Arizona, District of Columbia, Georgia, Idaho, Illinois, Indiana, Iowa, Kansas, Kentucky, Louisiana, Maryland, Maine, Mississippi, Missouri, Montana, Nebraska, New Mexico, New York, North Carolina, North Dakota, Puerto Rico, South Carolina, Utah, Vermont, Virginia, West Virginia and Wisconsin.

STATE BONUSES

Traditionally some states have paid bonuses to residents for wartime military service. As of the time of this writing seven states have enacted Vietnam-era state veterans' bonuses. They are:

1. Connecticut—claim forms may be obtained from the Office of the Treasurer, Vietnam Bonus Division, 15 Lewis St., Hartford, CT 06115. Deadline to apply for the bonus will be three years after the official termination of the Vietnam era.

2. Delaware—claim forms may be obtained from the Veteran's Military Pay Commission, 1224 King St., Wilmington, DE 19801. Deadline to apply for bonus will be one year after the cessation of hostilities in Vietnam.

3. Illinois—claim forms are available from the Illinois Veteran's Commission, 221 W. Jefferson St., Springfield, IL 62705. 1 July 1971 is the present application deadline but it may be extended again.

4. Louisiana—applications will not be available until the cessation of Vietnam hostilities.

5. Massachusetts—application forms may be obtained from the Vietnam Bonus Division, 23 Beacon St., Boston, MA 02133. There is no application deadline.

6. Pennsylvania—application forms may be obtained from the Vietnam Bonus Bureau, 900 Market St., Harrisburg, PA 17120. Deadline to apply will be two years beyond the date Congress sets as the end of the period of service to earn the Vietnam Service Medal.

7. South Dakota—claims will be processed by the South Dakota Veterans Department, Old Post Office Building, Pierre, SD 57501. Al-

though a Vietnam bonus has been approved, no payments can be made until funds are provided by the legislature. There is no application deadline.

Massachusetts is the only state with Korean War or World War II cash bonuses still payable. In all cases determination of eligibility rests with state authorities. To be eligible for a bonus, Armed Forces members and veterans must meet both service and residence requirements. When an enlisted person does not or cannot himself collect the bonus, the bonus to which he was entitled, or a larger sum, can be paid after his death to an eligible survivor. Even though there may be some doubt of eligibility, application should be made so that the responsible state authorities can pass on the claim.

Many states that do not traditionally authorize cash bonuses for veterans of periods of armed conflict do, however, offer other benefits, such as property tax advantages, special farm or home loans, and job preferences.

The purpose of the previous discussion on taxation and bonuses was to illustrate some of the advantages to which the Service member is entitled in the various taxing authorities. Obviously, state and local laws change frequently and the Service member should use the latest available data that he can obtain from state and local authorities.

Chase Manhattan Bank. *A Guide to U.S. Taxation of Foreign Nationals and Americans Abroad*. New York: The Chase Manhattan Bank, 1968.

Commerce Clearing House. *U.S. Master Tax Guide*. Chicago: Commerce Clearing House, Published annually.

Headquarters, Department of the Army. *State Bonuses for Wartime Service*. DA Pamphlet 360-609. Washington: U.S. Government Printing Office, 1969.

Internal Revenue Service. *Your Federal Income Tax*. Washington: U.S. Government Printing Office, Published annually.

J.K. Lasser Tax Institute. *J.K. Lasser's Your Income Tax*. New York: Simon and Schuster, Published annually.

Kohler, Heinz. *Economics: The Science of Scarcity*. Hinsdale, Illinois: Dryden Press, Inc., 1970. (Refer to Chapter 11 for an overview on government spending and taxation.)

Samuelson, Paul A. *Economics*. 8th ed. New York: McGraw-Hill, Inc., 1970. (Refer to Chapters 8 and 9 for an overview on government spending and taxation.)

*Let us all be happy and live within
our means, even if we have to borrow the
money to do it.*

—Artemus Ward

CHAPTER 5

CONSUMER CREDIT

MOST FAMILIES use debt at one time or another. In the past, going into debt for any reason was frowned upon. Later the use of consumer credit was grudgingly accepted. Today, the majority of American families use some type of installment credit. After all, how many Americans would own their own homes and automobiles today if they had not been able to finance these purchases through borrowing?

It is important to know how to make some basic decisions involving the use of credit. The major choices to make when obtaining credit involve its purpose, kind, source, and cost. You must also know and keep in mind the effect of indebtedness on your long-range financial plans, such as your active-duty survivorship plan.

PURPOSES OF CONSUMER CREDIT

Cash has always been the least expensive way to purchase. Yet credit is commonly used. There are two general purposes for using credit: convenience and necessity.

The use of certain forms of credit can bring added convenience to family financial operations. If you use interest-free 30-day charge accounts and credit cards, you can, without adding to the cost of goods purchased, reduce the amount of cash required in your wallet, use the telephone to order goods, and get a monthly statement of your purchases, a valuable aid to family record-keeping. In addition, sellers are generally more willing to accept returned goods when you have not paid cash. As long as you shop for goods at the lowest price, avoid the temptation to buy things just because credit is easy, and pay the bills soon enough to avoid service charges, the use of convenience credit can greatly simplify family financial operations.

The second purpose of credit is to meet financial emergencies which cannot be met with accumulated savings. Also, unless credit is used, several higher-priced durable goods simply could not be purchased. With credit, families can enjoy the advantages of durable goods while still paying for them.

When you constructed your Family Income and Expenditure Chart, you should have included a category of expenditure entitled "Set-asides for Future Expenditures." While there might be some families that can provide all needed goods out of accumulated savings, most younger families have insufficient accumulated savings to purchase everything they think they need. Thus credit must be used. To retire debts and pay interest charges, income allocated for set-asides must be used.

It is thus imperative that you integrate your purchases of expensive durables into your budget process. Usually, this will involve making a long-range plan for the acquisition of such goods. Your problem is to evaluate the benefits per dollar of durable goods along with those of all other budget items. You must ask whether the benefit derived from the income spent on payments for a car, refrigerator, washing machine, etc., exceeds the opportunity cost in terms of other purchases possible with the same funds.

Your evaluation of the benefit per dollar of the durable good can be weighed in the balance with the benefit per dollar—of food, clothing, security in retirement, etc., to determine the optimum allocation of your income. For example, the purchase of a washer-dryer combination might be under consideration. One family might decide that the convenience, time saved, and the addition to family net worth fully justifies the purchase of the combination. Another family, however, may decide that a weekly allocation of income for laundry service better suits its needs.

Still another family might decide that it should get the washing machine, but that a clothesline will suffice until the family has satisfied needs having a higher priority than the dryer. In each case, however, the family has balanced at the margin to determine the best allocation of income given the needs of that individual family. This is what your family must do, whether or not the use of credit is involved.

Before leaving this phase of our discussion, one factor bearing on marginal analysis should be pointed out. It is certainly easier to justify a credit purchase when use of the good can lead to savings in other budget areas. For example, a sewing machine may lead to savings on clothing costs that soon exceed the purchase price and interest charges on the machine.

Whenever you can determine that the purchase of a durable good will produce savings in excess of its cost within a reasonable length of time, the use of credit is justified. You must be careful, however, that you don't go broke saving money. Thus your long-range plan for acquiring durables should take into consideration the productivities of the goods planned for purchase. By purchasing the most productive ones first, the whole group can be acquired sooner.

KINDS OF CONSUMER CREDIT

From the consumer's point of view, indebtedness can be either mortgage debt (real estate debt) or short-term debt. Mortgage debt will be discussed in Chapter 7.

Of the short-term debt, there are two kinds: installment debt and non-installment debt. Installment debt, such as the typical automobile loan, is debt to be repaid in a series of installments. Non-installment loans are such things as charge accounts (such as those with gasoline companies), service credit (such as that extended by dentists, utility companies, and dry cleaners), and single-payment loans that are repaid in a single lump sum at the end of a specified time period.

Note that the distinction between installment and non-installment loans is not based upon how they *are* paid off, but upon how they legally mature. Thus a six-month single payment note from a bank could be paid off in equal monthly installments with interest computed on the unpaid balance, even though the borrower has the right to keep the full amount of the loan for the full six months. And on the other hand, the borrower should always retain the right to pay off the remaining balance of an installment loan without penalty and with an appropriate adjustment in interest charges.

There is tremendous variation in the kinds of credit contracts offered the consumer. An elaboration of the various types of loans and loan contracts is beyond the scope of this text. Therefore, only a few of the major characteristics of some of the most common types of credit are discussed along with the sources of credit below. The sources referred to in the bibliography contain more detailed information on these aspects of consumer credit. If at any time you cannot understand the provisions in a credit contract, ask your Legal Assistance Officer to help you before you sign the agreement.

There are a considerable number of persons and institutions in any community that stand ready to offer the officer credit. You, as an officer, are generally considered a good credit risk. But in the final analysis a credit rating is an individual thing.

You should attempt to cultivate as good a credit rating as possible by always promptly paying your bills. But do not allow any creditor to bully you into unjustified payments by threatening to destroy your credit rating. For example, some phonograph record clubs have been notorious for sending records after a member resigns from the club. Even after the ex-member returns the records to the sender, the bills keep rolling in. Chances are, the written requests of the now irritated ex-member to stop sending records and bills will be ignored, at least in so far as the sending of bills is concerned. Finally, the record company threatens to turn your account over to a collection agency unless you pay up immediately. Do not weaken!

If you have advised them of the situation once, that is sufficient. Even when the letters from the "collection agency" come rolling in, do not weaken! They will finally give up because they do not have a legitimate case. And they cannot destroy your credit rating. Only you can do that with a pattern of defaulting or delinquent payments of loans and bills. If any creditor attempts to treat you unethically or illegally, take the matter to your Legal Assistance Officer for advice.

SOURCES OF CREDIT AVAILABLE

Some sources of cash loans follow.

Commercial banks have become the largest source of consumer credit despite their late entry into this field. The money loaned by a commercial bank is obtained from the capital invested in it by its owners and from re-tained earnings, but most of it comes from the depositors.

Generally, banks have low loss rates on loans because of their strict credit standards. Usually, the more secured by collateral a loan is, the lower the interest rate is. For example, a personal loan, secured by the signature of the borrower, will carry a higher interest rate than a loan secured by col-lateral such as an automobile, securities, a life insurance policy or a savings account in the same bank. Rates of 8% to 18% are typical.

Industrial banks initially specialized in making loans to industrial em-ployees. However, they now make loans to all types of borrowers. In addi-tion, industrial banks today perform all of the functions of a commercial bank except checking accounts and trustee services. Generally, their loan rates of interest from 12% to 30% are higher than those of commercial banks, credit unions and life insurance companies, but lower than those of the small loan companies.

Mutual savings banks are found in only 18 states, primarily in New England. The various states differ in the services they allow the savings banks to perform. For example, New York limits its savings banks to ex-tending real estate, student, and passbook loans while some other states allow them to handle personal loans and even checking accounts as in commercial banks. Loan rates are typically 9% to 20%.

Savings and loan associations extend loans primarily on local real estate and are discussed in the chapter on housing.

Credit unions are cooperatives that lend to their members and operate under a federal or state charter. Eligibility for membership is usually reserved to those who work on or in a certain post, base, factory, institution, etc. Thus, most credit unions operating on military posts open their membership to only the post employees (and their dependents). When a member departs the post he may continue his membership account in the credit union but cannot open any new accounts at the station he has departed. However, he can begin new accounts at his present station if a credit union is available. The greatest advantage of borrowing from a credit union is its low 9%-12% interest rate. The loss experience is generally low because of the personal relationship between borrower, savers and the managers. Costs are low because the credit unions do not make profits, thus receiving tax advantages. Overhead costs are usually low because their office space is provided free.

Consumer finance companies specialize in making small personal cash loans to be repaid in installments. Household Finance Corporation and Beneficial Finance Corporation are examples of these companies. While state laws do regulate the rate of interest that finance companies may charge, the maximum interest permitted in many states is 42 percent, usually stated as 3.5 percent per month on the unpaid balance. The cost of servicing small loans, such as finance companies make, is often very high. However state laws usually prohibit additional charges such as fees, fines, or handling charges.

In some cases, lower interest rates are given to those with higher military rank reflecting the companies' preference in lending to those it thinks have the character and ability to repay the loan. Annual rates are typically 24%-42%.

Insurance companies will make loans against the cash surrender value of life insurance policies (other than term insurance). The cash surrender value of a policy may also be used as collateral in obtaining loans from other sources. A life insurance loan is attractive to the lender because little or no risk is involved; the money can be readily collected from the insurance company if the borrower defaults on the loan. If the borrower dies before the payment of the debt, the insurance company pays the debt and gives any remaining balance to the beneficiaries.

By law the insurance company must lend the cash surrender value to the insured if he so desires (but state laws also allow the companies to delay 3 to 6 months before giving up the money). Generally, the companies do not procrastinate in lending the money.

The company cannot force the borrower to pay the loan. As a result many people do not repay the loan and merely pay the low interest payments (or have the interest deducted from any remaining cash surrender value). Many consumers detest having to pay the company interest on their own money. However, the company quickly points out that the size of the premium is based on the assumption that the company will have the investment use of the money and that an interest charge is necessary if the premiums are not to be raised. Upon the death of the insured the beneficiary receives the face value of the policy less the amount of any loan outstanding. Annual loan rates are typically 4% to 6½% or at the "prime rate."

Pawnbrokers usually deal with people whose credit worthiness is very low. Borrowers pledge some type of collateral, such as jewelry or a camera in return for a small loan. The customers receive pawn tickets as evidence of their collateral. These must usually be redeemed within 2 months. Upon redemption, the loan, plus a fee of about 3% to 3.5% per month or 36% to 42% per annum must be paid in a lump sum. Sometimes a borrower may, by paying the pawn fees, extend the redemption deadline. If the collateral is not redeemed by the redemption date, the pawnbroker may sell it.

Rarely will the pawnbroker lend as much as 60 percent of the resale value of an item. The pawnbroker particularly likes the middle-income spendthrift who borrows prior to each payday, repays the loan, and borrows again. Then the pawnbroker can earn large fees by receiving and releasing the same jewelry or camera every few weeks. Obviously, a person who has learned how to budget will not fall into this trap.

Remedial loan societies were initially founded to counter the excesses of loan sharks and pawnbrokers. However, the remedial loan society is basically a pawnshop operated on a non-profit basis. The societies grant loans using pledged personal property as collateral. Although no credit investigations are used their rates of 12% to 24% are comparable with some bank loans. While the loans are generally made for a year, they may be renewed on request. If the loan is in default the collateral is auctioned. Any loss on the auction of the collateral is assumed by the society, but any surplus is returned to the borrower.

Loan sharks, also known as unlicensed or benevolent lenders, rely upon the need for hasty borrowing outside the law. Often a loan shark is a member of an organization to whose members he extends credit. Loan sharks in the armed services will often accommodate the needs of their "buddies" who require more money prior to payday or to cover gambling losses. For example, the loan shark may loan 4 dollars in return for a 5 dollar return on payday in 2 weeks. This 5 for 4 arrangement results in approximately a 650 percent annual rate.

The loan shark seldom puts the agreement in writing but uses a cover story such as a wager or supposed sale of an item to disguise the loan. The loan shark has a low loss rate due to strong-arm tactics and the reluctance of his customers to report him because they may wish to borrow again in the future. Loan rates of 1200% are not uncommon.

Credit may also be secured in ways other than through cash loans.

Charge Accounts. One of the major sources of credit is the seller from whom you buy goods or services. Many stores offer a variety of charge accounts to choose from. You should always arrange your credit so as to minimize the amount of interest or service charges you must pay. It is usually possible to purchase goods and services for which you will be billed on a monthly basis. If the bill is paid within a specified period of time, no service charge is made. In addition to charge accounts, many sellers offer conventional installment loans. Frequently, however, you can arrange to pay for a durable good at the cash price if you pay given installments within a 60 or 90-day period. In other words, systematic payment within 60 or 90 days is considered to be a cash purchase.

Revolving Charge Accounts. Many large retail stores offer revolving charge accounts on which no service charge is made when the monthly statement is paid within 30 days of the billing date. A service charge of 1 to 1½% per month is made on balances remaining over 30 days. Note that 1 to 1½% per month is equivalent to 12 to 18% per year.

Credit Cards. There are numerous types of credit cards in use which offer credit arrangements similar to the revolving charge accounts of retail stores.

1. *Limited Purpose Credit Cards* are offered by numerous airline and oil companies as an inducement to purchase their services and products.

2. *General Purpose Credit Cards* such as those issued by American Express and the Diners Club are also available. The above named charge an annual fee (approximately $15). Others such as Bankamericard and Unicard offer their cards free.

3. *Community Credit Cards* have been established by local banks. Under this arrangement, several merchants in the community agree to honor a credit card issued by the local bank. The bank will then bill the consumer for his various purchases just as a national credit card company would bill the user of its card, no matter where the purchases have been made.

Besides the risk of overspending as a result of the ease of credit using credit cards, there are other risks just as serious. If you lose your credit card, notify the store *immediately* so you are not held liable for unauthorized purchases by someone else using your card. A credit card can easily be used by anyone who finds it, regardless of the name on it. Therefore, the finder of your card might run up a large bill for which you are responsible unless you notify the company. Some companies hold you responsible for any such unauthorized use up to 30 days beyond your notification to them of the loss. When possible send the company a telegram.

This will give both the store and you a written record of the time and date of your notification.

The fact that there are several alternative sources of credit should make the necessity for shopping around obvious. It doesn't make much sense to shop for the best price on a new refrigerator and then finance it with an expensive installment loan. Why not get both the most favorable price *and* the most favorable financing?

There are three primary factors to consider when choosing the source of your credit: the reliability of the lender, the terms or conditions of the loan, and the cost of the loan. You can usually tell if the lender is unreliable. If there is doubt in your mind, consult the loan department of a commercial bank or your Legal Assistance Officer.

Normally, you should offer the best security possible, since the best lenders give the lowest rates on good security. For example, one of the most favorable loans available is a commercial bank demand note (promissory note payable on demand of the lender) secured by stocks or bonds. This note is callable which means that the bank may cancel it; but if this should happen you can then use your securities to get another although more expensive loan. In the meantime you will have saved money. Such a loan has the additional virtue of simplicity. The less complicated your loan arrangement, the better off you usually are.

TRUTH IN LENDING

Many loans have carried "add on" interest rates generally between 6 percent and 7 percent. Converting "add on" rates to "simple interest" meant the consumer actually paid roughly double the "add on" rate or about 12 or 14 percent.

Fortunately, Congress has helped clarify credit costs for the consumer. Under Title I of the Consumer Credit Protection Act of 1968 (the Truth in Lending Law), detailed in Federal Reserve Regulation Z effective 1 July 1969, the lender must tell the customer in writing how much he is paying for his credit and its relative cost in percentage terms. If the lender fails to inform the consumer of the *finance charge* and the *annual percentage rate,* the lender may be sued for twice the amount of the finance charge—for a minimum of $100.00, up to a maximum of $1000.00—plus court costs and attorney's fees. Lenders who willfully and knowingly violate the law are also subject to criminal penalties ranging up to a $5,000 fine and a year in jail. The finance charge is the total of all costs which the customer must pay for obtaining credit and normally includes:

1. Interest.
2. Loan fee.
3. Finders fee or similar charge.

4. Time price differential.

5. Amount paid as a discount.

6. Service, transaction, or carrying charges.

7. Points.

8. Appraisal fee (except in real estate transactions).

9. Premium for credit or other insurance, should this be a condition for giving credit.

10. Investigation or credit report fee (except in real estate transactions).

However, some costs may be excluded from the finance charge, such as:

1. Taxes.

2. License fees.

3. Registration fees.

4. Certain title fees and other legal fees.

5. Some real estate closing fees.

The importance of the finance charge statement cannot be overemphasized. It helps you choose the best alternative among the following courses of action:

1. Wait until you can buy for cash, thereby saving the entire finance charge.

2. Determine if a loan from your bank or credit union might cost less than the store's finance charge.

3. Buy at another store where the finance charge is lower.

The law also requires lenders to tell you, in most transactions, the annual percentage rate you are being charged. For example, if a store says it will charge you 1.5 percent per month on the balance of the amount you owe, it also must tell you that 1.5 percent per month really amounts to 18 percent a year. This is a common department store interest charge.

Also, the law requires that the lender tell you the number of payments you must make, the amount of each payment, and the date each is due. In addition, if you mortgage your house (to make repairs or for any other reason, except to buy it) you have 3 working days to think over the transaction before it becomes final. If you decide to back out, you must notify the lender in writing within those 3 days. In buying a house, the lender doesn't have to tell you the amount of the finance charge, but he does have to tell you the annual rate of interest he is charging.

Where To Direct Complaints. Occasionally it is possible that a merchant or lender may make a mistake. However, should you point out his actuarial error or disregard of the regulations and still receive no satisfaction, you should direct your complaint to the appropriate agency.

From the list that follows, you will be able to tell which Federal Agency covers your particular complaint. Any questions you have should be directed to that agency. These agencies are also responsible for enforcing the Truth In Lending Law.

1. National Banks (banks that use "national" in their name).
   Comptroller of the Currency
   United States Treasury Department
   Washington, D.C. 20220

2. State Member Banks (members of the Federal Reserve System).
   Federal Reserve Bank serving the area in which the State member bank is located: Boston, New York, Philadelphia, Cleveland, Richmond, Atlanta, Chicago, St. Louis, Minneapolis, Kansas City, Dallas, San Francisco.

3. Nonmember Insured Banks (non-members of the Federal Reserve System).
   Division of Examination
   Federal Deposit Insurance Corp.
   550 Seventeenth St., N.W.
   Washington, D.C. 20429

4. Savings Institutions Insured by the FSLIC and Members of the FHLB System (except for Savings Banks insured by FDIC).
   Office of the General Counsel
   Federal Home Loan Bank Board
   101 Indiana Ave., N.W.
   Washington, D.C. 20552

5. Federal Credit Unions.
   Division of Examination and Accounting
   Bureau of Federal Credit Unions
   633 Indiana Ave., N.W.
   Washington, D.C. 20201

6. Creditors Subject to Civil Aeronautics Board.
   Director, Bureau of Enforcement
   Civil Aeronautics Board
   1825 Connecticut Avenue, N.W.
   Washington, D.C. 20428

7. Creditors Subject to Interstate Commerce Commission (interstate trucking companies and railroads).
   Office of Proceedings
   Interstate Commerce Commission
   Washington, D.C. 20523

8. Retail, Department Stores, Consumer Finance Companies, and All Other Creditors.
   Truth in Lending
   Federal Trade Commission
   Washington, D.C. 20580

Generally, number 8 above will be the agency involved in enforcing the complaints of the average consumer.

COMPUTING CREDIT COSTS

In certain situations where there are finance charges of $5.00 or less, loans of under $75.00 or for more than $25,000, or credit not covered by Regulation "Z" (such as securities accounts), the annual percentage rate does not have to be stated. Therefore, practice in computing the interest rate is still valuable.

First, let us consider come of the basic terms used in the mathematics of finance. Money paid for the use of money is called *interest*. The *principal* is the amount of money borrowed, the *time* is the period during which the borrower has use of the money, and the *interest rate* is the percent of the principal which is charged for its use per unit of time. *Simple interest* is interest computed entirely on the outstanding principal. The interest would be called *compound interest* if it were based on a principal which was increased each time interest was earned. To compute simple interest, simply multiply together the principal, rate, and time. Thus the simple-interest formula is stated as:

I = Prt where I is the simple interest in dollars;
  P is the principal in dollars;
  r is the rate per year expressed as a decimal; and
  t is the time expressed in years.

Now we can consider how to calculate the cost of a single-payment loan on which interest is computed on the unpaid balance. All we need do is apply the simple-interest rate formula to find the unknown quantity. For example, if we borrow $100 from a bank for 3 months, and then must pay to the bank $103, I = $3, P = $100, t = 3/12, and r = I/Pt = 3/100 (3/12) = .12 or 12%. Thus we know the total dollar cost of the loan including all charges is $3, and the effective interest rate is 12%.

Now let us consider the slightly more complicated problem of an installment loan on which interest becomes part of the amount of the loan. In this situation, any quoted interest rate could represent one of a number of things. Therefore, we must obtain other information before we can accurately compare loan costs. Specifically, we must know the cash price of the good being purchased, or the amount (principal) being loaned. Next, we must know the dollar cost of the credit, the number of equal payments to be paid, and the rate of payments expressed as a number of payment periods in one year. All these figures can be obtained from the lender. Do not let any lender avoid giving you all the information you request.

Here is an example of why this is important. Suppose you purchase a new reclining chair which has a stated cash price of $120. Suppose also that the seller offers to let you pay for the chair in six monthly installments with a carrying charge of "only 6%" added. He then computes the carrying charge as .06 ($120) = $7.20.

Note that the first misleading aspect of this procedure is that the 6%

quoted rate is equivalent to 12% per year; but there is a second factor involved. Since you must pay off the loan in installments, you do not have the use of the full principal for the full six months. The full amount of the loan will be outstanding for only one month. Thus the effective rate of interest is obviously greater than 12% per year.

What is the effective interest rate being charged for this loan? There are a number of ways we could answer this question. We will use what is called a "constant ratio formula" to calculate an effective interest rate which approximates the simple interest rate used above. The formula is:

$$R = \frac{2MI}{P(N+1)} \quad \text{where}$$

R is the effective interest rate per year expressed as a decimal;

M is the number of payment periods per year (12 for monthly payments, 52 for weekly payments, regardless of the number of payments actually made);

I is the interest charge (total cost of the loan) in dollars;

P is the net amount of the loan (cash price less any down payment); and

N is the number of monthly payments to be made after any down payment.

Applying this formula to our example above, we find the effective interest rate is:

$$R = \frac{2 \times 12 \times 7.20}{120(6+1)} = \frac{24 \times 7.20}{120 \times 7} = 20.6\%.$$

This, obviously, is considerably more than the quoted rate of 6%! By knowing both the dollar cost of the loan ($7.20) and the effective interest rate (20.6%), we are in a position to compare this offer of credit with other alternatives.

Let us, for example, compare it with the alternative of a 6% simple-interest installment loan obtained from our bank by putting up stock certificates as security. The bank stipulates that interest payments on the secured loan are payable monthly. Therefore, our monthly payments will be equal to $20 (1/6 of $120) plus the interest due. The payment schedule would look like this:

1st month:	$20 +	120 x .06 x 1/12	=	$20 +	$.60	=	$20.60
2nd month:	20 +	100 x .06 x 1/12	=	20 +	.50	=	20.50
3rd month:	20 +	80 x .06 x 1/12	=	20 +	.40	=	20.40
4th month:	20 +	60 x .06 x 1/12	=	20 +	.30	=	20.30
5th month:	20 +	40 x .06 x 1/12	=	20 +	.20	=	20.20
6th month:	20 +	20 x .06 x 1/12	=	20 +	.10	=	20.10
	Totals =			$120 +	2.10	=	122.10

Thus we see that instead of accepting the seller's offer of an installment loan quoted at 6% (but actually having an effective interest rate of 20.6% with a dollar cost of $7.20), we should borrow from our bank at 6% simple interest since the dollar cost over the six-month period is only $2.10. Thus we save $5.10 in interest.

This saving would be even greater if the installment loan were a "discounted" loan instead of an "add-on" loan. Since the proceeds of a discounted loan equal the principal minus the interest charge, a higher amount must be borrowed to net the cash needed for the purchase price. In our example of the $120 chair, $127.66 must be borrowed to receive $120 to pay for the chair.

$$(P - .06P = \$120; \text{ thus } P = \frac{\$120}{.94} = \$127.66).$$

In this case, we see that the dollar cost of the loan is $7.66, and that the effective annual interest rate would be:

$$\frac{2 \times 12 \times 7.66}{120 (6 + 1)} = 21.89\%.$$

Note that the effective interest rate on an "add-on" loan is almost double the quoted rate, and the rate on a discounted loan is even higher.

Chart 5-1 emphasizes these points by indicating the total dollar cost of three loans quoted at 6%. The 12% line (1% per month) is exactly double the 6% simple rate. Chart 5-2 shows the effective interest rate of the same loans. Both charts show that the total dollar cost of all the loans increases as the length of the loan period increases. Both also show that the cost differential between the 6% simply-interest loan and the add-on and discounted loans widens as the length of the loan period increases. This is especially true of the discounted loans which quickly become very expensive.

CREDIT LIFE INSURANCE

One more item should be pointed out before summing up this matter of the use of credit. Whenever you take on any significant indebtedness, you are not only affecting your short-term budget, but also your long-range financial plans. Assume, for example, that you take out an automobile loan for $3000. Any survivorship plan made out before incurring this debt would now be short of your life insurance goal by $3000. How can you prevent this from happening?

One alternative is to take out credit life insurance with the loan provided such insurance has no exclusions such as war or aviation clauses. In some cases, the insurance may already be included in the cost of the loan. In other cases, it can be added for an extra charge. If the charge for credit insurance from the source of your loan appears too high, you have the alternative of purchasing a declining-term insurance policy for the

COMPARATIVE DOLLAR COST OF
A $1000 INSTALLMENT LOAN

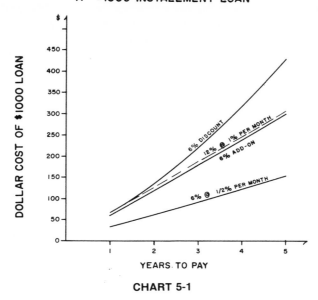

CHART 5-1

EFFECTIVE INTEREST RATES
FOR VARIOUS QUOTED RATES

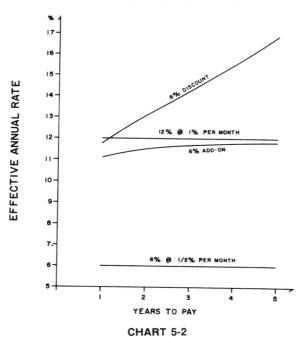

CHART 5-2

period of your indebtedness. In any event, be sure that assuming indebtedness does not hurt your family's long-range financial plans.

CHECKLIST ON BORROWING

Here is a checklist of rules on borrowing which is offered as advice on use of consumer credit.

(1) Never borrow unless you are sure of your ability to repay the loan. Integrate all of your loan payments into the set-aside portion of your budget.

(2) Borrow the smallest amount of cash which will cover your need.

(3) Shop for cash just as you would for any other commodity.

(4) Compare the costs of your alternative sources of credit.

(5) Offer the best security you have available to get the lowest possible cost.

(6) Avoid unlicensed or otherwise unreliable lenders.

(7) Know the exact borrowing terms; avoid undesirable clauses in your contract, and reserve the right of prepayment without penalty.

(8) Use convenience credit in such a way as to avoid service charges.

(9) Make all payments on time.

(10) Be sure your loan does not adversely affect your insurance program.

(11) If you are applying for a loan but do not need the funds until April, June or November—remember that interest costs start to accumulate when the loan starts—wait until you actually need the funds. Don't let interest accumulate needlessly.

The careful and planned use of consumer credit can add a great deal of additional satisfaction to your family's economic life. The irresponsible use of credit can bring financial disaster to a family and discredit to the officer. Take the time to be the master and not the slave.

Appropriate chapters in the standard personal finance texts listed in the bibliography for Chapter 3.

Credit Research Foundation. *Credit Management Handbook.* 2nd ed. Homewood, Illinois: Richard D. Irwin, Inc., 1969.

Federal Reserve Bank of Philadelphia. *Truth in Lending — What It Means For Consumer Credit.* Series for Economic Education (n.d.)

Federal Reserve Board. *What You Ought to Know About Truth In Lending, Consumer Credit Cost Disclosure.* (Federal Reserve Regulation Z) (n.d.)

Hart, William L. *Mathematics of Investment.* 4th ed. Boston: D. C. Heath and Company, 1969.

Bankers are just like anybody else,
except richer. —*Ogden Nash*

CHAPTER 6

BANKING SERVICES

FROM A personal finance point of view, you should understand the services offered by commercial banks, how to use those services and what they cost. Since commercial banks are competitive financial institutions, you should also have a reasonable method of deciding which one to do business with. The purpose of this chapter is to discuss briefly those factors which influence your selection of banking facilities. The mechanics of properly completing financial instruments such as checks, etc., are thoroughly explained in most standard texts in personal finance and will not be covered here. However, any commercial bank should be happy to give you a free copy of the American Bankers Association booklet, *Using Banking Services,* which would be a valuable aid in understanding the principles of using banking services.

THE AMERICAN BANKING SYSTEM

Commercial banks are owned by stockholders and are in business for profit. They are, however, subject to regulation by State and Federal Governments. A commercial bank chartered by the Federal Government has "National" in its name and must be a member of the Federal Reserve

System. It must operate in accordance with the rules and regulations prescribed by the Board of Governors of the Federal Reserve System and the Comptroller of the Currency who conducts examinations of National Banks to appraise their financial condition, soundness of operations, quality of management and compliance with existing laws, rules, and regulations.

State banks are regulated by state banking authorities which normally are not so demanding. If, however, the state bank is a member of the Federal Reserve System, it is subject to the System's regulation and examination. Approximately 45 percent of all commercial banks in the United States, holding approximately 85 percent of all deposits, are members of the Federal Reserve System.

Approximately 97 percent of the commercial banks in the United States are insured by the Federal Deposit Insurance Corporation. The FDIC pays off depositors up to $20,000 per account deposited in any insured bank that fails. All members of the Federal Reserve System are FDIC-insured. The safety of your money is enhanced if your bank is insured by the FDIC and is a member of the Federal Reserve System as well.

FUNCTIONS OF A BANK

Commercial banks perform a wide variety of services although not all banks provide as complete a range of services as others. The following functions are performed through commercial bank services:

1. *Safeguarding money and valuables* by providing checking accounts, savings accounts, and safe-deposit boxes;

2. *Transferring funds* using checking accounts, certified checks, official checks, travelers checks, money orders, bank drafts, and telegraphic or cable transfers;

3. *Making loans* such as personal, secured, installment, and mortgage loans;

4. *Providing trust services* by managing trusts and estates and providing financial and investment advice;

5. *Providing miscellaneous financial services* such as supplying currency and coin in denominations needed by the public, selling and redeeming U.S. Savings Bonds, and preparing cash payrolls for local business.

In addition, a number of enterprising banks are developing new services such as managing central charge accounts, offering automatic bill-paying systems and even travel bureau services. Some services, such as having funds transferred through use of a checking account, you will use quite frequently. Other services you will seldom or never use. On occasion your bank will be used as a reference if you are the subject of a credit investigation. The reference it gives, of course, will depend upon your demonstrated financial reliability. There are other worthwhile benefits through achieving a long-standing record of financial soundness and good character in your dealings with your bank. Many Servicemen, for example, go into business for themselves after they retire. Usually, such a venture requires a good deal of bank cooperation.

CHECKING ACCOUNTS

Commercial banks are financial institutions empowered to accept demand deposits—deposits subject to withdrawal by check. Generally no other financial institution can perform this function.

Most officers have no difficulty deciding that they want to establish a checking account with a commercial bank. Paying your bills by check has many advantages:

1. You avoid carrying large or bulky amounts of cash on your person.

2. You can pay the exact amount due in a convenient manner.

3. Checks provide you an automatic receipt useful as a legal document.

4. A checking account furnishes you with a record of receipts and payments.

5. Checks can be sent safely by regular mail.

6. Banks serve as collection agencies for deposit items.

The safety and convenience provided by checking accounts makes their use by the officer almost mandatory.

SELECTION OF A BANK

Traditionally, the selection of a bank involves four criteria.

1. *Your Money Must be Safe.* It is a good practice to review the most recent financial statements of a bank to judge for yourself whether the bank is in a sufficiently sound financial condition. In addition, it is advisable to consider only those banks which are subject to Federal regulation and in which your account is insured up to $20,000 by the FDIC.

2. *Convenience.* Years ago, convenience meant proximity—you had to have a local bank. Now, most banks are as close as your mailbox, and convenience involves having complete bank-by-mail facilities of all the services that you wish. Service families are frequently moved from place to place. The benefits derived from a continuing relationship with a full service bank no matter where you are stationed, coupled with the convenience and reliability of allotting your pay to one bank, seem to outweigh any advantages of dealing with a local bank. Some Servicemen prefer out-of-town banks even if they are less convenient for the reason that the bank has less

proximity to the Serviceman's Commanding Officer in the event of a misunderstanding or error by either party. This, however, is a value judgment you must make for yourself.

3. *Quality Service and Efficient Management.* Many banks are more familiar with the sometimes unusual requirements of Servicemen and are more eager than others to satisfy your needs. Some banks, for example, will not bounce a check without contacting you first. Others simply leave it to computers and clerks. Some military commanders place individuals who write a bad check on a control roster which can adversely affect promotion. Getting off a control roster can be difficult even if the bank bounced a check erroneously. Other qualitative measures of service are the speed with which your deposits are acknowledged, the ease with which loans may be obtained, and the efficiency with which any unusual problems are handled. Normally, competition among banks keeps the quality of service high, but if a particular bank does not provide high quality service, seek a better place to do business.

4. *Cost.* The cost of checking account services for any given account could run from nothing to $4 or more per month. No officer should feel "obligated" to maintain his account at a bank historically tied to his Service branch if the bank is costly or lacks quality service. A few "nonmilitary" banks now offer free checking accounts exclusively to military officers. Other banks also offer free checking accounts but usually only if you agree to maintain a minimum or average balance in the checking account or in a savings account. Certainly you should consider the saving account interest you could earn on any minimum or average balance required in a checking account solely to avoid service charges.

Barring qualitative differences, the selection of a bank should be on a least-cost basis. If all the banks you are considering are judged the same in regards to safety, convenience and efficiency, then you should select the one which provides the benefits you desire at the least cost. If there are discernible qualitative differences, then you must judge whether any additional benefits are worth the additional costs involved. If you find that the least-cost bank also provides unexcelled quality, then the decision required on a cost-effectiveness basis is obvious.

COST OF BANKING SERVICES

The dollar figures that you must consider in estimating the costs of banking services are:

1. The service charges on checking accounts.
2. The special service charges on individual services that you plan to use such as safe-deposit boxes, certified checks, etc.
3. The interest and charges you must pay for credit.
4. The interest you can earn on savings deposits.

The service charges applied to checking accounts can be calculated by the bank in a number of ways. Usually, however, the charge will vary with the number of transactions in the account and the average or minimum balance maintained in the account. One bank, for example, may charge a fixed fee depending on minimum balance. Another may simply charge a few cents for each check. Some banks have complicated schedules giving the charge to be applied at different combinations of minimum balances and transactions. Other banks give free checking accounts when the minimum balance in the account is maintained at a certain level, such as $200 or $300. Still other banks now offer free checking accounts with no minimum balance required. This might even include free personalized checks and postage both ways. In many foreign countries banks are permitted to pay interest on balances left in checking accounts. You might consider this when stationed outside the U.S. where even the branches of U.S. banks are allowed to follow the procedures of foreign countries and some pay interest on checking account balances. This practice, however, is illegal for banks within the United States.

To calculate the cost of maintaining a checking account, assume the number of monthly transactions you will make (usually 20 to 30), and the minimum or average balance you will maintain in your account, depending upon the criteria used by the bank to compute the service charge. Do not neglect the cost of the checks themselves (which may be $1 or more per 100) and the postage, if you bank by mail.

Special charges for individual services do not vary significantly from bank to bank. Unless you have an unusual requirement, such services will be used so seldom that their costs, when comparing banks, are negligible.

As pointed out in Chapter 5, most Service families have occasion to borrow money from time to time. You should thus examine the costs of:

1. Loans secured by stocks, bonds or life insurance cash values.
2. Personal (unsecured) loans.
3. Automobile or other special installment loans.
4. Callable loans.

Usually one of the most favorable rates available will be that offered by commercial banks. However, do not neglect the lending facilities of other financial institutions such as industrial banks, savings banks, savings and loan associations, etc. mentioned in Chapter 5.

Commercial banks are regulated in the amount of savings deposit interest they can pay. But, since there are several ways to apply the same interest rate, you should check the bank's practices. For example, if the bank computes interest on all funds from day of deposit to the day of withdrawal, it is more favorable than that computed on the minimum balance during each quarter. We shall delay our discussion of savings media, however, until Chapter 10. Suffice it to say at this point that any savings deposit interest you forego by using any particular bank account as opposed to another bank or financial institution must be considered a cost of doing business with your particular bank.

BANK ACCOUNTS AND MONEY MANAGEMENT

The balance you keep in your checking account should be sufficient to meet your monthly operating requirements. Keeping too much in your checking account incurs the opportunity cost of foregone interest. Keeping too little runs the risk of overdrawing the account or incurring undesirable service charges.

It is good procedure to have only one checkbook in the case of a joint account to preclude bouncing a check. Or it may be best for you to have two separate joint accounts even if each person writes checks on only one account. The growth of free checking accounts with no minimum balance makes this practice more desirable.

A savings account should be maintained as both an emergency fund and a depository for set-aside funds which will be withdrawn as your schedule requires. Funds thus have the opportunity to draw interest while they are being reserved for specific purposes. Your bank can transfer funds from one account to the other at your request.

The size of your savings account will also depend on your family's individual needs. Once it becomes larger than your needs require, you should then consider the alternative savings and investment media discussed in Chapter 10.

Appropriate chapters in the standard personal finance texts listed in bibliography for Chapter 3.

American Bankers Association. *Using Bank Services.* New York: ABA, 1969.

Board of Governors of the Federal Reserve System. *The Federal Reserve System Purposes and Functions.* Washington: U.S. Government Printing Office, 1963.

Department of Defense, Armed Forces Information Service. *Your Personal Affairs.* DOD Pamphlet PA-6A. Washington: U.S. Government Printing Office, 1968.

*The goodness of a house does not con-
sist in its lofty halls, but in its
excluding the weather.*
                         —Chinese Proverb

CHAPTER **7**

HOUSING

MOST SERVICEMEN change duty station several times during a career and thus are frequently confronted with the necessity of finding a place to live.

When Servicemen are about to retire from active duty, they normally want to settle down in a particular community. In this situation, the housing problem is somewhat different from the one they have faced throughout their active-duty careers. Nevertheless, the process by which the housing problem is solved remains basically the same.

Active-duty Servicemen have three alternative solutions to their housing problem: government housing, renting, or buying. At some stations, excellent government housing will be available. At other stations, you may be forced to decide whether to rent or buy. What you can rent ranges from small apartments to single-family houses. What you can buy ranges from mobile homes to cooperative apartments to single-family houses.

Your decision will be based upon what the housing market has available, your family's housing needs and wants at the particular time, and the amount you can reasonably afford. The available housing may be so limited that you may face little more than picking the lesser of the evils.

The purpose of this chapter is to point out very briefly some of the major economic factors to consider if you decide either to rent or buy housing facilities. The starting place for any analysis of the problem of housing is the family budget. When you constructed your Family Income and Expenditure Chart in Chapter 3, you integrated the values you placed upon housing with the values placed upon other family needs to come up with the allocation to housing.

This is a troublesome problem for the military family that moves from a low-cost to high-cost area. Comparable living conditions cost much more in the New York metropolitan area than in Eagle Pass, Texas. After several moves you may be forced to pay more for a reduced standard of living. Thus you must take a new look at your budget each time you change duty station. Generally, you should avoid allocating more than 25% of your monthly income to housing. If you are buying a house, you should try to avoid a cost greater than 2-1/2 times your annual income.

Once your range of alternatives becomes clear, you must select the best of the housing alternatives offered at the time you need the housing. In light of your determination of what constitutes adequate housing and what can be reasonably spent, you must choose the housing that offers the greatest anticipated benefit per dollar. This requires you to consciously examine your housing goals and the full net costs involved in any alternative, including in your comparisons any differentials in transportation, utility and maintenance costs, as well as tax advantages.

For additional information, refer to the sources listed in the bibliography. You should consult your Legal Assistance Officer before you sign any agreements to rent, lease, buy or sell housing facilities. If a check is given in deposit, do not write any notations on it; if you give a cash deposit, take only a receipt for the amount with no stipulation noted. Otherwise you may be legally liable to buy or rent the property.

RENTING

Generally, renting is more advantageous than buying if:

1. You expect the size of your family to change.

2. You do not have the initial down payment usually necessary when buying (or do not wish to lower your cash resources).

3. You do not wish to incur a large constant demand debt for 15 or more years fixed housing expenses.

4. You want lighter responsibilities regarding housing and do not wish to concern yourself with the worries caused by tax collectors, fuel bills, landscaping and yard maintenance, painters, insurance agents, etc.

5. You prefer to spend a larger portion of your income on new cars or entertainment.

6. You prefer to move frequently.

CHECKLIST FOR HOME RENTERS

At the end of this chapter we present a checklist for home-buyers. Much of the investigation buyers should perform is also applicable to the renter, especially that listed under NEIGHBORHOOD. In addition, the renter should make sure that he and the landlord agree in writing regarding the following technical details.

1. Who pays for utilities (water, gas, oil, electricity, garbage collection, etc)?

2. Who pays for the repairs that become necessary?

3. How much notice must be given before moving?

4. Is the rent fixed or can it be suddenly increased after you have moved in?

5. Do you have the right to sublet?

6. To what extent are you liable for damages to the house or property?

7. Is a deposit required, what does it cover, and how and when will you get it back?

8. Who pays for the taxes or the insurance covering damage to the building?

9. Are pets, pianos, etc. allowed?

10. Can you alter the house or apartment? If so, do the added cabinets, toolshed, etc. become the landlord's property?

11. Does the lease give the landlord unrestricted access to the property at any time?

12. Can the landlord put the property on continual public exhibition to prospective renters or buyers? You should try to limit this to 30 days before you vacate.

13. Is a military clause releasing you from your lease in the event of transfer or other Government reason included in your contract? A Serviceman should never sign a lease unless it includes a so-called military clause. A suggested wording is:

In the event the Tenant is or hereafter becomes a member of the United States Armed Forces, the Tenant may terminate this lease on thirty days written notice to the Landlord in any of the following events:

1. If the Tenant received permanent change of station orders to depart from the area where the premises are located.

2. If the Tenant is relieved from active duty.

3. If the Tenant has leased the property prior to arrival in the area and his orders are changed to a different area prior to occupancy of the property.

4. If the Tenant is assigned government quarters.

5. Other:

Be sure all the details are in writing. Do not rely on verbal promises. In addition, it is wise to check with former tenants or other people living in the neighborhood to find out the landlord's reputation regarding character, building maintenance, etc.

Also, you should check that there is an area for your washer and dryer if you have one. If you have to have your clothes done commercially you will have an added expense in the rental. The storage of a washer and dryer may also be an expense if they cannot be accommodated. If you own a refrigerator, range or dishwasher and these units came with the rental, will you have to pay to store appliances elsewhere?

BUYING A HOUSE

Unless you find the house that you want to live in after retiring, you usually must buy a house with the knowledge that you must sell it within a short period of time. Normally, reselling a house less than three years after purchase is a very costly operation, unless the market value of the house significantly appreciates. The required mobility needs of the Service member often outweigh the reasons most people consider the purchase of a house. These reasons consist of:

1. *A Form of Forced Savings.* Many people find it difficult to save, and building equity in a house is one means of saving.

2. *A Feeling of Security and Independence.* Rarely will the military man own a house that is fully paid and owned. However, if he owns a house, he will become a landlord for at least a portion of his career and bound up in the problems inherent in renting to others besides his own current housing problems.

3. *Tax Advantages.* The interest and property taxes paid by the buyer are deductible on his federal income tax form. Thus, the buyer can pass some of his housing costs on to the government.

4. *Neighborhood Environment.* Better neighborhoods tend to be located in areas where the houses are occupied by their owners.

5. *Space.* A homeowner usually has more privacy and space than a renter.

However, the disadvantages of home ownership are also important. The buyer should consider the inconvenience and added work and expenses of house maintenance as well as the possibility of losing money on the sale of a house either while it stands vacant or because prices may fall.

If you decide that buying a house is the best solution for a temporary housing problem, be sure to consider the following factors carefully.

Buying For Quick Resale. When you get your next PCS orders, you will probably want to sell your house quickly. Few officers can afford to make payments on a vacant house while paying for housing at a new location. Thus you should buy a popular style of house in a section of town where houses turn over quickly. Such a choice might conflict with some other considerations, but usually the necessity for a quick resale is over-riding.

If you were buying your retirement home, you would probably want to minimize your net cost by making a large down payment and paying off the mortgage in as short a period as possible. As a short-term buyer interested in quick resale, however, your situation is quite different.

Normally, you should put down as small a down payment as possible so that you will not have trouble getting your equity out when you want to sell. At the same time, you will want to extend your mortgage term as long as possible to hold down your monthly payments. In this manner, you will be in a position to offer your house to a larger number of prospective buyers. If they can pay you the down payment you ask, and then take over the payments on the loan already on the house, it is normally less expensive than obtaining completely new financing on the house.

Sometimes, however, your situation may be such that you would prefer to have the house refinanced. For example, you may want to buy a house from an individual having a considerable equity position in a home financed with a mortgage having an unusually low interest rate. If your financial situation is such that you can afford the large down payment and assume the low-cost loan, you may be able to achieve significant savings.

The only problem is that few other people are in a position to purchase outright your large equity in the house. Thus you must either face a greatly reduced buying market or force the buyer to completely refinance the house.

Unless you pay cash or make special arrangements with the seller, you will need a mortgage loan to finance your house. The most common type of mortgage today is the amortized or direct reduction loan. This type of loan requires the borrower to make a fixed monthly payment which includes interest on the loan, a partial reduction of principal, and, in many cases, an escrow payment which is a prorated portion of the annual taxes and insurance charges. As time passes, the interest portion of the monthly payment decreases and the amount applied to the principal correspondingly increases so that the entire loan is paid off at the end of the agreed upon period of time.

Types Of Mortgage Loans. Eligible Servicemen have four types of mortgage loans available:

1. The conventional loan.
2. The Federal Housing Administration (FHA) regular loan.
3. The FHA In-Service loan.
4. The Veterans Administration (VA) loan.

Before you purchase a house in any given area, you should fully investigate the availability and cost of each type of loan. The best one to use depends upon a large number of factors which include the prevailing interest rates, your long-range plans for buying homes in the future, and the willingness of lenders and sellers to deal with government bureaucracies. The following paragraphs will briefly describe these four types of loans. You must, of course, bear in mind that this information is based upon laws and regulations which are subject to change and, in some cases, also subject to local conditions. Get the advice of your Legal Assistance Officer and that of at least two available lending agencies before finally signing a mortgage note.

1. *Conventional Loans*. If you get a conventional loan, you offer two kinds of security: the mortgaged property and your own credit or investment worth. The great majority of single-family homes are financed with conventional loans. In this type of loan a financial institution lends its own money and takes the entire risk of loss. As a result, conventional loans are usually limited to 75 percent of the appraised value and run for shorter terms, rarely as long as 25 years.

The rate of interest on a conventional loan tends to be higher than an FHA or VA loan because the lender is assuming the entire risk. At the time of this writing conventional loans are carrying interest rates nationwide of 7 to 12 percent as against 8½ percent for FHA and VA loans. However, a strict comparison on this basis alone is not possible due to various factors including the charging of "points" (discussed later).

When comparing such loans, be sure to consider the loan provisions as well as the interest rates. Some lenders seek to include undesirable escrow arrangements, stiff penalties for late payments, and a large penalty for prepaying the mortgage. Make sure you understand the terms of the contract before signing it.

2. *FHA Loans*. An FHA loan is a private loan insured by the FHA. The FHA does not actually loan money. FHA merely insures the lending institution against loss on insured loans. The borrower pays .5 percent annually of the unpaid premium. If the borrower defaults, the FHA pays the lender certain losses—not in cash but in long term government bonds.

The most advantageous loan available to Servicemen is the FHA "In-Service" loan.

3. *FHA "In-Service" Loans*. To be eligible for such a loan, a Serviceman must be on active duty in any branch of the U.S. Armed Forces or Coast Guard and have at least two years' service. To obtain his loan, the Serviceman must follow the following procedure:

a. Obtain 3 copies of DD Form 802, "Request for and Certificate of Eligibility" from the commander in charge of his personnel records. When he decides on the house he wants to buy, he is ready to apply for the FHA loan.

b. Apply at any lending institution that makes FHA loans in the area in which the desired property is located. If the institution is willing to lend the money, it will submit the 3 copies of DD Form 802 and other required documents to the FHA for approval.

    c. Wait for FHA approval. The FHA will process the application in two steps:

        (1) Determination of property eligibility.

        (2) Determination of purchaser eligibility.

    Step c.(1) involves inspection and appraisal of the property. Step c.(2) requires determination of whether the Serviceman's income is adequate to carry the monthly payment load incidental to owning and occupying the house. When the lender receives FHA's commitment to insure the mortgage, it notifies the Serviceman that the funds are available for him to complete the purchase of the home.

    An FHA In-Service loan may be used for the purchase of an existing home or the construction of a new home, but may not be used to refinance a home already owned. The mortgage must cover a single-family dwelling. The Serviceman or his family must live in the house or certify that failure to do so is the result of military orders.

    The highest mortgage amount that FHA can insure is $30,000. The amount of the loan is also limited to 97% of the first $15,000 of FHA-appraised value, plus 90% of the next $5,000, plus 85% of FHA-appraised value over $20,000, up to the maximum amount of $30,000, if the property was approved for mortgage insurance prior to the start of construction or is more than one year old. If the property was not approved for mortgage insurance prior to the start of construction and is less than one year old, loan limits of 90% of the first $20,000 of FHA appraised value plus 85% of FHA appraised value in excess of $20,000 ($30,000 maximum) apply.

    Although the maximum loan is $30,000, no limit is placed upon the value of the house than can be purchased. The Serviceman, however, must make a large enough down payment to cover the difference between the maximum allowable loan and the cost of the house. This minimum cash investment required by law is $200, although initial payments for future taxes and insurance premiums can be credited toward this $200. Normally, the longest period for repayment of the loan is 30 years.

    The interest rates on FHA-insured mortgage loans vary from time to time according to the availability of funds. Since 1967, this rate has varied from 5¾ to 8½. Once a mortgage is insured, it continues to bear interest at the originally established rate.

    On all mortgages that it insures, the FHA charges a mortgage insurance premium of 1/2% annually on the average scheduled balance of premiums outstanding during the year. On In-Service loans, these premiums are paid by the Department of Defense as long as the Serviceman is on active duty during his period of ownership and occupancy of the home. The Serviceman may have more than one FHA loan on which DOD pays the insurance premium provided that he certifies that he cannot live in his other FHA-insured home(s) as a result of a military-directed transfer or move. Obviously, this implies that he has also been unable to sell the former houses at a reasonable price.

The government will pay the insurance premiums for two years after the death of the Serviceman or until his widow remarries or sells the property, whichever happens first.

One possible extra cost results from the fact that FHA does allow the buyer to pay an initial service charge, if the lender requires it. This charge cannot be more than 1% of the mortgage amount unless, for property under construction or to be constructed, the lender makes inspections and partial disbursements during construction, in which case the charge can be as much as 2½%.

It is easy to see that the lender and seller can make the cost of an FHA loan uncompetitive with that of the conventional loan. When this is done, the major reason for financing with an FHA loan becomes the lower required down payment, assuming that the extra charges have not nullified that advantage too.

If the Serviceman becomes ineligible for the FHA Section 222 loan by selling his house, be reason of death, retirement, or etc., his personnel unit must complete and process SS Form 803, Certificate of Termination. The individual is required to pay the 1/2% premium as soon as he becomes ineligible for the Section 222 loan.

Whenever a Serviceman retains an FHA loan after he becomes ineligible under Section 222, or whenever a Serviceman wants to finance additional property with FHA loans, he can apply for a regular FHA loan under Section 203 of the National Housing Act. Such a loan is basically the same as the Section 222 loan, except that the 1/2% insurance premium is paid by the individual instead of by the Department of Defense.

4. *VA Loans.* To those Servicemen who are eligible, the VA home loan is often the best of the four types of home financing. The principal advantages of VA loans (also referred to as GI loans) are the low or no downpayment, a reasonable maximum interest rate (varies with credit conditions as does the FHA interest rate), long maturity (up to 30 years), and no prepayment penalty.

The VA guarantees home loans made by private lenders to the extent of $12,500 or 60%, whichever is less. On other loans, VA guarantees the lender against loss up to 50 percent of the loan, with a maximum guarantee of $4,000 on real estate and up to $2,000 on non-real-estate loans. Under certain conditions, the VA will make direct loans to veterans. Note that although the VA requires no downpayment on a VA loan, private lenders may insist that one be made.

There are various classes of veterans and Servicemen eligible for VA loans. The eligibility for World War II veterans expired 25 July

1970. Korean veterans (those with at least 90 days active service or discharge by reason of disability between 27 June 1950 and 31 January 1955) are eligible for VA loans for 10 years from the date of discharge or release from active duty plus one year for each 3 months of active service. The eligibility of Korean veterans began expiring on 31 January 1965.

Post-Korean and Vietnam veterans (those with at least 181 days of active duty after 31 January 1955) and Servicemen who have served at least 2 years on active, even though not yet discharged, may be eligible for VA home loans.

Eligibility for post-Korean and Vietnam veterans will continue for 10 years from the date of discharge or release from the last period of active duty, plus one year for each 3 months of active duty not to exceed 20 years. If eligibility is based upon 2 years active duty, entitlement is available so long as the Serviceman remains on active duty without a break. The maximum terminal date for the use of eligibility is 20 years from the date of discharge or release from the last period of active duty.

If you believe that you are eligible for a VA loan, you should submit a VA Form 26-1800, "Request for Determination of Eligibility" with required documents to the VA to obtain a Certificate of Eligibility. This Certificate of Eligibility must be shown to the lender before he will commit himself to a VA loan.

If you believe that your eligibility for a VA loan is about to expire, apply for the loan even though a Certificate of Eligibility has not yet been obtained. Application from the lender must be received by the VA on or before the day your eligibility expires. The five steps in arranging a VA guaranteed loan are as follows:

1. Find the property suitable for your needs. Make your final decision to buy only if you are sure the price is right, the house is right, and you are completely satisfied in all respects.

2. Apply to a lending institution (such as a bank, savings and loan association, insurance company, or mortgage company) that makes the type of loan you wish to obtain.

3. Present your plan to the lender with your papers relating to all qualifying service and/or a Certificate of Eligibility. Lenders generally have the forms and other necessary papers required for the loan. If the lender turns down your request for a loan, see another lender. The fact that one lender is not interested in making the particular type of loan does not preclude the possibility that another may be.

4. If the lender accepts your application, the VA, at the request of the lender, arranges for an appraisal of the property to be sure that the price you pay is not excessive in the housing market prevailing at the time appraisal is made and also determines if the property meets acceptable standards of good construction. A point to remember is that the appraisal cannot indicate whether the purchase is wise or unwise, or what the resale

value may be at some future time. The VA-appraised value may not be the same as that made by the FHA or the lender.

5. As the result of the appraisal, VA will forward to the lender a Certificate of Reasonable Value which is the medium by which the reasonable value established by the VA for the property is made known to the lender. At this point, the lender will either make the loan or send the loan application, including the credit report, employment verification, copy of the executed sales contract, etc., to VA for approval. Closing costs must be paid in cash on all homes for which VA has issued appraisals after April 27, 1955. Closing expenses include items such as title evidence (search) costs, hazard insurance premiums, prepaid taxes, recording and the one percent fee required by lenders in lieu of other costs.

Post-Korean Conflict veterans must pay a fee of one-half of one percent of the amount of the loan to the lender who will remit to VA. Under certain conditions, the fee will not be required if the veteran or Serviceman, at the time of application, was also eligible for a loan based on World War II or Korean Conflict service. VA determines whether a fee is payable at the time the veteran applies for a certificate of eligibility. The certificate issued will indicate whether the fee is payable. If so, the fee may be paid in cash or included in the loan.

If you sell the property which secures your VA loan, remember that you will still be legally liable on that loan, even though you no longer will be the owner of the property, unless (a) your loan is paid in full in connection with the sale, or (b) the Veterans Administration releases you in writing from all future liability on the loan.

When you compare the costs of available loans, be sure you get all the costs involved. Ask each prospective lender to provide you with a written statement containing the following information:

Preliminary fees	$..........	
(appraisal, credit investigation, etc.)		
Down payment	....	
Closing Costs	....	
(Title search, legal fees, etc.)		
Total initial cost		$..........
Monthly mortgage payment	$..........	
Escrow payments for taxes	....	
Escrow payments for home insurance	....	
Other escrow charges		
Total monthly payments		$..........

Be sure the costs are fully itemized and complete. And again, have them in writing.

Also you should consider the monthly or annual costs of heating, services, utilities, repairs, redecorating, remodeling, assessments, etc., in deciding whether you will be able to consistently meet the payments each month or when due and in deciding on how much to borrow and for how long.

When credit conditions are tight, VA and FHA loans may be difficult to get. A lender cannot be compelled to make a particular kind of loan. But some lenders will offer better terms than others, and some will make VA or FHA loans when others will not. Therefore, systematically shopping around can save you a considerable amount of money. On commercial loans you may discover that mortgage companies and savings and loan associations require smaller down payments than insurance companies, commercial banks and savings banks. The lowest interest rates are usually given by insurance companies followed by savings banks, commercial banks, mortgage companies, and savings and loan associations in this order. The longest loan length is extended by insurance companies, followed by mortgage companies, savings and loans and then commercial banks. The different lending institutions also favor different priced houses—insurance companies preferring high-priced housing and savings and loan low-priced housing, the others preferring middle-priced housing. Obviously, the above comparisons are generalities which will differ depending upon the availability of money that the various institutions have in the geographical area in which you wish to borrow. You should also consult as many lenders as possible to find the best source of a loan. A home is probably the largest single expenditure you will have. A mistake here can cause you financial difficulties for life.

Points. There is an item of particular importance to the Serviceman in comparing the cost of the different types of mortgage loans. At times the rate of interest that lenders can charge on FHA, VA and conventional loans is lower than the rate required by lenders in the market. The lender thus charges discount points to make up the difference between the FHA or VA or legal maximum conventional interest rates and the yield he can get elsewhere in the market.

A point is one percent of the amount of the mortgage. For example, let us assume that the seller must pay 8 points on the mortgage or the lending institution will not agree to give the borrower the loan to buy the seller's house. If the borrower needs a mortgage of $20,000 then the seller must pay the bank 8% of $20,000 or $1600. If the buyer only needs $10,000, then it costs the seller $800. In such a situation, it is easy to see that the seller must either suffer a large loss in equity if he must pay points, pass on the point cost to the buyer by raising the price, or find a cash buyer. In some cases the buyer must pay all the points; in other cases, both parties pay some.

Remember that the point charge is over and above the interest rate and other charges on a loan. Also note that points are payable in advance—not on a pay-as-you-go basis as is the interest. Even if the points are paid off by the seller, you should consider this factor before becoming a buyer because it may affect your ability to resell the house at a reasonable price.

The VA does not permit buyers to pay points. Under FHA rules, points may not ordinarily be collected from home buyers. Thus they are collected from the seller or builder. To prevent their costs from increasing in this way, sellers or builders will often demand a higher price for the property if it is financed with an FHA loan. In this manner, the points are actually shifted to the buyer.

HOMEOWNERS ASSISTANCE PROGRAM

This program provides benefits to eligible Department of Defense (DOD) military and civilian personnel as well as to eligible personnel of other federal agencies serving or employed at or in connection with a military base or installation that has, subsequent to 1 Nov 64, been ordered to be closed in whole or in part. In accordance with established procedures, an eligible person may elect to:

a. Receive a cash payment as partial compensation for losses sustained in the private sale of his home,

b. Sell his home to DOD, or

c. Receive compensation for liabilities resulting from foreclosure action commenced by 3 Mar 67.

DOD requires that all applications for assistance under the program be given full consideration and that benefits under the program be extended to all homeowners who are determined to be entitled to assistance. The Personal Affairs Officer provides information on the program to military personnel.

A CHECKLIST FOR HOME-BUYERS

We close this chapter with an amended Veterans Administration check-list recommended for prospective home buyers.

CHARACTERISTICS OF PROPERTY (Proposed or existing construction)

NEIGHBORHOOD
Consider each of the following to determine whether the location of the property will satisfy your personal needs and preferences:
Convenience of transportation
Stores conveniently located
Elementary school conveniently located
Absence of excessive traffic noise
Absence of smoke and unpleasant odors

Play area available for children
Fire and police protection and garbage collection provided
Residential usage safeguarded by adequate zoning
Community taxes and assessments

LOT
Consider each of the following to determine whether the lot is sufficiently large and properly improved:

Size of front yard satisfactory
Size of rear and side yards satisfactory
Walks provide access to front and service entrances
Drive provides easy access to garbage
Lot appears to drain satisfactorily
Lawn and planting satisfactory
Septic tank (if any) in good operating condition

EXTERIOR DETAILS
Observe the exterior detail of neighboring houses and determine whether the house being considered is as good or better in respect to each of the following features:

Porches	Storm Sash
Terraces	Weather stripping
Garage	Screens
Gutters	Breezeway

INTERIOR DETAILS
Consider each of the following to determine whether the house will afford living accommodations which are sufficient to the needs and comfort of your family:

Check and double check the probable cost of heating and utilities
Rooms will accommodate desired furniture
Dining space sufficiently large
At least one closet in each bedroom
At least one coat closet and one linen closet
Convenient access to bathroom
Sufficient and convenient storage space (screens, trunks, boxes, off-season clothes, luggage, baby carriage, bicycle, wheel toys, etc.)
Kitchen well arranged and equipped
Laundry space ample and well located
Windows provide sufficient light and air
Sufficient number of electrical outlets

CONDITION OF EXISTING CONSTRUCTION
Resale value

EXTERIOR CONSTRUCTION
Inspect to see that the following appear to be in acceptable condition:

Wood porch floors and steps
Windows, doors, and screens
Gutters and wood cornice
Wood siding
Mortar joints
Roofing
Chimneys

Paint on exterior woodwork
General design and architecture

INTERIOR CONSTRUCTION

Check to see whether:

Plaster is free of excessive cracks
Plaster is free of stains caused by leaking roof or sidewalls
Door locks are in operating condition
Windows move freely
Fireplace works properly
Basement is dry and will resist moisture penetration
Mechanical equipment and electrical wiring and switches adequate and in operating condition
Type of heating equipment is suitable
There is adequate insulation in walls, floor, ceiling or roof
Floors are level and without cracks

The following appear to be in acceptable condition:

Wood floor finish
Linoleum floors
Sink top
Kitchen range
Bathroom and papering
Exposed joists and beams

ARE YOU SURE ...

That the basement will stay dry after heavy rains?
That the foundations are sound?
That there has been no termite damage?
That the title is free, clear and unencumbered?
You'd better get expert advice on the condition of existing construction, if you want to be sure the house is a good buy.

Appropriate chapters in the standard personal finance texts listed for Chapter 3.

Headquarters, Department of the Army. *Your Personal Affairs Handbook*. DA Pamphlet 608-2. Washington: U.S. Government Printing Office, August 1969.

Hoaglund, Henry E. and Leo D. Sloan. *Real Estate Finance*. 4th ed. Homewood, Illinois: Richard D. Irwin, Inc., 1969.

Marshall, Robert A. *Before You Buy a House*. Maplewood, N.J.: Hammond, Inc., 1969.

Smith, Carlton and Richard P. Pratt. *The Time-Life Book of Family Finance*. New York: Time-Life Books, 1969.

U.S. Savings and Loan League. *Savings and Loan Fact Book*. Chicago: U.S. Savings and Loan League Headquarters, Published annually.

Veterans Administration. *Home-Buying Veteran*. VA Pamphlet 26-6, Revised. Washington: Veterans Administration, January 1970.

————. *Pointers for the Veteran Homeowner*. VA Pamphlet 26-5, Revised. Washington: Veterans Administration, January 1969.

Except the American woman, nothing interests the eye of American man more than the automobile, or seems so important to him as an object of esthetic appreciation.
—A.H. Ban, Jr.

CHAPTER **8**

AUTOMOBILE COSTS AND INSURANCE

GRANTED THAT ownership of at least one automobile is essential in most families today, the attendant costs must be provided for in every family budget. For an indication of what portions of the personal income and consumer expenditure dollar were used for this in 1970 refer to Chart 3-3.

PURCHASE CONSIDERATIONS

How Expensive A Car? Generally, the higher the price of a car, the less return or benefit from the extra dollars spent. The lower-priced or compact vehicle provides comfortable transportation, safety and some style at lower operating cost. As you spend more money on larger automobiles you pay for greater weight, better upholstery, fancier trim and sometimes better mechanical features. However, the marginal return from each extra dollar spent tends to decrease, the more expensive the car becomes. While there is an increase in comfort, mechanical engineering, performance, and durability, marginal benefits do not increase as quickly as marginal costs.

The trade-in allowance on the larger cars is a smaller percentage of the original purchase price than on the medium or small-sized automobile. This reflects the fact that used car buyers tend to prefer less expensive and less complex automobiles. In general, used car buyers reflect the belief that the more costly and heavy a car is, the more expensive it is to maintain and repair.

For example, sample cost estimates in a garage mechanic's estimates manual were obtained. The replacement costs of a radiator grill on cars costing approximately $2200 (2900 lbs.), $3100 (3800 lbs.), and $6000 (4700 lbs.) averaged $25, $100, and $160 respectively. On fender replacement, the average costs were $100, $150, and $210. In some cases where the design of the car complicated the repair, the cost of labor far exceeded the cost of the materials used. This discussion will be pursued again later in this chapter in the discussion on automobile insurance.

What Options and Accessories? For each basic car shell, automobile makers offer several lines. Be careful to observe the real difference in specifications—you may find that the only difference between the Slushpump and the Slushpump Slinger is a $200 difference in paint, trim and upholstery.

Before you buy a model, sit in it. You may find yourself unable to sit up straight in a lower slung, more rakish and luxurious hardtop version costing $300 more than the sedan. If you like wearing a "wheel-type" military hat in your automobile, try wearing one while driving the contemplated low-slung model. You may find you need a lower slung hat or a higher slung model.

One of the most significant and costly options is the array of engines available. The higher the horsepower, the higher the engine price. At one point on the horsepower spectrum, the engines offered will need to be run on high-test gasoline. This results not only in a higher initial cost of the engine and car but also adds 4 cents to 7 cents cost to every gallon of gasoline during the life of the car. Furthermore, the cost of higher octane gasolines can be expected to rise as antipollution measures force the elimination of relatively inexpensive octane boosters such as lead.

Automatic transmissions and radios are usually sold as extras but are considered standard by many buyers and dealers. Together they add $250 to $300 to the cost of the car. The price of the car rapidly escalates when you add air conditioning at $300, power brakes at $50, power steering at $100, tinted glass, etc. You may find that the same options cost more at the bottom of the manufacturer's medium-priced line than at the top of his low-priced line. Try to limit yourself to only those extras that are genuinely useful. Remember, the cost of options will be increased further by the additional costs of insurance on these options.

Resale Values. You should be aware that only a few accessories add to the normal resale value of a car. The dealer will assume the car has a radio and subtracts from the resale value if a car does not have one. While air conditioning and power steering may add a few dollars to the resale value, most other accessories will not and are considered merely frosting on the cake. Generally, the more "normal" your car is, the better will be your percentage return at trade-in or resale.

One common dealer ploy is to describe the high demand on the Coasts for snappy and low sports models, hinting that he is selling the car to you so cheaply that you can easily drive it awhile and resell it for a quick profit. He may add that the car is being put out as a limited edition of only 15,000. The implication is that the price will stay up (or even rise) because the supply is limited and the demand is great. You should question the assumptions behind this analysis. The demand may not be so great—if it were, why hasn't the "so-called" limited edition already been fully subscribed? Manufacturers are in business to earn profits. Car manufacturers in our competitive markets can most readily do this through economies of mass. If the demand is greater than forecast, they will merely produce more at a larger profit since the dies of a car model are already a sunk cost.

Perhaps the car *is* a good seller on the Coast. Is it also a good seller at Fort Benning, Ga. or Fort Hood, Texas where other young officers may also be attempting to sell similar models? What will be the costs of getting the car to the Coast for resale if you are transferred directly from Fort Benning to Southeast Asia? Let us assume that you are able to sell the car on one of the Coasts. Will a dealer give you more than you paid for the car? Remember, he can order an unused one at cost directly from the factory. If you can sell the car to a private party you may be able to recoup most of your costs and possibly even turn a profit. Generally, few non-dealers turn a profit on car resales.

Officers going to Southeast Asia may be wise to avoid buying a car—or at most should consider an inexpensive used car that can be sold with small loss when they depart. A car left sitting in storage not only depreciates but deteriorates as well. The costs of storage can be high and unless you are dealing with a reputable company, you may find the battery, radio and wheels gone on your return. In some cases, graduates going to SEA may be wise to consider renting a car when needed for a weekend and using taxis for normal fare time.

FINANCING AUTO PURCHASES

For those who are able to pay cash, there is no problem. For the majority, however, financing the purchase of a car through monthly payments will be the only solution. Credit arrangements vary; shopping for the best terms available may result in a considerable saving. You should refer to the discussion on consumer credit in Chapter 5. The automobile dealer himself may offer you a financing plan, however, these are rarely as good as you can obtain through a bank or credit union. Automobile clubs and associations often make loans to members at rates just slightly higher than those of banks. Generally, a loan on a used car will carry an annual percentage rate of interest 2% to 3% higher than a new car loan. A car over 2 years old usually carries the highest rate.

It pays to shop for financing. For example, on a 3-year auto loan for $3000 the difference between a credit union or bank and a dealer loan may easily amount to $300. Some dealers make more money on the financing of a car than on its sale. There should never be any requirement that you must finance a car through the dealer.

Normally the lender will insist that you carry the normal insurance on the car he finances, since it is his collateral on the loan. In addition, the car buyer usually is forced to buy credit life insurance; this pays the lender the unpaid balance on the car if the buyer dies before completing all the payments.

AUTOMOBILE INSURANCE

Automobile insurance is a major factor in the present-day economy. Its impact is as widespread as the increased use of automobiles; it has cushioned or eliminated financial stress in countless accident cases. While the cost of this insurance to the individual is considerable, it is not out of proportion when the hazards of today's driving and the increased costs of repairs and of claims settlements are taken into account. Several items emphasize the importance of automobile insurance to the Serviceman.

First, financial responsibility and related laws in all the states have been enacted to protect the innocent victims of automobile accidents by requiring drivers to maintain an ability to furnish proof of financial responsibility. Failure to furnish proof of financial responsibility when required usually leads to a suspension or revocation of driving and registration privileges. The most practical way to meet the requirements is to have automobile liability insurance in at least the required limits.

Second, the states of Massachusetts, New York, and North Carolina require proof of liability insurance prior to the issuance of registration.

Third, the owner of a car is not permitted to operate a vehicle on most military posts or bases without a specified minimum of liability insurance.

Fourth, the owner of a car may have his car and other property attached in payment of damages, unless insurance is available to satisfy a judgment against him.

Fifth, if he is unfortunate enough to be subjected to the adverse publicity because he has hit a child or an aged person, or caused severe injury or damage, the resulting stigma can be relieved, at least in part, by an appropriate insurance payment.

Lastly, automobile insurance is important because of its appreciable cost. For a young unmarried male owner, annual cost may range from a low of approximately $50 to a high of over $1,000, depending on the coverages selected, the location of the car, his age, and driving record. This is the equivalent to the cost of $3,000 to $48,000 of life insurance taken out at age 21.

Unless the insurance is carried by a reliable company, the money spent for insurance is worse than wasted because of the lack of real protection. A good company provides adequate protection, and as a company policy, stands ready to assist the insured to the best of its ability within the terms of its contract. For these reasons, as much care should be exercised in selecting a company and the coverages for automobile insurance as for any other major insurance program.

Basic Coverages. There are 6 basic coverages of automobile insurance. Chart 8-1 summarizes these coverages.

1. *Bodily Injury Liability Insurance.* This coverage applies when your car injures or kills pedestrians, persons riding in other cars, or guests in your car. It is in force as long as your car is driven by you, members of your immediate family or others who drive your car with your permission. You and all members of your family are covered even while driving someone else's car if you have the owner's permission. When claims or suits are brought against you, Bodily Injury Liability Insurance provides protection in the form of legal defense, and if your insurance company agrees—or a court decides—that you are legally liable for the injury, the insuring company will pay bodily injury damages assessed against you up to the limits of the policy.

The minimum amount for which Bodily Injury Liability is written is $5,000/$10,000 which means that the insurance company assumes liability up to $5,000 in the case of the death or injury of one person, and up to

---

A SUMMARY CHART OF AUTOMOBILE INSURANCE COVERAGES

COVERAGES	PRINCIPAL APPLICATIONS	
Bodily Injury Coverages	Policyholder	Other Persons
— Bodily Injury Liability	NO	YES
— Medical Payments	YES	YES
— Protection Against Uninsured Motorists	YES	YES
Property Damage Coverages	Policyholder's Automobile	Property of Others
— Property Damage Liability	NO	YES
— Comprehensive Physical Damage	YES	NO
— Collision	YES	NO

SOURCE: Insurance Information Institute.

CHART 8-1

$10,000 in the case of the death or injury of two or more persons in each occurrence for which the insured is held liable.

Since the financial responsibility laws of most states require Liability insurance of at least $10,000/$20,000, this is the minimum coverage which should be carried by any Serviceman. However, since court awards are often much higher than this, car owners are advised to carry Bodily Injury limits of not less than $50,000/$100,000. The premium is usually about one-third higher than that for $10,000/$20,000. Still higher limits such as $100,000/$200,000 are available at rates so little higher than for $50,000/$100,000 that they may be considered well worth the cost.

2. *Medical Payments Insurance.* Medical Payments coverage provides for the payment, up to the limits of the policy, of all reasonable expenses incurred within one year from date of accident for medical, surgical, X-ray and dental services, including prosthetic devices, and necessary ambulance, hospital, professional nursing and funeral services:

a. To the named insured, spouse, and each relative resident in the same household who sustains bodily injury caused by accident while in, upon, entering into, alighting from or through being struck by an automobile or trailer; or

b. To or for any other person who sustains bodily injury caused by accident while occupying an insured car.

Medical Payments coverage is not written unless Bodily Injury Liability coverage is included in the policy. It is commonly written in limits of $1,000, $2,000 or $5,000 per person. In order to have Medical Payments insurance for accidents in all cars owned by an individual, it is necessary to have the coverage for each owned car.

Unlike liability insurance, medical payments are made by the insurance company to guests and friends injured in the insured car, regardless of legal liability. Also, the insured, spouse, and relatives resident in the same household are protected in case of accidental injuries or death while occupying or being struck by any automobile.

The advisability of Service personnel carrying Medical Payments insurance may justifiably be questioned in view of the Civilian Health and Medical Program of the Uniformed Services (CHAMPUS) and the availability of medical care at Service hospitals and clinics. However, there are several points which also should be considered.

First, the cost of the Medical Payments coverage is generally less per annum than the $25 deductible provisions of the CHAMPUS program. Second, the CHAMPUS provisions do not include coverage for persons other than legal dependents. Third, there are limitations on the type of treatment authorized under the CHAMPUS program. The coverage is, therefore, desirable but not a necessity.

3. *Protection Against Uninsured Motorists.* This coverage applies mainly to bodily injuries for which an uninsured motorist, or a hit-and-run

driver is legally liable. It applies to the policyholder and family whether occupying their car, someone else's or while walking. It also applies to guests occupying the policyholder's car. The insuring company agrees to pay damages to injured persons up to the limits required by the financial responsibility laws of the state.

The coverage is written in only specified limits varying by state. In most states the limits are $10,000/$20,000. This coverage is available in the United States, its territories and possessions, and in Canada. It is presently required by law in over one-half of the states.

4. *Property Damage Liability Insurance.* This coverage applies when your car damages the property of others. More often than not the property is another car; but it also covers damages to other properties such as lamp posts, telephone poles, or buildings. It does not cover damage to your car. It is in force as long as your car is driven by you, members of immediate family or others who drive your car with your permission. You and all members of your family are covered even while driving someone else's car if you have the owner's permission. When claim or suits are brought against you, this coverage provides protection in the form of legal defense, and if your insurance company agrees - or a court decides - that you are legally liable for the damage, the insuring company will pay damages assessed against you up to the limits of the policy.

Property Damage Liability is available in the limit of $10,000 at very little more premium than the $5,000 limit.

5. *Comprehensive Damage Insurance.* This coverage provides protection against financial loss resulting from breakage of glass, falling objects, fire, theft or larceny, missiles, explosion, earthquake, windstorm, hail, water, flood, vandalism or malicious mischief, riot or civil commotion, or collision with a bird or animal. It does not cover damage resulting from collision with other vehicles or objects or by upset of the car, or those due and confined to wear and tear, freezing, mechanical or electrical breakdown, or radioactive contamination. Comprehensive insurance can be written with a deductible clause which provides for a $50 deduction from payment for each loss. However, no deduction is made from payment for losses caused by fire. The $50 deductible premium is 25% to 50% less than for full Comprehensive.

Under Personal Effects insurance, the insuring company agrees to pay for loss caused by fire or lightning to robes, wearing apparel and other personal effects which are the property of the insured, his spouse and relatives resident in the same household, while such effects are in or upon the owned automobile. Payment will not exceed $100 for any one occurrence. The Personal Effects insurance is written without additional charge whenever Comprehensive coverage is included in the policy.

6. *Collision Insurance.* Collision insurance provides for reimbursement to the insured for damages to his car caused by accidental

collision of the car with any moving or stationary object or by upset of the car. Loss or damage to the insured car by a moving object (other than a falling object or missile) is also covered. The insured car does not have to be in motion to sustain collision damage.

The insured car is covered for the loss up to the actual cash value of the car (depreciated value at the time and place of loss) less the deductible amount. The coverage is usually available with $50, $100, $250 or $500 Deductible.

It is possible to purchase this coverage in higher deductible amounts, but such amounts are certainly a questionable buy for the junior officer. In effect, the insured is his own insurer up to the deductible amount. As an example, let us assume that a policy provides $100 Deductible Collision coverage and the car is damaged in a collision. The amount of damage determined is $173. The insurance company would pay the excess over $100, that is, $73.

Similarly, in the event of a total loss due to collision, the settlement is made on the basis of the actual cash value of the car at the time of the accident less the deductible amount. The deduction applies to every collision accident which occurs during the life of the policy. However, in most locations, there is no deduction when the collision is with another automobile insured by the same company.

Because small collision claims are numerous and almost as expensive for the company to handle as larger claims, there is a a marked saving in premium when a higher deductible amount is carried. The rate decreases as the deductible amount increases. Many Servicemen carry the $100 Deductible Collision coverage as the form which offers the best relation between the premium charged and the protection afforded. However, you should weigh very carefully the amount of deductible you can afford; realize fully that $100 deductible, for example, means that you pay the first $100 for any repairs or losses.

Additional Coverages. The following coverages are provided within many policies without additional charge except where stated below.

1. *Coverage For Borrowed Automobiles.* Where the term "non-owned automobile" is used in the regular policy, it refers to borrowed cars which are not owned by the insured, his spouse, or any relative resident in the same household. The Family Automobile Policy provides coverages of insurance for non-owned or borrowed cars as follows.

a. Without additional premium charge the insured and his wife have the same coverages, as for the owned car, for borrowed cars which are not furnished for their regular use and not used in the automobile business. They also have liability coverages for borrowed cars which are other than private passenger cars as long as such cars are not used in their business or occupation nor furnished for regular use.

b. Relatives of the insured and spouse who are resident in the same household are insured for the same coverages as for the owned car while driving borrowed private passenger cars which are neither furnished for their regular use nor used for business purposes.

c. *For an additional premium* the Liability coverages may be extended to cover any vehicle borrowed by the named insured and spouse or by a relative resident in the household. The additional coverage, termed Extended Non-owned Automobile Coverage, is recommended for officers who drive or, as passengers, direct the driving of government-owned vehicles. Slightly lower rates and an endorsement to exclude the government as an insured and to exclude damages under Public Law 87-258 apply in almost all states.

d. Coverage for a borrowed car applies only if the car was used with the owner's permission.

e. Insurance for borrowed cars is excess insurance over any other valid and collectible insurance.

f. In general, companies consider dependent sons and daughters who are attending school away from home to be residents of the same household as their parents.

2. *Trailer Coverage.* Luggage, utility and home trailers are covered by the policy without additional charge for Bodily Injury, Property Damage and Medical Payments, provided like coverages are carried on the insured car. Medical Payments coverage is excluded for accidents occurring in a trailer which is used as a residence or premises. Collision, fire, theft and miscellaneous coverages, such as windstorm, hail, flood, etc. are available for owned home trailers or owned utility trailers for an additional premium or by separate policy.

3. *Supplementary Payments.* In addition to the provisions explained above the insurance company will:

a. Pay all expenses incurred by the company, all costs taxed against the insured in any suit alleging bodily injury or property damage and all interest on the entire amount of any judgment therein which accrues after entry of the judgment and before the company has paid or tendered or deposited in court that part of the judgment which does not exceed the limit of the company's liability.

b. Pay premiums on appeal bonds required in any such suit, premiums on bonds to release attachments for an amount not in excess of the applicable limit of liability of the policy, and the cost of bail bonds required of the insured because of accident or traffic law violations arising out of the use of an insured automobile, not to exceed $100 per bail bond, without any obligation to apply for or furnish any such bond.

c. Pay expenses incurred by the insured for such immediate medical and surgical relief to others as shall be imperative at the time of an accident involving an insured automobile.

d. Pay all reasonable expenses, other than loss of earnings, incurred by the insured at the company's request.

e. Reimburse the insured for transportation expenses not exceeding $10 per day or totaling more than $300, incurred during the period commencing 48 hours after a theft of the automobile covered by the policy has been reported to the company and the police, and terminating when the company tenders settlement for such theft or when the car is returned to use.

f. Pay general average and salvage charges for which the insured becomes legally liable, as to the automobile being transported.

4. *Automatic Coverage*. The coverages as written in the policy extend automatically to a newly acquired automobile, provided (1) it replaces the car described in the policy or (2) the company insures all automobiles owned by the named insured and is notified during the policy period or within 30 days of purchase. Under a condition of the policy, premiums are to be adjusted as of the date of acquisition.

HOW AUTOMOBILE INSURANCE PREMIUMS ARE DETERMINED

Automobile insurance premiums are computed and published by underwriting and rating organizations, such as the National Bureau of Casualty Underwriters, where the total premiums and losses of all member companies are tabulated by classes of risks and locations. Since the companies affiliated with these organizations write a large portion of the automobile insurance in effect in the United States, there are sufficient data available for the computation of reliable premiums.

The premiums for an automobile insurance policy are determined by the location, use and description (make, model, age, etc.) of the car, the age, marital status, and driving record of the drivers, and the coverages requested. As an example of the value of the car having an impact on the cost of insurance, all other considerations equal, one recent insurance rate table quoted a collision premium of $100 per year on a compact car versus $160 for an XKE and other high cost cars; an increase of 60%.

Driver Training Credit. Driver training credits of approximately 10% of the premiums are allowable in the majority of states where a certificate (or copy) signed by a school official is presented that an operator under 21 years of age (male operators under 25 in some states), resident in the household, has successfully completed a Driver Education Course, provided the course:

1. Was sponsored by a recognized secondary school, college, or university and conducted by certified instructors and had the official approval of the State Department of Education or other responsible agency; and

2. Was composed of a minimum of thirty clock-hours of classroom instruction plus an average minimum of six hours actual driving time.

Insurance and Driving Skill. Although at first it may appear that a discussion of driving skill is out of place in a chapter on insurance, examination of the facts shows a definite relationship between driving ability and automobile insurance. For example, lack of skill in driving causes accidents, which in turn cause increased rates. This is especially apparent in the high rates for cars with youthful operators. The increase over the rates for older drivers is based on widespread statistics gathered from the experience which automobile insurance companies have had.

Contrary to popular belief, a relatively small proportion of the serious accidents from this group are caused by "juvenile delinquents." Rather it is the young man of good character, who has never been in any kind of trouble, whose enthusiasm, overconfidence and daring sometimes allow him to take chances that should not have been taken and which may result in serious injury to himself or others. This is true regardless of the fact that the young man may have passed driver tests with high scores.

The cost of automobile insurance varies from one group, or classification, of drivers to another. In some states all single male operators under 25 are bracketed in one group and pay the same rate regardless of whether they are 17, 20, or 24. In many other states, a driver classification plan developed by a large segment of the automobile insurance business and used by many companies went into effect early in 1965. Under this plan the price continues to be highest for young unmarried men, but it is scaled downward year by year from age 17 through 29. In addition, the new plan includes a separate classification for the young unmarried female driver who pays more than the base rate with the cost decreasing each year from age 17 through 20. Chart 8-2 shows the relative cost of automobile insurance for youthful drivers under the classification plan introduced in 1965.

Some other results, often overlooked, of lack of skill in driving should be noted. If a driver has too many accidents, the insurance company may refuse to renew his insurance in self-defense. A careless driver may find it difficult to get insurance with any reliable company. His only recourse may be to apply for insurance under the Assigned Risk plan. The companies to which Assigned Risks are allotted are not required to accept any coverages other than Bodily Injury and Property Damage. Under most circumstances, a driver pays higher rates under the Assigned Risk classification.

The worst results of careless or unskilled driving are, of course, the direct and often serious injury to the Service member, to his wife or family. Insurance does not compensate for serious disabilities which may remain for life to hamper or cancel out one's military career or to cloud the life of a wife, son or daughter.

IN THE EVENT OF AN ACCIDENT

Every person should realize that the policy which he holds is a private contract between himself and his company. For this reason, no information

RATES GO DOWN
AS YOUNG DRIVERS GROW OLDER*

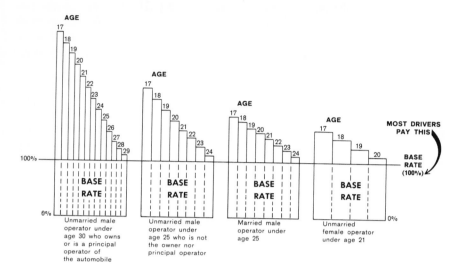

* Based on a driver classification plan developed on behalf of a large segment of the business and effective in many states beginning in 1965. These comparisons are for private passenger cars used for pleasure where all operators have "clean" driving records. Adjustments in premiums are made for cars used to drive to work, used for business, or used on a farm. Adjustments are also made for youthful operators with driver training credit, drivers with "unclean" driving records, and owners of more than one car.

SOURCE: Insurance Information Institute.

CHART 8-2

should be given to any outside person regarding the limits of coverage afforded. The policy itself should not be exhibited nor kept in the car. A disclosure of high liability limits is often disadvantageous to both the insured and his insurance company in that it results in excessive demands being made, thus precipitating a lawsuit and increasing the costs, as well as causing the policyholder considerable inconvenience in being required to appear in court as a witness.

Every automobile policy contains a provision that the insured shall do nothing, after an accident or loss, to prejudice the subrogation rights of the insurance company. Subrogation rights are the legal rights of an insuring company, after paying the insured for a claim, to attempt to recover all or part of the amount from the other driver or persons whose negligence caused the damage. Therefore, one should not give a statement to a third party, nor accept settlement covering only a portion of his damages, and then make claim under his own insurance policy.

If the car owner accepts payment from the owner of the other vehicle, or from the insurance company of the other owner, he cannot later look to his own company for payment under the Collision coverage because he has signed away all subrogation rights.

In the event of accident while driving a borrowed car, it is important for an insured to determine immediately if the legal or registered owner of the borrowed car has insurance and the type of insurance afforded. If there is no insurance on the car, he should report the accident immediately to his insurance company or to the company's adjusting office in the locality where the accident occurred.

Where the owner carries Liability coverages, the borrower of the car should report the accident at once to the owner's company and give the company full cooperation. If the accident involves serious injury or death of a third person, he should file a full report with his own insurance carrier without delay in order that he might claim protection if the claims and demands exceed the coverage carried on the borrowed vehicle. The same holds true if his wife, or children who are residents of his household, should become involved in an accident while operating a borrowed vehicle.

At The Scene of an Accident. In the event of an accident the insured owes a duty to his insurance company to obtain all possible information at the scene of an accident. This includes:

1. Securing the names and addresses of all persons involved in the accident.

2. Learning the names and addresses of all witnesses.

3. Describing the damaged vehicle and/or property.

4. Measuring the length of skid marks left by each car.

5. Stating whether or not the accident was investigated by the police.

6. Reporting on any statement made by the driver of the other vehicle immediately after the accident.

All available data should be placed in the hands of the insurance company as quickly as possible, regardless of who is responsible for the occurrence. Furthermore, every person involved in an automobile accident should look after his own interests by noting and recording all pertinent facts at the scene of the accident. If serious property damage and personal injuries have been sustained by the insured or members of his family, he may later wish to make claim against the other party for substantial damages.

Checklist of Minimum and Recommended Automobile Coverages

Coverage	Minimum	Recommended
Bodily Injury Liability*	$25,000/$50,000	$50,000/$100,000
Medical Payments	None	$1,000
Uninsured Motorists	As Required by Law	$10,000/$20,000
Property Damage Liability	$5,000	$10,000
Comprehensive**	$50 deductible	$50 deductible
Collision**	$100 deductible	$100 deductible

*Re this checklist, automobile owners who also own substantial amounts of property in the form of real estate, bank accounts, stocks and bonds, etc., which might be attached by a court to settle a judgment, should carry appreciably higher liability coverage in order to protect themselves against loss of their estates. Although publicity indicates that higher awards are made in metropolitan areas, the recommended average limits of $50,000/$100,000 are ordinarily sufficient. Service personnel, regardless of station, face the continued likelihood of being required on short notice, because of leave, temporary duty, or change of station, to drive in metropolitan areas. This fact should be taken into account when selecting coverages. Possible sources of information on recommended liability coverage in different localities are the automobile club to which the insured may belong and his insurance company.

**Also re this checklist, Comprehensive and Collision coverages can be dropped altogether when the value of the car falls below $300.

AUTOMOBILE COSTS

Insurance. In general, count on insurance costs of anywhere from $200.00 to $500.00 for the first year. Rates for the same coverage may vary significantly among companies. For example, mutual automobile insurance rates and stock company rates differ by as much as 25% in some areas. However, unless you insure with a good, sound and reliable company, your money may be wasted. Your analysis should consider those associations which cater exclusively to military officers, as these groups often have advantages over other companies. (See Appendix A.) In any event, select your coverage carefully. Here are some of the factors you should consider.

1. Consider insurance costs when you purchase the automobile. Within the same price range of automobiles, insurance costs run higher for the sportier and "muscle" models than for the more staid variety. Compact cars receive lower rates in some areas; however, a compact car with a high horsepower engine may require higher rates than a larger car with the same horsepower.

2. Do not omit buying Comprehensive insurance if you have a relatively new car. Imagine yourself in the position of a young officer who did not buy Comprehensive coverage, whose new "Vette" was stolen and who was still liable for 42 months of payments to the bank.

3. Neither should Collision coverage be ignored. The cost of replacement parts has increased drastically. The USAA 1969 Annual Report presented an interesting example of this increase. A new 1969 car listed for $3500. Yet, to buy all of the car's individual replacement parts and the labor to assemble them would cost $15,000. Thus, when a car is only 25% damaged, it must be written off as a total loss.

The same report cited crash damage costs at low speeds. At only 5 mph front or rear crashes caused over $200 average damage among Chevrolet, Ford, Plymouth and Ambassador cars tested. At 10 mph the average damage cost exceeded $650. Clearly, it is not only the young engineer trying to move a bridge abutment with a sports car at 100 mph, who can easily "total" a car.

Licensing and Registration. Vehicle licensing and registration fees vary widely from state to state. Some states charge a flat fee; others base their rate on the type of automobile, its rated horsepower, or its weight. Some states, if your domicile, also require payment of a purchase tax on new automobiles, or make registration the occasion to collect a personal property tax. These taxes may run as high as 5% or more of the assessed value or purchase price of the car. Investigate fully all of your licensing and registration options; compare your present residence with your state of domicile, or the state in which you will be stationed. For planning purposes, discounting a property tax, you can expect to pay an average of $15 to $35 yearly for registration fees.

The Soldier's and Sailor's Civil Relief Act permits you to retain your home state registration on your motor vehicle as long as you have paid the license fee or excise required by your home state. Since the Act exempts only the Serviceman and not his dependents, title to the vehicle should usually be in your name alone.

If the vehicle is registered in your home state and title held in your name alone, you may retain your home operator's license. If you register your vehicle in the state where you live rather than your home state, you may be required to obtain an operator's license from the jurisdiction in which you reside. Many states require the surrender of all out-of-state drivers licenses as a condition of issuing their own. Regardless of where you register your vehicle, your dependents may be required to obtain a driver's license from the state in which they reside.

Operating Costs.

1. *Fuel.* The normal assumption is that gasoline accounts for the largest portion of car expenses. However, fuel bills amount to less than a quarter of the total car expenses. But gasoline is the largest single item deriving from the actual driving of the car. The national average gasoline prices are 34 cents per gallon for regular and 39 cents for premium. If you are driving a 6-cylinder engine, you can expect to average 17 miles per gallon; if you've got a V-8 you should figure less than 15 miles per gallon. Don't disbelieve these figures because you have heard reports of better performance; these are not just trip mileages, these are averages; including local driving to and from work, shopping, and weekends, averaging about 12,000 miles per year.

2. *Oil.* Oil costs for the average car come to about one-tenth of a cent per mile, and include the cost of periodic oil and oil filter changes.

3. *Tire.* Tire costs are difficult to figure. So much is dependent upon the size and weight of your car, the terrain, and your driving habits. You can count on the factory-installed tires lasting 20,000 miles, unless you persist in fast starts and hard stops. Generally, it should cost about $150 to replace your tires.

Maintenance. Maintenance costs, even for a new car with a warranty, are a significant item in the operating budget. In all of the required services at various mileage intervals, the warranty will cover replacement of faulty parts; it may not cover all the labor involved. Also included in maintenance costs are such items as polish and wax, anti-freeze, lubrication, wheel balancing, etc. You should plan on a *bare minimum* of $80 per year as maintenance costs; if you exceed 12,000 miles driving per year, add another $20 to this amount. Some states also require you to have and pay for vehicle inspections at least once each year.

Depreciation. Depreciation is the largest single item of fixed expense. As a planning figure, today's popular, medium-sized and low-priced car will lose approximately 25% of its remaining value each year during the first three years, assuming a trade-in at the time the car changes ownership. If you prefer a dollar planning figure, a $2,500 automobile will depreciate $50.00 a month for three years, if you trade it in at the end of that time. In actuality, the depreciation curve is steep for the first year, slightly flatter for the next two, steep in the fourth year, and then fairly flat and constant for the remaining life of the car. At about ten years, the automobile's value approximates its scrap metal value. An obvious corollary to the flattening depreciation curve is the increasing repair costs necessary to keep older cars running. In computing costs of operation you should not count both depreciation and monthly payments.

AUTO COST COMPUTATIONS

Now, let's assume a hypothetical Second Lieutenant with his newly purchased automobile, and estimate what it may cost him to pay for and operate this car during the average month. We will assume he negotiated a loan from a bank for $2,500 to be repaid in 36 monthly installments at approximately 6% simple interest.

Item	Remarks	Monthly Cost
Monthly Payments	— — —	$ 76.00
Insurance Premium	Normally paid annually; estimated cost $300 per yr.	25.00
License Fees	Normally paid annually; Average cost $24 per yr.	2.00

Gasoline Costs	Assumes an annual mileage of 12,000 miles, regular gas, and 15 miles per gallon.	20.65
Oil Costs	Again, assumes an annual mileage of 12,000 miles.	1.00
Tire Costs	Assumes a tire life of 20,000 (good luck) miles, and mileage of 12,000 miles per year.	7.50
Maintenance Costs	Based on the bare minimum of $80 per year.	6.66
Turnpike & Bridge Tolls	Impossible to estimate; however, should be considered if much long distance traveling is contemplated.	?

TOTAL COSTS/MONTH $138.81

Cost/mile (assume 12,000/yr or 1,000/month)   13.9 cents
Note: Depreciation is not counted here because of the monthly installment payments and because depreciation is not an out-of-pocket expense.

In summary, aside from the purchase of a house, the purchase of an automobile is usually the largest purchase many people make in their lifetime. Take the time to be sure of all of the implications inherent in the purchase, financing, and insuring of a car. A review of Chapters 3 and 5 may be helpful. Consult your Legal Assistance Officer if you are in doubt on any contract.

Appropriate chapters in the standard personal finance texts listed in the bibliography for Chapter 3.

Athearn, James L. *Risk and Insurance.* 2nd ed. New York: Appleton-Century-Crofts, 1969.

Insurance Information Institute. *A Family Guide to Property and Liability Insurance.* New York: Insurance Information Institute, 1967.

Insurance Information Institute. *Do You Know???* New York: Insurance Information Institute, 1968.

*To be alive at all involves
some risk.*
    —Harold Macmillan

CHAPTER 9

MANAGING PROPERTY AND LIABILITY RISKS

PLANNING WOULD be simple if it were not for uncertainty. One kind of uncertainty that must be faced is the uncertainty of financial loss. Such uncertainty is called risk. In this chapter, we will discuss the major kinds of financial risks that financial managers must integrate into financial planning. Then we will introduce the types of insurance protection available for guarding against property and liability losses.

CLASSIFYING RISKS

The source of risk (uncertainty of loss) is called a peril. Fires, auto wrecks, and liability judgments are sources from which losses emerge. They are perils that give rise to risks. But the perils are not easily avoided. The only way to avoid the peril of an auto wreck is to avoid all contact with automobiles. Avoiding the perils of life would probably lead to an unpleasant life.

A condition that increases the likelihood of loss is called a hazard. A fire is more likely if oily rags are piled in the garage. A liability judgment is more likely when a deep hole in the front walk is left unbarricaded.

One way financial risks can be classified is to distinguish between speculative risks and pure risks. Speculative risks are those involving both the promise of gain and the chance of loss. This is the kind of risk assumed when making an investment in a common stock or savings account. This type of risk will be examined in more detail in Chapter 10. This chapter will be concerned with pure risks, or those taken with the possibilities of either loss or no loss. For example, homeowners may or may not suffer damage to or destruction of their home. Either the calamity occurs or it doesn't.

A property risk is the uncertainty of loss resulting from damage to or destruction of property. Homes, personal property, automobiles, and other types of property are subject to damage or destruction through many perils such as fire, windstorm, explosion, criminal perils such as theft, transportation perils and so on. Three methods are commonly used to treat property risks: risk retention, prevention, and insurance. Insurance protection against property losses is discussed in the paragraphs below.

A liability risk is the uncertainty of financial loss which could result from being found personally liable for damages to others arising out of the ownership or occupancy of a building, personal responsibility for injury or damage caused by family members or pets, or the ownership or operation of an automobile. An important method of treating liability risks is insurance. This includes using both Personal Liability insurance (Comprehensive insurance) and Automobile Liability insurance which was discussed separately in Chapter 8.

As the head of a family, you must carry out the three functions of a risk manager, which:

1. Identify the sources from which losses may arise (risk analysis).
2. Evaluate the impact on the family if the loss should occur.
3. Select the most effective and efficient techniques to deal with the risks.

You, as the head of a family, have the responsibility of controlling the risks your family must face. All too often, however, the functions of risk management are not performed systematically. The remainder of this chapter concerns itself with the insurance method of protecting your family against financial losses resulting from property and liability risks.

INSURANCE AGAINST PROPERTY LOSS

All property which a person owns is subject to loss or damage by a variety of perils. Risk by some perils is either uninsurable or the insurance is prohibitively expensive. Risks by the most common perils are insurable under various kinds of property insurance policies. Such policies are written to cover homes (with possible extensions to the property within, other private structures such as garages, and consequential losses), personal property (property owned except homes, automobiles, and any other property excluded by the policy such as boats, aircraft, etc.), and automobiles.

Whenever you are considering the purchase of Property and Liability insurance, you should consider all coverages at once. Auto insurance policies are specialized policies which can be considered separately. But insuring the remainder of your property should be viewed as one problem, even though your choice of insurance coverages may be in separate policies.

Four factors must be considered whenever you are comparing alternative Property insurance coverages.

1. What property is covered? Policies can vary according to the breadth of property covered. Make sure you understand precisely which property is or is not included under the policy.

2. Against what perils is your property insured? You can select a variety of coverages according to the perils you desire to be insured against. The broader your policy, the more expensive it will be. Insurance against all perils to your property is not available. Thus you must retain risk to some extent. But you have considerable choice of how much risk to retain and how much to transfer to the insurance company.

3. To what extent will any loss be reimbursed? Does the policy provide for full coverage of any loss, or is there a deductible clause? What maximum amounts are payable on any kind of loss?

4. How much does the insurance cost? Be sure you know why the costs in alternative policies are different. Does the one policy cost less because protection is less or is the rate structure less? You should recognize what cost you are paying for any alleged benefit and decide for yourself whether or not the benefit is worth the cost. This is true whether you are trying to decide how much risk to retain versus how much to transfer to the insurance company, or whether you are trying to decide between comparable coverages offered by different companies. Note that the principle of indemnity requires that the policyholder be reimbursed for actual losses only—he is not permitted to make a profit. Thus, it is nonsense to insure a $20,000 house for $30,000, since only the actual value of the property loss can be paid (unless the state requires that the face amount of the policy be assumed the value of the property under a "valued policy" law).

Some insurance policies are written to cover property in a given location only. A policy covering a house is an obvious example. Other insurance policies, however, cover personal property on a Floater basis. The Floater policy covers the property wherever it may be within the territorial limits of the policy. You should understand any geographical limitations written into your policy. This is particularly important if you expect to be assigned to a duty station outside the Continental United States.

One more characteristic of Property insurance should be pointed out before we briefly consider the individual types of policies. Property insurance policies can be classified as either Named-Peril policies or All-Risk policies. A Named-Peril policy is one that stipulates the particular causes of loss (perils) for which the insured may be indemnified. Thus, unless property is damaged or destroyed in a manner specifically named in the policy, no recovery is possible.

An All-Risk policy protects the insured against all perils of loss to covered property except those specifically excluded in the contract. Note that an All-Risk policy does not protect your property against all risks. It will cover "all risks of physical loss of or damage to the described property except those herein excluded." Nevertheless, the All-Risk policy is fundamentally broader in coverage and will therefore pay a greater range of claims than will the Named-Peril type.

Insurance on the Home. The home and its contents are exposed to direct damage by a tremendous number of perils. Some are uninsurable. Depreciation, or the gradual physical decline which takes place because of wear and tear and the effect of the elements, is an example. Normally, such perils as war and nuclear radiation damage are excluded from coverage. But many perils are insurable, and there are three basic standard policies from which to choose the coverage that best suits your needs.

First, there is the Standard Fire policy which normally insures the policyholder against losses due to fire and lightning. Secondly, Extended Coverage may be purchased for a small extra premium to cover such perils as cyclones, tornadoes, hurricanes, hailstorms, windstorms, motor vehicles, aircraft, explosion, riots, or smoke. Finally, Additional Extended Coverage can be purchased to cover such perils as water damage from plumbing and heating systems, vandalism and malicious mischief, glass breakage, ice, snow, freezing, fall of trees and collapse.

Both of these latter types of coverages are normally sold only with deductible clauses which require the policyholder to assume the first few dollars of loss (usually $50 or $100) on specified perils. By accepting a deductible clause, substantial premium dollars can be saved, since the high cost of paying frequent small losses is eliminated. In a number of states a deductible clause is mandatory by law.

Factors Affecting Home Insurance Costs. Although the loss experience of the insurance companies determines in large measure what you pay for insurance on your home, there are additional factors that must be considered. These include the firefighting equipment of your fire department and the efficiency of its personnel, the dependability of the fire alarm system, and the nearness of a water supply suitable for fighting a fire. The type of material used in constructing your home is a factor. It costs more to insure an all-wood house than it does to insure one made of brick. And, of course, the cost is affected by the amount of coverage. The homeowner whose house is insured for $28,000 pays more than a neighbor whose smaller house is insured for $18,000.

As you would expect, the price you pay for home insurance varies with the number and kind of perils you are insured against. For example, if you are covered for damage resulting from fire and lightning only, you will pay less than if you have extended coverage which insures you against a number of perils in addition to fire and lightning. Likewise, you pay less for the Standard Form of the homeowners policy with its eleven perils than you do for the Broad Form which insures against nineteen perils.

With so many factors affecting the cost of home insurance, the cost varies considerably from time to time, from one part of a state or city to another.

Personal Property Insurance. Most Armed Forces officers live in either government quarters or rented houses and thus have no need for insurance on a house. However, they should have insurance on the contents of any home in which they live. This is called Personal Property insurance. Such insurance can be of either the Named-Peril or the All-Risk variety. Usually it is written on a Floater basis which means that the property is insured anywhere within the territorial limits of the policy.

There are a variety of ways in which coverages can be applied to personal property. Again, the buyer must determine the extent of property coverage, perils insured against, amounts of protection and costs of protection if he is to choose rationally among alternative policies.

Homeowners Package Policies. The packaging of insurance is designed to provide the homeowner with all the Property and Liability insurance he needs with the exception of automobile insurance. Thus the Homeowners Package policy is a combination of a Home insurance policy, a Personal Property insurance policy, and a Comprehensive Personal Liability insurance policy.

Normally, a package policy is cheaper than the sum of the costs of the separate policies included therein, since writing costs are lower for the company. But you still must be sure that the coverages in the Homeowners policy give you all the protection that you desire. You may still want to purchase additional protection, although you should avoid duplication. Again you should note that overinsuring just costs you money since you cannot collect more than the actual financial losses experienced. Thus owning a Homeowners package plus a duplicating Personal Property insurance policy would be a waste of money.

This situation also suggests that you should give some thought to your property insurance each time you change stations, since the kind and amount of coverages you need may change. Moving time is also a good time to update your inventory of personal property which would be used to itemize any substantial claim you might have. An inventory form is available from your insurance company.

When you purchase a homeowners policy the number of perils your property is insured against depends on whether you choose the Standard

Form, the Broad Form, or the Comprehensive Form of the policy (See Chart 9-1).

The STANDARD FORM of the homeowners policy insures your property against the first 11 perils shown in Chart 9-1. The most popular form of the policy, the BROAD FORM, insures your property against all 19 perils listed in the chart. The COMPREHENSIVE FORM, sometimes referred to as an All-Risks policy, insures against the same 19 perils—and many more. Generally speaking, an All-Risks policy is one that insures you against all perils *except*—and then it lists the exceptions. Perils excluded under the Comprehensive Form are shown at the bottom of Chart 9-1.

A Homeowners Policy For Renters. Even though you live in an apartment or rent the house you occupy, a homeowners policy is available in the RESIDENCE CONTENTS BROAD FORM or TENANTS FORM. Such a policy insures your household contents and personal belongings against the same perils as those included in the Broad Form, all 19 of which are shown in Chart 9-1.

This policy form also provides coverage for additional living expenses and Comprehensive Personal liability coverage. These coverages are discussed next.

PERILS AGAINST WHICH PROPERTIES ARE INSURED
HOMEOWNERS POLICY

Forms				Perils	
C O M P R E H E N S I V E F O R M **(5)**	**B R O A D** **F O R M** **(2)**	**S T A N D A R D** **(1)**	**F O R M**	1. fire and lightning	7. vehicles, if not owned or operated by the insured
				2. loss or damage to property removed from premises endangered by fire	8. sudden and accidental damage from smoke
				3. windstorm or hail	9. vandalism and malicious mischief
				4. explosion	10. theft
				5. riot, riot attending a strike, civil commotion	11. breakage of glass constituting a part of the building
				6. aircraft	
				12. falling objects	17. sudden and accidental tearing asunder, cracking, burning or bulging of appliances for heating water for domestic consumption
				13. weight of ice, snow, sleet	
				14. collapse of building(s) or any part thereof	
				15. sudden and accidental tearing asunder, cracking, burning, or bulging of a steam or hot water heating system	18. freezing of plumbing, heating and air-conditioning systems and domestic appliances
				16. accidental discharge, leakage or overflow of water or steam from a plumbing, heating or air-conditioning system	19. sudden and accidental injury to electrical appliances, devices, fixtures and wiring (TV and radio tubes not included)

All perils **EXCEPT:** earthquake, landslide, flood, surface water, waves, tidal water or tidal wave, the backing up of sewers, seepage, war, and nuclear radiation.

SOURCE: Insurance Information Institute.

CHART 9-1

COMPREHENSIVE PERSONAL
LIABILITY INSURANCE

The head of a household is liable if the actions or negligence of any member of his household, including pets, cause bodily injury or property damage to others. He may have this liability imposed on him if the milkman slips on Mary's roller skates; if Rover bites the newsboy; if mother's umbrella accidentally pokes out someone's eye while she is shipping downtown; or if he himself slices a golf drive and injures another player.

The likelihood of all or any of these occurrences in a given household may not be great. However, the liability imposed by any one of them happening can involve a claim that will strain family finances to the limit for many years.

A Comprehensive Personal Liability policy (also referred to as Comprehensive Personal insurance) covering your legal liability for bodily injury, illness, death, or property damages may be purchased for a small premium. A policy including $25,000 Personal Liability, $500 Medical Payments per person, and $250 Physical Damage to property can be obtained for as little as $10.00 a year, depending upon location. Doubling the limit of Personal Liability coverage to $50,000 costs only an additional $1.80. Doubling it again to $100,000 costs only an additional $1.20. This phenomenon is a characteristic of any Liability insurance. A large increase in protection can be purchased for a very small increase in premiums.

When you have a homeowners policy, it includes liability insurance that provides financial protection when a lawsuit or a claim is filed against you by persons who consider you responsible for their injuries or damage to their property. The three liability coverages that go with the homeowners policy and are included in a Comprehensive Personal Liability insurance policy are Personal Liability, Medical Payments, and Physical Damage to the Property of Others.

Coverage L - Personal Liability. Personal Liability insurance is designed to protect you against a lawsuit that could cripple you financially. Suppose, for example, that a visitor slips and falls on your property, suffers a head injury which impairs his vision, and eventually sues you for fifty, seventy-five, or a hundred thousand dollars. Or, suppose that while you are burning leaves in your back yard the fire spreads, your neighbor's property is damaged extensively, and he sues you. In either case, your insurance company will pay the legal costs of defending you. Furthermore, if it is agreed by the parties involved—or decided by a court if they cannot agree—that you are legally liable for the visitor's injury or the damage to your neighbor's property, your insurance company will pay the damages assessed against you up to the limits stated in your policy.

Minimum personal liability coverage under all forms of the homeowners policy is $25,000, but larger amounts can be purchased. The two situations described in the preceding paragraph deal with accidents occurring on or near your property. However, those occurring elsewhere are covered in the same way if they are caused by you, a member of your family, or your pets.

Coverage M - Personal Medical Payments. Many homeowners feel a moral obligation for a friend's medical expenses if they are connected with a minor accidental injury he suffered while on their property. Such expenses are paid by your insurance company under the medical payments coverage in your homeowners policy. The minimum amount of protection is $500 for each person, but larger amounts can be purchased. Your policy also covers injuries occurring off your premises, if they are caused by you, a member of your family, or your pets.

An important feature of this coverage is that payment is made regardless of who is liable or at fault. This feature makes possible the prompt payment of medical bills, because there is no need to go through the time-consuming process of establishing legal liability. Medical payments coverage is somewhat similar to the coverage of personal liability. It differs, however, in that it is designed for the small rather than the large claim—the minor rather than the major injury; also payment is made without concern for legal liability.

Coverage N - Physical Damage to Property. Physical damage to the property of others applies when you or any member of your family accidentally damages someone else's property. Damage caused by children under 12 years of age is covered, whether accidental or intentional; but your insurance company is not obligated to pay for damage caused intentionally by youngsters 12 years or older. Payment for damages or repair or replacement of the property is made regardless of who, if anyone, is at fault. However, the maximum amount that your insurance company pays for any one accident is limited to the amount stated in the policy, usually $250 in a homeowners policy.

EXTENSIONS OF LIABILITY COVERAGE

There are certain extensions of coverage, some of which are added by endorsement at an extra premium charge, or which may be available without charge in policies issued by Service-oriented insurers.

Additional Living Expense. In the event of loss to the residence of the insured this covers the increase in living expenses necessary to continue the normal living standard of the policyholder's household, for the time required to repair or replace the damaged or destroyed property, or for the household to be resettled in permanent quarters.

Boatowner's Insurance. Boatowners should verify whether or not their boat is covered under their basic policy. If horsepower, total value or other characteristics of your boat require an endorsement to your basic policy, it should be obtained. High limits of liability are desirable for the same reasons that apply to Automobile Liability insurance.

Fire Legal Liability. This extends Coverage L of the CPL policy to include all sums which the insured becomes obligated to pay because of property damage to the premises or furnishings, caused by fire, explosion, smoke or smudge caused by sudden unusual and faulty operation of any heating or cooking unit, providing the insurance does not apply to liability assumed by the insured under any contract or agreement. By this means liability for loss or damage to government quarters or rented quarters can be insured.

Credit Card Insurance. This policy covers the insured in the event an unauthorized person fraudulently uses the insured's credit cards and the insured is held liable for the expenses incurred.

CHECKLIST OF MINIMUM AND RECOMMENDED PROPERTY AND LIABILITY COVERAGES

The following checklist indicates what the writer believes are the minimum Property and Liability coverages acceptable to Armed Forces officers. Without these minimum coverages, the officer is dangerously exposed to financial disaster. The recommended coverages are those suggested for the typical junior officer. The recommended Liability coverages should be increased as the assets of the officer increase.

1. Insurance on Homes Owned.

    a. Minimum—A Homeowner's package policy (or Standard Fire and Lightning plus Extended Coverage if a package policy is unavailable when you do not occupy the home) on at least 80% of the value of the house.

    b. Recommended—A Homeowner's package policy (or standard form coverages if a package policy is unavailable when you do not occupy the home) of the broadest form available, covering the full value of the house.

2. Personal Property Insurance.

    a. Minimum—Value of property fully covered for major perils, 1/2 of its value covered by Broad or All-Risk insurance.

    b. Recommended—Fully insure with Broad or All-Risk coverage.

3. Comprehensive Personal Liability Insurance.

    a. Minimum—$25,000 Liability, $500 Medical Payments and $250 Property Damage.

    b. Recommended—$50,000/$1000/$250.

Those policies offered by Associations specializing in insurance for military officers should certainly be considered (see Appendix A).

Insurance Information Institute. *Insurance for the Home.* New York: Insurance Information Institute, 1968.

_____. *Sample Insurance Policies, Property Liability Coverages.* New York: Insurance Information Institute, 1969.

Magee, John H. and Oscar H. Serbein. *Property and Liability Insurance.* 4th ed. Homewood, Illinois: Richard D. Irwin, Inc., 1967.

Office of the Surgeon General U.S. Army. *Uniformed Services Health Benefits Information.* Denver, 1968.

I'm not so interested in the return on my money as in the return of my money.
—Will Rogers

CHAPTER 10

MANAGING SAVINGS AND INVESTMENT

BEFORE DISCUSSING various forms of savings and investment media, it is pertinent to consider the reasons for saving and the goals that can be achieved by savings.

REASONS FOR SAVING

The basic purpose of saving is to provide for future contingencies. There are two basic kinds of future contingencies: risks and opportunities. Certain kinds of risks were discussed in the previous chapter. Recall that risk is the uncertainty of financial loss as the result of some kind of peril. Opportunity, in the sense used here, means the financial ability to carry out certain desired activities such as sending your children through college, buying a home, or establishing a business in retirement.

It must be granted, however, that the distinction between these two basic kinds of future contingencies is not always clear. It should also be noted that the same funds that are at one time used to guard against a risk can later be used to exploit an opportunity. For example, a savings fund might be established as an emergency fund to provide for an unexpected financial need while raising a family. Later on, after the children have established families of their own, the emergency funds not actually used could be used to buy a retirement home. The following list gives some of the traditional functions performed by savings. Accumulated savings can provide:

1. For fluctuations in the actual pay-out of funds for set-asides, annual insurance premiums, taxes, vacations, Christmas gifts, and other near-term purchases.

2. A financial cushion for emergencies such as traveling on emergency leave, hospitalization of your wife, extraordinary dislocation costs, or unforeseen repairs on your home or automobile.

3. Funds for major long-term goals such as buying a home, sending the children through college, financing the daughter's wedding, etc.

4. A means of supplementing retirement income or survivor benefits.

5. The ability to take advantage of financial opportunities such as a business or major investment.

6. An estate for your heirs.

Examining the above list should shed additional light on the relationship between your Family Balance Sheet and your Family Income and Expenditure Charts (discussed in Chapter 3). Note that portions from several budget categories show up as additions to assets or net worth on your Balance Sheet. Thus a mortgage payment from your housing budget reduces a liability and therefore increases net worth. Money for annual insurance premiums can be accumulated in a savings account. If the premium is for an insurance policy which builds cash values, then that part of the premium which adds to cash value is savings and adds to family net worth.

Some families consider any income allocation that adds to net worth an investment. Other families prefer to reserve the term "investment" for the commitment of funds with the hope of gain. The definition used is not critical. The important things to determine are your purposes for saving, how much to save to accomplish each purpose, and the best form in which to invest your savings.

HOW MUCH TO SAVE

The determination of how much income should be allocated to a savings and investment program depends upon the purposes for which savings are accumulated, and the benefits you expect to derive from satisfying those purposes. In practice, your judgment of the benefits derived from accumulated savings is translated into a priority assigned to achieving savings goals. For example, you may be willing to sacrifice a good deal of current consumption in order to accumulate an emergency fund. Once that fund is accumulated, you might turn to the satisfaction of current wants until other reasons for saving become more pressing. Thus the amount you save is determined by your own value judgments, resources, and responsibilities.

You should establish a systematic savings plan which will initially provide for your short-range goals. Once sufficient reserves have been established for these, savings should be directed toward the achievement of longer-range goals.

Many families attempt to establish their programs by devoting a fixed percentage of their income to a systematic savings and investment program. The typical percentages run between 5 and 15%. The amounts established to provide for any given goals must also be determined based on individual priorities.

Your need for a specific emergency fund will decrease as the size of your net worth increases. Thus, if you have several thousand dollars invested in corporate securities, you can satisfy emergency needs by borrowing against them.

COMPOUNDING AND SAVINGS GROWTH

When you consider saving for long-range goals, some attention must be directed toward analyzing how rapid an accumulation is necessary to achieve various goals. Consulting standard interest tables will give you an idea of how funds accumulate at various interest rates. For example, if you invest ten dollars a month in a savings account accumulating at the rate of 4% compounded quarterly, it will grow to approximately $661 in five years, $1466 in ten years, and $2450 at the end of 15 years. If the amount saved per month is $100, the accumulations become $6610, $14,660, and $24,500 respectively.

Once you have a goal in mind, use an interest table to find out how much you will have to save at various interest rates in order to achieve it. Table 10-1 indicates how one $10 deposit will grow at various interest rates compounded annually. Notice that at 5% your money doubles in a little over 14 years. At 14% your money doubles in a little over 5 years, and at the end of your 30-year career, $10 would be worth $509.50. These figures make it obvious why a savings plan should be started early in your career.

A realistic savings plan consists of setting aside an amount systematically. Table 10-2 indicates how an annual deposit of $100 will grow at various interest rates compounded annually. Notice that the $3000 in 30 payments of $100 grows to almost $7000 at 5% in 30 years. Many savings accounts compound interest more frequently than on an annual basis, in which case these figures would be even larger.

Chart 10-1 indicates how systematic savings will grow if compounded quarterly. Chart 10-2 indicates how $1000 will grow if allowed to accumulate at various interest rates, compounded quarterly.

HOW ONE $10 DEPOSIT WILL GROW

INTEREST RATES (Compounded Annually)

AT END OF YEAR	4%	5%	6%	8%	10%	12%	14%
1	10.40	10.50	10.60	10.80	11.00	11.20	11.40
2	10.82	11.02	11.24	11.66	12.10	12.54	13.00
3	11.25	11.58	11.91	12.60	13.31	14.05	14.82
4	11.70	12.16	12.62	13.60	14.64	15.74	16.89
5	12.17	12.76	13.38	14.69	16.11	17.62	19.25
6	12.65	13.40	14.19	15.87	17.72	19.74	21.95
7	13.16	14.07	15.04	17.14	19.49	22.11	25.02
8	13.69	14.77	15.94	18.51	21.44	24.76	28.53
9	14.23	15.51	16.89	19.99	23.58	27.73	32.52
10	14.80	16.29	17.91	21.59	25.94	31.06	37.07
11	15.39	17.10	18.98	23.32	28.53	34.79	42.26
12	16.01	17.96	20.12	25.18	31.38	38.96	48.18
13	16.65	18.86	21.33	27.20	34.52	43.63	54.92
14	17.32	19.80	22.61	29.37	37.97	48.87	62.61
15	18.01	20.79	23.97	31.72	41.77	54.74	71.38
16	18.73	21.83	25.40	34.26	45.95	61.30	81.37
17	19.48	22.92	26.93	37.00	50.54	68.66	92.76
18	20.26	24.07	28.54	39.96	55.60	76.90	105.75
19	21.07	25.27	30.26	43.16	61.16	86.13	120.56
20	21.91	26.53	32.07	46.61	67.28	96.46	137.43
25	26.66	33.86	42.92	68.48	108.35	170.00	264.62
30	32.43	43.22	57.43	100.63	174.49	299.60	509.50

TABLE 10-1

HOW $100 DEPOSITED ANNUALLY WILL GROW

INTEREST RATE (Compounded Annually)

AT END OF YEAR	4%	5%	6%	8%	10%	12%	14%
5	563	580	598	634	671	711	753
10	1248	1321	1397	1565	1753	1964	2204
15	2082	2266	2467	2932	3495	4175	4998
20	3096	3472	3899	4942	6300	8069	10,376
25	4330	5011	5815	7895	10,818	14,932	20,732
30	5833	6976	8380	12,234	18,094	27,028	40,672

TABLE 10-2

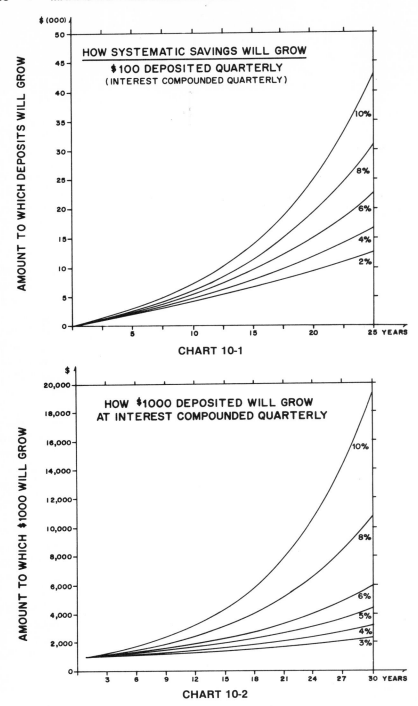

CHART 10-1

CHART 10-2

These figures are approximate because there are many ways in which interest on a savings account can be calculated. Nevertheless, all systems yield figures within a few dollars of those given above. These numbers indicate that accumulating $10 a month in a savings account for 15 years will scarcely provide the down payment on a home or one semester of Ivy League education for one child.

SAVINGS AND INVESTMENT MEDIA

Once you have determined your savings goals, and have an idea of how much you can save to meet them, you must decide on the form in which to hold your savings accumulations. You should be sure that the characteristics of the selected media suit your specific needs. All investments vary in their ability to provide convenience, safety of principal, liquidity (the ease and speed with which you can convert the investment to cash), and growth of principal.

Earlier, it was suggested that you allow funds accumulating for the purchase of set-asides and other short-run goals to accumulate in a savings account. The primary criterion for accumulating funds in this manner is convenience. Allowing funds to accumulate in the checking account would be even more convenient, but in the U.S. such funds earn no interest. You must decide how to divide the balances between these accounts so that they are most useful to you. You would probably do well to begin the accumulation of an emergency fund in the same savings account. Once a satisfactory balance is achieved, you should use an investment which yields a higher rate of interest.

Whenever the purpose of an investment is to meet near-term needs, a high emphasis on safety of principal and liquidity is required. Time deposits and U.S. Savings Bonds are fixed principal investments, which means that the investor is guaranteed that the principal will not reduce. They are also quite liquid, although a savings institution can delay payment of a time deposit for 30 days, and Savings Bonds are not redeemable until 60 days after purchase.

At the other end of the spectrum, we note that common stocks can decline in value quite rapidly, and investments in real estate are frequently difficult to convert quickly into cash without sustaining a considerable loss. Thus the latter investments would be inappropriate for satisfying short-term needs unless borrowing against their value were contemplated.

When you turn your attention to achieving long-term goals, the characteristics of safety of principal and liquidity become less important, and growth of principal should be emphasized. This is especially desirable in the case of Armed Forces officers. No matter what you do with your money, you face investment risks.

It is not our purpose to examine the detailed characteristics of savings media, each of which has its own advantages and disadvantages. The following is a list of the principal investment media and some of their key characteristics.

Checking Accounts. Banks in the U.S. are not allowed to pay interest on deposits kept in checking accounts. However, banks in foreign countries often can and do pay interest on checking account balances. For example, U.S. branch banks serving military personnel in South Vietnam pay 5% interest on checking account deposits.

Savings Accounts. There are numerous financial institutions that offer various types of savings accounts.

1. *Commercial Banks.*

   a. *Regular Savings Accounts.* Banks can require 30 days' notice for withdrawal, but this is rarely done. Your bank should be FDIC insured, which guarantees the safety of your account to $20,000. Commercial banks can pay you up to 4.5% interest on such deposits although not all pay this maximum.

   b. *Savings Certificates* vary in amount from $100 to $2500 and usually mature in 1 to 5 years. Usually you cannot redeem these prior to 90 days after purchase without being penalized on the certificate's value. The interest rate on a 1-year savings certificate may be as high as 5.5%; a 2-year certificate 5.75%.

   c. *Open Accounts* usually have an exotic title such as "Golden Passbook", or "VIP." These accounts normally require a large initial deposit ($500 or more) and often have a minimum for later deposits. They also require notice for withdrawal (usually 90 days).

   d. *Certificates of Deposit* are issued in large denominations such as $50,000 and earn higher rates of interest, depending on the length of time held and the dollar amount of the certificate.

2. *Mutual Savings Banks.* Generally, the government allows these banks to pay 1/2 to 1% more interest on passbook accounts. Most savings banks are FDIC-insured; others are state-insured. In a crisis these banks could require one to 3 months notice for withdrawal depending on the various state laws. Rarely have they required any notice. At the time of this writing, savings banks are allowed to pay 5% on passbook accounts, 5.25% on 90 days notice accounts, 5.75% on one year certificates, 6% on 2 year certificates, and higher amounts on certain certificates of deposit.

3. *Savings and Loan Associations.* Most S&L accounts are insured up to $20,000 by the Federal Savings and Loan Insurance Corp (FSLIC). Be sure the S&L you deal with has FSLIC or state insurance for the safety of your deposits. These associations specialize primarily in long-term home loans. They can, in a crisis, require depositors to give notice and can then pay off depositors by making partial payments in rotating order over a period of time. Generally, S&L's are permitted to pay 1/2 to 1% more than commercial banks on regular, notice, and certificate accounts.

4. *Credit Unions.* If your installation has a credit union, you are probably eligible for membership. Generally, there is a 25¢ membership fee per account. Some credit unions have their deposits insured and all are regulated by either the Bureau of Federal Credit Unions or a state agency. The majority of credit unions paid 5% or over in 1969 but there was a wide variation in rates. Some credit unions require notice for withdrawal and some restrict each member's savings to a few thousand dollars.

Credit Unions also give life insurance on savings without cost to their members. Let us assume that your credit union pays 5% on accounts and gives free insurance up to $2000 in each account. Should you—or the named insured on joint accounts—die, the credit union would "double your money" up to $2000 (some only insure up to $1000). This provides the depositor with free term insurance worth (let us assume) $5 per thousand. If the account is insured to $2000 and the member has this much in the account, then the value of the insurance feature may well add as much as .5 to 1% return on his savings, depending on his age, etc.

Soldiers Deposit. Under the Uniformed Services Savings Deposit Program (USSDP) any member of the Armed Forces overseas can save any amount of his unallotted pay and allowances and the government will pay 10% interest compounded quarterly on the average balance. Furthermore, the money may continue to earn interest up to 90 days following your return to the U.S.

Members of the Armed Forces assigned to duty stations outside of the 50 States, the Virgin Islands, Puerto Rico, the Canal Zone, Guam or American Samoa are eligible for USSDP. The maximum amount upon which interest may accrue is $10,000. Deposits made on or before the tenth of the month earn interest from the first of that month.

A Service member has three options for final settlement of his Savings Deposit account. Final settlements are not automatically made.

1. Routine repayment. If a member wishes repayment of deposits plus interest after return to the United States or its possessions, DA Form 2082 (Request for Repayment of Savings Deposits) should be processed through his finance and accounting office. Interest will be paid through the month of repayment but not beyond 90 days after the member's return.

2. Accelerated repayment. If a member wishes to receive repayment of deposits plus interest immediately upon arrival in the United States or its possessions, his application for final repayment must be forwarded by the member's overseas finance and accounting office after appropriate PCS orders are issued. Interest will accrue through the date the member is eligible for return from overseas.

3. Maximum interest accumulation. A member may choose to let his savings deposits earn the maximum interest payable (90 days after return to the United States or its possessions).

Emergency withdrawals of Savings Deposits are authorized only when:

a. The depositor's Commanding Officer has approved the payment (overseas only).

b. The health and welfare of a member of his dependents would be jeopardized if the withdrawal is not granted.

c. A member serving in Vietnam, who has extended his tour of duty there by at least six months, is granted a special 30-day leave in the United States or its possessions. (This does not include rest and recuperation leave.)

d. Directed by the Secretary of the Service concerned on behalf of the dependents of a member in a missing status.

e. A member returns from a status of missing, missing in action, beseiged or captured, detained or interned in a foreign country.

Few savings programs can compare with USSDP. For example, let us compare USSDP with a typical savings account paying 5% interest compounded semi-annually. On a 36-month tour, a $50 monthly investment would yield $297 interest in USSDP versus only $140 in the 5% account.

U. S. Government Savings Bonds. Series "E" Savings Bonds mature in 5 years, 10 months. These bonds can be redeemed 60 days from date of purchase, but, of course, must be held to maturity to realize the full 5 1/2% interest. The first-year rate is now 4%. When you buy "E" bonds, you pay 75% of face value, and the interest is paid in the form of a gradual increase in accrued value. "E" bonds may be held at interest for 10 years beyond maturity.

"H" bonds are current-income securities. You pay the full face value when purchasing these and the Treasury sends you interest checks semi-annually. "H" bonds earn 4.29% interest the first year and 5.1% thereafter until they mature in 10 years. The average earnings are the same as "E" bonds—5% with a bonus to 5 1/2% if held to maturity. The interest on "E" & "H" bonds is exempt from state and local income taxes and the federal income tax on "E" bond interest may be deferred until redemption.

An important thing to remember about your U.S. Savings Bonds is that if any are lost, stolen, mutilated, or destroyed they will be replaced free of charge by the U.S. Treasury. To report such a case, use application form PD 1048, available at most banks.

Treasury Bills, Notes, Bonds. Treasury bills, notes, and bonds are not a common method of savings or investment for the military officer, because of the large amount of cash necessary for their purchase. However, their high interest rate makes them worthy of consideration.

1. *Treasury Bills* are bearer obligations sold at a discount and redeemed at face value. The significance of the term "bearer" is that if they are lost or stolen another person can readily sell or redeem them. The

minimum-size bill issued the small purchaser has been raised to $10,000. Generally, the bills mature in 13 or 26 weeks, 9 months, or occasionally one year. Tax-anticipation bills may be used at face value to pay income taxes even though the bills may not fully mature for another week or so. Therefore, the yield is greater if used to make tax payments than if held for cash at maturity.

2. *Treasury Notes* have maturities of one to 7 years but are issued in bearer or in registered form. Interest is paid semi-annually.

3. *Treasury Bonds* are much like notes but mature in more than seven years.

Before continuing, a few points should be clarified regarding bonds. It is easier to buy bonds through a bank or broker than to do so yourself. However, before you place an order through a firm, ask what your effective yield will be. You may find that on small orders, the commissions and fees charged may wipe out any yield on the bond. In buying Treasury bills, etc., directly from the Federal Reserve you must provide "immediately available" funds, usually meaning cash or a check drawn on a Federal Reserve Bank by a member bank. Sometimes a certified check or a bank cashier's check is also acceptable.

Bond prices are stated as a percentage of their face value. A $1000 bond discounted (selling at less than its face value) to $900 would be quoted at 90. Government bonds are usually quoted in thirty-seconds of a point (a quote of 100.16 means 100 16/32, or $1,005); corporate bonds are usually quoted in eighths of a point (dollar).

Do not buy long-term bonds in the belief that your money can be gotten back at any time without significant loss. If you cannot invest your money for a long-term, you should confine yourself to short-term bonds. Generally, the shorter the term, the lower the yield (1969 and 1970 were exceptions), but the smaller the price swings in the market.

U.S. Government Agency Securities. Many agencies established by Congress also issue debt obligations (bonds). Their securities are not guaranteed by the government but it is unlikely that the government would allow them to default since it supervises them and is often a part-owner. Because of their relatively poorer backing, these bonds pay a higher yield than those of the Treasury. These agencies include the Federal National Mortgage Association (FNMA), the Government National Mortgage Association (GNMA), the Tennessee Valley Authority (TVA), the Export-Import Bank, The International Bank for Reconstruction and Development (World Bank), Federal Land Banks and others.

Municipal Bonds. The interest on state and local government bonds is exempt from federal income taxes and income taxes in the state where issued. Despite the generally good credit of municipal bonds (even during the Depression more than 98% met their payments without fail), one or two manage to be in danger of default almost every year. When a person passes the 30% tax bracket (which can happen on military pay) he should begin to consider these fixed-income securities.

Corporate Bonds. There are two major classifications. Secured bonds are guaranteed by a mortgage on the company's property, much like a mortgage on a home. Unsecured bonds are debentures backed by the general credit of the company, similar to a signature loan.

Both types promise to pay a specified sum at maturity and interest at a fixed rate regularly until maturity. The principal and interest are payable ahead of the dividends on stock. In the event the company goes bankrupt bondholders have a claim on assets ahead of the stockholders (but they may still suffer a loss).

Some bonds are convertible, allowing the holder to exchange them for common stock at predetermined prices. Thus, the holder has the safety and fixed income of a bond until he decides to share in the growth of the company.

Bonds generally offer a higher return than savings accounts.

Preferred Stock. The advantage of preferred stock is that if dividends are paid at all, the preferred stock must normally be paid dividends first. Usually any unpaid back-dividends owed to the preferred stock must also be paid before the common stockholders share in any dividends. Dividends on preferred stock are usually stated as a fixed rate. Bondholders, however, have a prior claim to earnings and liquidation assets.

Common Stock. This form of equity offers the greatest management control (each share normally has one vote) and participation in the growth of a corporation. Because its market value is subject to wider variation than that of senior securities, common stock offers greater possible returns and/or appreciation.

Dividends, if paid, are usually paid in cash, but may also be paid in extra shares of stock, sometimes in another company. The holders of common stock have the last claim on earnings or assets (in the event of liquidation).

All forms of stocks (as well as bonds) are usually purchased through brokers or brokerage houses, which can be found in the yellow pages of the telephone book. A commentary on equity returns is made later in this chapter.

Investment Companies. Many military officers have purchased or will purchase open-end (Mutual Funds) or closed-end funds. For this reason a separate section is devoted to this form of investment media later in this chapter.

Permanent Life Insurance Policies. Generally, permanent life insurance policies contain a cash value or surrender value or "savings plan." Rarely do insurance policies guarantee as much as a 4% return on the "savings" in the policy. Usually the guarantee is between 2½% and 3½%. Sometimes a company will pay more if its mortality rates are less than predicted. This is, however, essentially a rebate on the "insurance" part of a policy. Participating policies may also return the policyholder a greater return than guaranteed. Generally, the interest rate on the "savings plan" is less than that paid on savings accounts in commercial banks. The later chapters on life insurance cover these points on cash value in more detail and should be consulted.

Equity in a House. Chapter 7 on "Housing" should be consulted. The mobility of the military man usually precludes his living in a home for a sufficient length of time to build up in-residence equity in a home. As an absentee landlord he may lose control over the quality of his tenants, their payment of the rent, and the necessary upkeep and maintenance of the property. The anxiety caused by having remote property may offset the tax benefits and equity advantages of owning the house. Remember that real estate is often difficult to market quickly.

Real Estate Investments. Let us first consider an investment in raw land. Substantial care should be taken to insure that the land value will increase. Land is worth nothing until someone wants to live, play, work on it or invest in it.

Leverage is one possible advantage of this investment medium. Whereas a common stock purchase requires that you put 60% down, on land you may have to put down only 20% to 25%. For example, if you buy land for $1000 cash and sell it for $2000 a year later you have made a 100% profit. However, let us assume you bought the same land, put $200 down, borrowed the other $800 and still sold it for $2000 a year later. You would have been able to pay off the $800 (we will ignore interest in this example) and enjoyed a return of $1000 on your $200 investment. By using leverage you would have made a 500% profit.

If land (or a house) is held for 6 months the profit normally is subject only to a capital gains tax, never more than 1/2 of your ordinary tax rates. Other advantages are those that could accrue to you as a result of the acceptance of prepaid interest by the seller (resulting in tax advantages to you), or in the use of land as a hedge against inflation.

Notice however that all of the advantages hinge on major assumptions—that the land is well-selected or that it sells at a profit. In land investment, appearances can be very deceiving. The land may have geological problems (improper drainage, underground streams, no water, solid rock).

Legal problems may also be present. Easements giving others the right to your land for use as access to their property or for underground cables, etc. may restrict its use. Zoning may further restrict its use. As an absentee owner, the property next to yours may be rezoned for use as a junkyard.

Brokerage fees and taxes will decrease your profits. The land may be difficult to market quickly. A 50% gain on the sale after 10 years is less than you could have gained in many savings accounts. Your money is tied up until the land is sold.

Real Estate Investment Trusts invest in land as well as commercial buildings, dwellings, construction loans, and mortgages. In this case you might purchase stock in the trust. This stock can usually be bought and sold more readily than land and real estate. Also, the trusts are usually headed by professional managers, and historical data can usually be obtained from your broker regarding the trust's performance.

There are also other means of investing in real estate, such as Real Estate Syndicates and Real Estate Companies. The bibliography should be consulted for more depth in this subject area.

Direct Ownership in a Small Business. Few military men have much time to devote to such an outside activity unless it requires very little time and effort. Certainly, you will need to work out a schedule that does not detract from the accomplishment of your military duties.

Commodity Speculation. Very few military officers have the specialized knowledge required to deal profitably in commodities. Very few civilians have it either. A prominent and knowledgeable leader in a leading brokerage house told the writer that over 98% of those who enter the commodity markets "lose their shirts." He went on to marvel that there were always more people ready and eager to take the losers' places.

The major attraction of the commodity market is the chance to "make a killing" with a small stake by using "margin." For example, $400 on 8% margin will allow you to buy $5000 worth of a commodity. Assume, for illustration, a speculation in a standard contract of 60,000 pounds of soybean oil. If the price goes up only one cent per pound you make $600 on your investment of $400 (ignoring margin and brokerage expenses).

What risks do you run?

1. What if the price should drop? If it is a 1¢ drop, your $400 investment is wiped out, plus you owe the broker his fees, the margin rate charges, a new margin amount of $400 which he will be anxiously awaiting, plus the additional loss of $200 in the contract's value (remember, it dropped $600 in value).

2. Not all commodities are traded actively at all times. To control the wild gyrations in commodity prices somewhat, the exchanges place trading limits. Soybean oil prices, for example, can only go up or down 1¢ per day before trading ceases for the day.

Suppose you suddenly hear that a bumper crop of soybeans will be harvested and you call your broker to sell. Let us assume you are very lucky. Of 350 people who place hurried orders to sell you are in the first 5%—in fact, you are number 16—trying to sell. The commodity clearing house lists your order as number 16 in a list containing the other 349 sell orders. Only now the buyers also know that the price will fall and will not buy. As a result only 5 buyers (who desperately need soybean oil) buy before the price drops the full 1¢, the trading limit is reached, and trading stops. The next day only another 5 buy, the price drops 1¢ again and trading stops. The third day is a repeat performance. Finally, on the fourth day, you (in the lucky top 4 or 5%), sell your contract. In the meantime you have lost sleep and $600 per day plus fees and commissions. Note one important difference between the commodity and the major stock exchanges. You are not guaranteed a buyer (or seller) on the commodity exchanges.

3. At this point you may say—why sell at all, I will just wait until the price goes up again. Unfortunately, another difference between stocks and commodities must now be noted. All commodity contracts come due on a certain date. To avoid having the commodity shipped to you on that date, you must sell it prior to that date—unless you really want to have 60,000 pounds of soybean oil delivered to your front door in a tank car. If that should occur, you would of course have to pay the full $5000 or so value of the commodity plus shipping and storing expenses!

Even if you had a contract with a due date some time off, and did not sell, you would still have to cover your $600 losses per day during the price drops.

Only a few of the possible pitfalls have been discussed here. Hopefully the discussion is sufficient to make clear that speculation in commodities is extremely risky for the military officer. He has neither the specialized knowledge nor the proximity to the markets necessary to speculate successfully in commodities.

INVESTMENT COMPANIES

Officers have several advantages which are conducive to sound savings patterns. Relatively fixed pay scales and job security enable the officer to budget his income. If he can save money as a junior officer, his savings should increase with each promotion. Service benefits free the officer of the need to build up a large cash reserve for emergencies. He is young and can afford a limited amount of risk. On the other hand, the constant relocation of his family inhibits his ability to turn a profit on real estate investment or to participate in other local business ventures since he must either forego necessary supervision of his investment or suffer the expense of hiring someone to do it for him.

The basic problems confronting the officer are time, technology, money, and risk. The dedicated officer does not have time to explore the financial world around him. He has neither the time for proper investment analysis nor the time to supervise his investments. He has not the money to hire experts to share their knowledge with him. Finally, he cannot accept the risk associated with the speculator or gambler and he wants some guarantee of success.

Investment companies were instituted to meet the needs of the small investor and they offer one possible solution to the needs of the officer. These companies were predicated on the idea that a lot of small investors could pool their money thereby attracting professional financial analysts who could devote their time and technical knowledge to the management of the "pool". Most funds offer diversification which no small investor could hope to achieve without excessive expense and, therefore, limited protection against unusual degrees of risk. In return, the investors reward the management with a percentage of the assets but at a much lower fee than they, as individuals, would have to pay for the same personal attention.

The types of investment companies are commonly described as "closed-end" and "open-end" (Mutual) funds.

Closed-end Investment Companies. A closed-end fund has a fixed number of shares outstanding whose price is determined by the value of the securities it holds and the demand for its own stock on the market. The number of shares outstanding is constant. The stock of these funds is traded on the national exchanges and on the over-the-counter market just as are shares of railroads, manufacturing companies and utilities. A broker's commission is charged both when the closed-end stock is bought and when it is sold. Depending on supply and demand, these stocks may sell at a "discount" (less than their net asset value) or at a "premium" (more than their asset value).

Open-end or Mutual Funds. Open-end means that the fund is always ready to sell new shares or redeem old ones. Thus the number of its shares is always changing. These transactions are usually made through a broker or salesman rather than on the market. Price is determined by the net asset value of the fund plus the salesman's commission.

Load and No-load Mutual Funds. The eager fund buyer often overlooks the costs associated with purchases. These costs easily may vary from less than 1% to 15%. Two basic types of mutual funds are LOAD and NO-LOAD funds. LOAD funds are mutual funds which have hired salesmen to seek investor money. In exchange for these services, the fund pays the salesman a commission which is usually around 8½% but varies depending upon size and method of investment. The commission of 8½% is based upon the total amount paid but is actually a larger percentage of the amount that is actually invested for the buyer. For example, on a $1000 sale the salesman would receive 8½% or $85. However, only the difference or $915 would be placed in the fund for the investor. Therefore, the investor has paid $85 to invest $915—a commission on the actual amount invested in the fund of almost 9.3% ($85 ÷ $915). NO-LOAD funds, on the other hand, do not have salesmen, but rely upon inexpensive advertisement to attract investment dollars. The expense is relatively insignificant to the investor.

The other expenses associated with the purchase of mutual fund shares are handling, or service charges, and the management fee. Most funds employ a bank to handle their accounts, mail receipts, and do their bookkeeping. Some banks associated with these funds may charge as much as $.50 per deposit while others charge nothing. Other service charges might be for quarterly statements, disbursement from your account, or for the reinvestment of dividends or capital gains distributed to you.

One fee common to all funds is the management fee. This fee is usually less than one percent annum and is unavoidable. Naturally, the LOAD funds are aggressively seeking new accounts with salesmen since this will increase their assets and in turn their management fee. NO-LOAD funds are generally smaller and have a lower salaried management. They can do this because their management group usually is engaged in other business ventures and as a result has additional sources of income. The performance of both groups appears similar. During the period 1 January 1965 to 31 December 1969, the top four mutual funds (assuming all distributions reinvested in stock) were comprised of 2 Load and 2 No-Load funds.

There are some ways to avoid excessive costs if you decide to buy a LOAD fund. Since salesmen are working for a commission, many of them will steer you toward the type of program that will net them the most commission. There are three basic types of investment programs: Systematic Accumulation, Voluntary Accumulation, and Single Payment Plans.

The salesman would like you to buy the Systematic Accumulation plan. The Systematic Accumulation or "Front-End Load" is an arrangement under which the investor makes monthly or quarterly payments into the fund for a stipulated period ranging up to ten years or more. The commissions are bunched heavily into the first year and sharply reduced in subsequent years, so that the investor who buys a contractual plan and discontinues it in the early years will find he has paid a very high rate of commission on the amount invested. By law, commissions on a front-end load plan may never exceed 9 percent of the total dollars to be invested, and no more than half of any periodic investment during the first year may go for sales commissions. For example, in a $6000 plan spread over a ten-year period, the shareholders would put in $50 per month for a total of $600 the first year. The commission of 9% amounts to $540 of the total $6000 contracted. Of the $540, $300 would go to pay sales commissions from the first year's payments ($600). The remaining commissions would be deducted at a lesser rate during the remainder of the payments over the next nine years. Clearly, if the officer had to discontinue his contract at the end of one year he would have paid in $600 but receive only $300 in return. Also, since more money is taken out early, less goes to work for the investor at the very start.

The alternative plan, Voluntary Accumulation, eliminates the "front end loading" and the salesman's commission is spread evenly over the entire investment period. This plan gives the investor a better equity relationship over the first few years and allows more freedom. He is no longer paying commissions in advance and can terminate his plan with little or no loss during the early years. The voluntary plan does not offer insurance coverage but still permits dollar cost averaging and will attain the same investment objectives.

The third plan is the Single Payment plan. This is for people who have large amounts of cash that they would like to invest in one lump sum. The commissions are scaled depending upon the amount. This plan does not facilitate dollar cost averaging and is not encouraged for those people who will worry about minor fluctuations in the stock market. A more conservative approach would be to open a voluntary account and invest your savings in equal amounts over a period of months or even years.

Both Load and No-Load funds offer various options such as reinvestment plans, retirement plans and periodic accumulation plans.

Performance is probably the key consideration in selecting a fund; however, potential performance is hard to measure. Among both LOAD and NO-LOAD you will find much variation in fund performance, a key element in any investment decision. No one should pick a fund solely because it charges no sales commission. Certainly, a well-managed LOAD fund would be better for an investor than a NO-LOAD with consistently inferior performance. However, given similar investment objectives and performance, the investor's income will be higher and his capital results better in the fund that invests the entire amount of his purchase.

The performance ratings, objectives, costs, fees, and addresses of both LOAD and NO-LOAD funds may be found in the bibliographical references at the end of this chapter. Refer especially to *Fundscope* magazine and Wiesenberger's *Investment Companies*.

INFLATION

The value of the dollar in terms of purchasing power has declined for the past 30 years. This is inflation. There have been times in our country's history when the value of the dollar has increased in terms of purchasing power. The Great Depression is the most recent example of a period of deflation. An investment program must guard against both risks to the value of the dollar. The officer already has certain built-in protections against deflations which include his retirement pay, Social Security and medical benefits. Thus the main risk your long-term investment program should be designed to treat is inflation.

Inflation (a rise in the general level of prices) has occurred at an annual compound rate of over 3% since 1940. The purchasing power of the consumer dollar of 1958 shrank to less than 75c by 1970. Such inflation means that the dollar's purchasing power is decreasing; to buy a standard of living costing $500 a month today is apt to require $1000 a month 30 years from now.

This should be kept in mind when you are setting long-range goals such as a retirement income fund. We recommend that officers base their long-range investment program on equity investments, so that the effect of inflation can be nullified by growth in the value of investments. This program, of course, should be initiated only after adequate insurance programs and reserves for all short-term needs have been established.

RETURNS FROM EQUITY INVESTMENTS

It is legitimate to ask what kind of return can be expected from equity investments. It is not necessary to assume high risks through speculative techniques in order to achieve attractive rates of return in the long run. This fact is pointed up by studies made by Professors Lawrence Fisher and James H. Lorie of the University of Chicago. Their extensive research is summarized in two articles in the *Journal of Business:* "Rates of Return on Investments in Common Stocks" (July 1968) and "Outcomes for 'Random' Investments in Common Stocks Listed on the New York Stock Exchange" (April 1965). Free reprints are available from Merrill Lynch, Pierce, Fenner & Smith, Inc.

Among other things, the authors discovered that the median rate of return on the 1,856 NYSE common stocks from 1926 to 1965 was 9.3% per year compounded annually. The chance of making money by purely random investments on the New York Stock Exchange during the period was 78%.

Another study made at the University of Michigan covering the 1937-1960 period of NYSE listed stocks assumed a regular investment in each of the 92 stocks that had a trading volume of a million shares or more in 1936. All dividends were assumed to be reinvested. The compound growth rate of these 92 stocks for the entire period was 14%. Between 1950 and 1961 their compound growth rate was 14.2%.

From 1950 to 1965 the Dow-Jones Industrial Average showed a growth rate of over 10% a year compounded. This is growth in value only, dividends are not included.

The writer believes that if reasonable selection techniques are used, the typical investor in high-quality growth issues can expect an average rate of return of 10% per year when both dividend yield and capital appreciation are considered. Naturally, equity investment always includes the chance of loss and the opportunity for much greater returns than 10% per year. The typical returns, however, certainly make direct investment in the stock market attractive to the officer.

Remember that you receive a $100 tax-free income deduction from dividends on stock (up to $200 on a joint account). You may wish to purchase dividend producing stocks initially to take advantage of this tax deduction.

No text of this scope can hope to cover all of the area of savings and investments, but the readings in the bibliography have been selected for your information, pleasure, and perhaps profit.

Appropriate chapters of the standard personal finance texts listed in Chapter 3.

'Adam Smith' (Goodman, George). *The Money Game.* New York: Random House, 1968.

Barnes, Leo. *Your Investments.* New York: American Research Council, Published annually. (This inexpensive but comprehensive book is highly recommended as a starting place to study.)

D'Ambrosio, Charles A. *A Guide to Successful Investing.* Englewood Cliffs, N.J.: Prentice-Hall, Inc., 1970.

Department of Defense, Armed Forces Information Service. *Uniformed Services Savings Deposit Program.* DOD Pamphlet FS-39A. Washington: U.S. Government Printing Office, 1968.

——————. *Spending and Saving While Overseas.* DOD Pamphlet FS-56. Washington: U.S. Government Printing Office, 1968.

Engel, Louis. *How To Buy Stocks.* New York: Bantam Books, 1969.

Fundscope. Los Angeles: Fundscope, Inc., Published monthly.

Hazard, John W. *Choosing Tomorrow's Growth Stocks Today.* Garden City, New York: Doubleday & Co., Inc., 1968.

How to Read a Financial Report, What Everybody Ought To Know About This Stock and Bond Business, and other pamphlets available free from Merrill Lynch, Pierce, Fenner and Smith, Inc., 70 Pine Street, New York, N.Y. 10005.

Investment Company Institute. *1970 Mutual Fund Fact Book.* New York: Investment Company Institute, Published annually.

Know, Harvey A. *Stock Market Behavior, The Technical Approach to Understanding Wall Street.* New York: Random House, 1969.

Polakoff, Murray E. (ed.). *Financial Institutions and Markets.* New York: Houghton Mifflin Co., 1970.

Schwartz, Robert J. *You and Your Stockbroker.* New York: Macmillan Co., 1968.

Understanding the New York Stock Exchange and other free pamphlets published by the New York Exchange, 11 Wall Street, New York, N.Y. 10005.

Weston, J. Fred and Eugene F. Brigham. *Managerial Finance.* 3rd ed. New York: Holt, Rinehart and Winston, Inc., 1969.

Wiesenberger, Arthur. *Investment Companies.* New York: Nuveen Corporation, Published annually.

PART **TWO**

GOVERNMENT SURVIVOR AND RETIRED BENEFITS

The first years of a man must
make provision for the last.
—Samuel Johnson

CHAPTER 11

MANAGING PERSONAL RISKS

IT WAS POINTED out in Chapter 9 that, as a risk manager, you should identify the perils that can cause financial losses, evaluate the impact such losses would have on the family, and select the most effective and efficient techniques to treat them. In addition to property and liability risks, your family faces the *personal risk* of financial loss through:

1. Accident or sickness.
2. Disability.
3. Superannuation (living beyond the years of economic productivity).
4. Premature death (death of a person while others are dependent upon him for income).

As an Armed Forces officer, you must evaluate these risks in light of the government programs which are available to offset the effects of losses due to each of the risks. This chapter will briefly present the nature of the first three risks and the major government programs to include in your plans. Analysis of the fourth personal risk—that of loss of income through premature death—will be presented in succeeding chapters.

ACCIDENTS OR SICKNESS

Accident or sickness is a source of two types of financial loss; the loss of income caused by a period of disability and the cost of medical care. Many civilian workers must rely on insurance protection against these risks. Armed Forces officers, however, receive government assistance which usually eliminates the need for additional protection whether on active duty or retired.

Your risk of loss of income through accident or sickness is non-existent since pay continues as long as an officer is on active duty. Retirement pay also continues for retired officers. Relative to the situation that arises when sickness or accident results in disability retirement see a later heading—Disability Retirement.

MEDICAL EXPENSES

Officers On Active Duty. The risk of loss through extraordinary medical expenses has been largely eliminated for most officers by government medical care programs. The active-duty officer is always entitled to medical and dental care at government expense except where illness or injury occurs "not in line of duty." Normally this care is provided in a Uniformed Services medical facility.

Retired Personnel. Eligible retired personnel will be furnished medical and dental care to the same extent provided active-duty officers in any Uniformed Services facility, but on a space-available basis. Retired personnel may also be eligible for various medical benefits administered by the VA. Such benefits could include treatment in a VA hospital, domiciliary care, out-patient medical and dental treatment, medical examinations, and treatment by approved private physicians in the veteran's home community, depending upon the retiree's eligibility under current provisions of law. In addition, retirees are eligible for civilian medical care under the CHAMPUS program briefly discussed below.

Treatment In Facilities Of The Uniformed Services. Medical care may be furnished for qualified dependents of active-duty, eligible retired or deceased officers in Uniformed Services facilities. The precise services provided are determined by current provisions of law, the capability of the facility involved, and the extent that providing such services does not interfere with the primary mission of the facilities. Since the families of Servicemen are often separated from adequate Uniformed Services facilities, obtaining proper medical care has frequently been a serious problem.

Medical Care Under CHAMPUS. The Civilian Health and Medical Program of the Uniformed Services (CHAMPUS) has significantly alleviated this situation by providing a complete range of medical care in civilian facilities with civilian doctors. Also eligible for care are dependents of active-duty, retired and deceased members of the Uniformed Services.

When seeking civilian health benefits, eligible persons are encouraged to seek care from sources who will participate in the program. When a person obtains care from a participating source of care, the source of care signs a certificate on the claim form that except for the amount payable by the patient in accordance with the terms of CHAMPUS the amount paid by the government will be accepted as payment in full for the authorized services and/or supplies furnished. Thus, the patient is not obligated to pay any disallowed portion of the charges for authorized care.

If an eligible person elects to obtain care from a source who will not participate in the program, the patient must first pay and thereafter submit a claim for reimbursement. In such cases, reimbursement can only be made in the amount that would have been payable had the source of care participated in the program; any disallowed portion of the charges remains the responsibility of the patient.

The scope of medical and dental care under CHAMPUS can be expected to change through amending legislation. Therefore, you should always consult current official directives to determine the precise benefits available to you. Keeping this fact in mind, the following paragraphs briefly outline the major provisions of CHAMPUS.

CHAMPUS expands the scope of services authorized for dependents in Uniformed Services facilities to include hospitalization and out-patient treatment for chronic conditions and diseases and nervous, mental, and emotional disorders; artificial limbs and eyes; loan of durable equipment; and family planning services.

The civilian health benefits established by CHAMPUS for dependents and retirees include:

1. Hospitalization in semi-private accommodations for all types of medical care.

2. The following services and supplies on either an in-patient or out-patient basis:

   a. Services of a physician (or dentist when appropriate) for treatment of medical and surgical conditions; nervous, mental and emotional disorders; chronic conditions and diseases; contagious diseases.

   b. Maternity and infant care.

   c. Diagnostic tests and services.

   d. Anesthetics and oxygen and their administration.

   e. Blood, blood plasma, and blood plasma expanders.

   f. Radiation therapy.

   g. Physical therapy.

   h. Orthopedic braces (except orthopedic shoes) and crutches.

   i. Dental care required as a necessary adjunct to medical or surgical treatment.

   j. Artificial limbs and eyes.

k. When ordered by a physician, the services of persons specializing in a science allied to the practice of medicine, such as anesthetists, psychologists, physical therapists, optometrists, speech therapists, etc.

i. Immunizations when required as a part of medical treatment.

m. Use of out-patient treatment and facilities.

n. Family planning services and supplies.

o. Insulin, drugs and medicines obtainable only by written prescription.

p. Rental of durable equipment such as wheelchairs, iron lungs, and hospital beds.

q. Home calls when medically necessary.

r. Necessary services and supplies ordered by the attending physician except those excluded by law.

s. Routine physical examination and routine immunizations only when required by active duty dependents who are under orders to perform travel outside the United States as a result of their sponsor's duty assignment.

t. Certain non-government ambulance service.

u. Certain Christian Science services.

Health benefits *not* authorized from civilian sources under CHAMPUS are:

1. Domiciliary or custodial care.

2. Routine physical examinations and immunizations (except as in u. above) not for diagnostic purposes and routine immunizations.

3. Routine care of the newborn and well-baby care.

4. Spectacles or examinations for them.

5. Prosthetic devices (other than artificial limbs or eyes), hearing aids, and orthopedic shoes.

6. Dental care except when required as a necessary adjunct to medical or surgical treatment.

7. The services of chiropractors.

Payment for *in-patient services* in civilian facilties under CHAMPUS is authorized as follows:

1. Dependents of active-duty members will pay the first $25 of the hospital's charges or $1.75 a day, whichever amount is greater. The government will pay the remainder of the hospital's charges for authorized services and the fees of professional personnel.

2. Retired members and their dependents and dependents of deceased members will pay 25% of the hospital's charges and the fees of professional personnel. The government will pay the remainder of the hospital's charges for authorized services and fees of professional personnel.

Payment for *out-patient services* from civilian sources under CHAMPUS is as follows:

1. Dependents of active-duty members will pay the first $50 of ex-

penses incurred for out-patient services each fiscal year (not to exceed $100 per family), plus 20% of the charges in excess of the $50 or $100-deductible as appropriate. The government will pay 80% of the charges for out-patient services in excess of the amount deductible.

2. Retired members and their dependents and the dependents of deceased members will pay the same deductible as above, plus 25% of the charges in excess of the deductible. The government will pay 75% of the amount exceeding the deductible.

These medical benefits require the typical officer to maintain the type of emergency fund discussed in previous chapters, but make the purchase of insurance protection against accident and sickness unnecessary.

In fact, individuals (except active duty dependents) enrolled in any other insurance, medical service, or health plan provided by law or through employment are not eligible for reimbursement for civilian care under CHAMPUS unless the benefit claimed is not payable under the other plan.

At age 65 most beneficiaries will be eligible for civilian care under the Social Security Medicare Program. Consequently they will transfer to that program and will no longer be eligible for civilian care under the Uniformed Services Civilian Health Program. (This does not apply to active duty dependents.) Beneficiaries, however, may continue to receive space-available care in Uniformed Services facilities. Whether or not one should elect to participate in the Social Security Health Program for the Aged or commercial insurance programs upon reaching the age of 65 depends on, among other things, the availability of adequate Uniformed Services or VA facilities, and existing family conditions. You should seek the advice of your Service's Retired Activities Branch and commercial health insurance agents when the time approaches for making the decision.

DISABILITY RETIREMENT BENEFITS

If the Service Secretary decides that a disability disqualifies an officer for active duty, the Secretary can place him on either a permanent or temporary disability retirement list, or can grant a disability discharge either with or without severance pay. Anyone disabled while on active duty will be fully informed, before he retires, of the various rights and benefits to which he is entitled.

The important point to note is that purchase of protection against disability, in addition to that already afforded by government programs, does not appear to be warranted. Funds so allocated would probably bring greater benefits if allocated to savings and investments. Although the typical healthy officer need not take any action to protect himself against disability risks, a brief outline of the protection presently afforded by government programs is in order. In addition to the medical benefits mentioned above, certain income benefits are available to officers retired for disability.

Disability Retired Pay. If an officer with a 30% or more disability is permanently retired for disability, his Service will pay him a fixed monthly sum between 30% and 75% of his basic pay for the rest of his life. The amount paid will depend upon the degree of his disability and his choice of one of two formulas that can be used to compute it.

These formulas are:

1. Monthly base pay x number of years of service x .025.
2. Monthly base pay x percentage of disability.

In neither case can the pay benefit exceed 75% of his base pay. If the second formula is used, his income will be entirely tax exempt. If the first is used, that part of it equal to the amount computed by the second formula is tax exempt; only the remainder is taxable.

If the Secretary of the officer's Service rules that he has a disability rated 30% or more that may be permanent, but which cannot definitely be classified as permanent at the time, he can be placed on the Temporary Disability Retired List (TDRL) for up to five years. While on the TDRL, he will receive monthly payments of at least 50% but not more than 75% of the basic pay for his retired grade.

An officer having 20 years active duty can be permanently retired or placed on the TDRL with a disability rated at less than 30%. In this case, his retired pay would be calculated using the first formula above, since it would always result in a higher amount. Years of service on the TDRL count for basic pay computation but do not count as creditable service for retirement.

Severance For Disability. If an officer with less than 20 years service has a less than 30% disability which was not caused by his own intentional misconduct, willful neglect or while AWOL, his Service Secretary can discharge him with severance pay. Severance pay is equal to two months basic pay for each year of qualifying service up to 12 years.

VA And Social Security Benefits. A fact of vital importance is that any separation from active duty with the Armed Forces under conditions other than dishonorable, makes an officer a veteran and thus usually eligible for benefits administered by the Veterans Administration (VA). Any officer who believes that he has a disability, even if his Service disagrees with him, should investigate his eligibility for a VA disability compensation award.

The Services and the VA do not necessarily give an individual the same disability rating and they do not make the same payments for the same percentage of disability. The Service disability rating is based on the physical condition of the member at the time of his retirement and is permanent. The VA disability rating may also be decreased or discontinued, but if this happens, a retired member may always elect to resume receipt of his retired pay.

Payment received from the VA as compensation is exempt from Federal taxation, whereas Service retired pay, except for disability pay, is subject to taxes. Some (but not all) retired members can effect a tax saving by receiving part of their pay in the form of disability compensation.

Also note that a person retired from the Service is entitled to certain VA-administered readjustment benefits which may be received concurrently with retired pay. If retirement is due to disability, one may be eligible for vocational or educational rehabilitation benefits. In addition, those who can establish a Service-connected disability, even if it is 0% disabling, qualify for "Service Disabled Veterans' Insurance." The major point is to review VA benefits with a VA representative before you retire, whether because of disability or not. The VA will be able to give you up-to-date information upon which you can base your election of benefits, and will assist you in applying for those that are available.

If an officer is disabled under the definition contained in the Social Security Act (unable "to engage in any substantial gainful activity"), he may be eligible for Social Security disability benefits. Such officers should have their case presented to the Social Security Administration for determination of eligibility for benefits.

VOLUNTARY RETIREMENT BENEFITS

The retirement system established for the Armed Forces officer is unique in many respects. Of particular note is the fact that while retirement and superannuation usually go hand in hand for the civilian worker, voluntary retirement from a Uniformed Service often means the beginning of a second career. Mandatory retirement around the age of 65 is becoming more and more common for the civilian worker. From that point on, employment opportunities are quite limited.

Armed Forces officers are permitted to retire as early as after 20 years of active duty. Thus a man commissioned at age 21 could retire from active duty at age 41, with more than 20 years remaining before he reaches age 65. Even after 30 years of service, many retired officers make valuable contributions to industry and the nation's economy through civilian employment for several years. Each officer facing retirement must make his own decision regarding a second career.

In this chapter we will consider only those factors necessary to demonstrate the construction of the Retirement Income Plan. Only after you have constructed this Retirement Income Plan, the Retired Survivorship Plan (discussed in Chapter 13), and the Active-Duty Survivorship plan (discussed in Chapter 12) can you tell how well you are prepared for future contingencies.

In this chapter we will illustrate the monthly income of a retired officer of an assumed age and rank. There are two governmental sources of income available to the retired officer: retirement pay and Social Security retirement benefits. The retired officer can supplement these benefits with his savings and investments and earnings from employment.

Let us first examine the current retirement pay computations, keeping in mind that the retired pay structure is subject to change. Be sure to use current pay scales when you develop your own plan.

Retirement Pay. Upon your retirement, final pay and allowances will be paid you. You will also receive a lump-sum settlement for unused accrued leave up to a maximum of 60 days. Your retired pay is usually 2½% of the base pay of the highest rank you held for at least six months multiplied by your number of years of service (not to exceed 30). Thus your retirement pay will fall somewhere between 50% and 75% of your basic active-duty pay.

All retirement pay is made by U.S. Treasury checks, mailed directly to your bank if you so desire. Retirement pay cannot be attached or garnisheed by order of any court. Only the U.S. Government can control or take such pay. Allotments in effect at the time of retirement may be continued; new allotments from retired pay are authorized for life insurance premiums, indebtedness to the United States, U.S. Savings Bonds and bank account deposits. Retirement pay based on length of service or age is taxable.

If you are eligible, you may waive an equivalent portion of your retired pay in order to receive non-taxable VA compensation. Doing so will not affect your entitlement to such benefits as Commissary and Exchange privileges, medical care, etc. You may, at any time, subsequently re-elect to receive all your retirement pay through the Service.

Once your retirement pay has been established and you retire, increases in retired pay are tied to the Consumer Price Index. Increases are authorized whenever the CPI advances to and remains for at least 3 consecutive months at a level of 3% (or more) higher than the point in the Index from which a previous pay increase was granted. Thus, if you are planning for retirement, you can assume that your retired pay will keep pace with inflation.

Dual Compensation. Under the most recent Dual Compensation Act (Public Law 88-448), Regular officer retirees can receive the full salary of any Federal civilian office held.

However, if certain Federal civilian offices (as defined in the Act) are held, the Regular officer retiree's retirement pay is reduced to an annual rate equal to the first $2000 of retirement pay plus 1/2 the remainder, if any. This $2000 amount, however, will be increased according to increases in the CPI as described above, and by April 1970 had already increased to $2360.

This reduction in retirement pay does not apply to certain types of disability retirement pay. Neither does it apply when retirees hold certain offices exempted by U.S. Civil Service Commission regulations whenever appropriate authority determines such exceptions are warranted on the basis of special or emergency employment needs. Non-regular officers and enlisted retirees, including those advanced to a higher temporary grade upon retirement, are exempt from this restriction.

Assumptions For Making A Retirement Plan. For the remainder of this chapter, let us consider the situation of a hypothetical 0-3 with 9 years service, making out a Retirement Income Plan in June 1971. Let us assume that he plans to retire in 1982 with 20 years service with a basic pay of $1300 per month. The most conservative approach to planning retirement income is to assume retirement at the earliest possible date, with a pay grade reasonable for that period of service. This allows calculation of the lowest likely income for the longest anticipated period of retirement. When you reach the point of qualifying for retirement, you should of course use data appropriate to your individual case.

For the purposes of planning, we assume that military pay will increase just enough to keep pace with inflation. To calculate the retired pay, recall that you merely multiply base pay by 2.5% and the expected number of years service. For our example:

$$1300 \text{ x } 2.5\% \text{ x } 20 = \$650$$

This figure can be plotted on the Retirement Income Chart as indicated in Chart 11-1. To retirement pay we must then add Social Security retirement benefits. Before computing this benefit for our illustration, a brief introduction to the Social Security system is in order.

SOCIAL SECURITY

The Social Security Act establishes a number of programs having various social objectives. These programs are:

1. Retirement insurance.
2. Survivors insurance.
3. Disability insurance.
4. Hospital and supplementary medical insurance for the aged.
5. Unemployment insurance.
6. Various public assistance and welfare services.

The first four programs are operated by the Federal Government; the remainder are operated by the states with grants from the Federal Government. Retirement, survivors, and disability insurance benefits are cash benefits paid directly to beneficiaries by the Social Security Administration. The remainder of this chapter will outline some general aspects of the Social Security system as applied to Servicemen, summarize the retirement insurance program and illustrate the calculation of retirement benefits. A

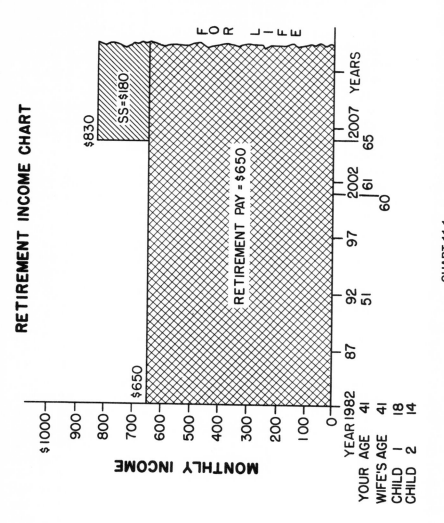

RETIREMENT INCOME CHART

MONTHLY INCOME

$1000 — 900 — 800 — 700 — 600 — 500 — 400 — 300 — 200 — 100 — 0

$830

SS=$180

$650

RETIREMENT PAY = $650

FOR LIFE

YEAR 1982   87   92   97   2002   2007 YEARS
                      51   61   65
                                  60

YOUR AGE   41
WIFE'S AGE 41
CHILD 1   18
CHILD 2   14

CHART 11-1

discussion of Social Security survivors benefits is presented in Chapter 12. The remaining Social Security programs will not be discussed in this text.

Basics of the System. From the individual's point of view, it is necessary to know whether or not his employment is covered by Social Security, how much his participation in the Social Security program costs, and what benefits he or his dependents are eligible to receive under the system.

Each individual covered by Social Security is given an account number and a record of his earnings is maintained by the Social Security Administration, Baltimore, Maryland 21235. A statement of your Social Security earnings is available upon request.

Active-duty members of the Uniformed Services have been covered by Social Security on the same basis as individuals working in civilian life since 1 January 1957. Prior to 1957, under certain conditions, members were granted free wage credits of $160 per month for service from 17 September 1940 through 31 December 1956.

Your statement of earnings does not include wage credits for service before 1 January 1957, but if you are eligible for them, they will be considered when a claim for benefits is made. Social Security taxes are withheld from the active-duty Serviceman's pay. Retired pay is not subject to Social Security tax and unless otherwise engaged in covered employment, a member will not earn Social Security credits after retirement.

Social Security programs are financed out of taxes paid by employers and employees. The rates each must pay are indicated in Table C-10, Appendix C. This table also indicates the amount of annual income subject to the Social Security tax rates and the consequent maximum amount of tax payable in any one year. Only the Serviceman's basic pay is taxable for Social Security purposes. Note also that the rates and amounts shown in Table C-10 for 1971 forward are subject to legislative change. Be sure you are using current data.

Eligibility for Benefits. To be eligible for cash benefits under the Social Security system, Servicemen must accumulate a specified number of credits (quarters of coverage). For the purposes of our analysis, there are two kinds of Social Security insured status: *fully insured* and *currently insured*. To receive retirement benefits, a Serviceman must be *fully insured*. For his widow age 60 to receive survivor benefits, he must be *fully insured*. For his widow caring for his child under age 18, or his child either under age 18, or age 18-21 and a full-time student, or qualified under disability provisions, the Serviceman can be either fully or currently insured in order for them to be eligible for survivor benefits. Regardless of the benefit payable, the individual upon whose earnings record the benefits are based must have attained a certain insured status by acquiring quarters of coverage. Note also that insured status determines only the eligibility for certain benefits, and has nothing to do with the amount of benefits that can be paid.

To earn a quarter of coverage, a Serviceman must receive at least $50 in basic pay during a calendar quarter of three months. However, even though an individual does not receive sufficient pay in a quarter to be credited with a quarter of coverage, he will be credited with four quarters of coverage for any year in which his base pay received exceeds the taxable base indicated in Table C-10.

To be *fully insured*, a person would normally be required to earn one quarter of coverage for each year elapsed after 1950 (or after the year in which he attained age 21, whichever is later) and before:

1. In the case of a woman, the year in which she died or attained age 62, whichever is earlier.

2. In the case of a man who has died, the year in which he died or the year in which he attained age 65, whichever is earlier.

3. In the case of a man who has not died, the year in which he attained or would attain age 65. In any case, however, no one can be *fully insured* if he has less than 6 quarters of coverage. A person who has 40 quarters of coverage is *fully insured* for life.

A person is *currently insured* if he has at least 6 quarters of coverage during the full 13-quarter period ending with the calendar quarter in which he either died or became entitled to retirement benefits.

Quite clearly, the typical officer who has been on active duty until his voluntary retirement in 1968 or thereafter, is *fully insured* and is thus eligible for both retirement and survivor benefits. It is also clear that anyone who now graduates from a Service Academy and remains on active duty is *fully insured* since he will always have at least one quarter of coverage for each year elapsed after the year in which he attained age 21.

Noncontributory Wage Credits. Members of Uniformed Services are given noncontributory wage credits (deemed wages) in addition to credit for their basic pay for calendar quarters after 1967. The amount of deemed wages that may be credited for a quarter is:

1. $100 if the basic pay in the quarter is $100 or less.
2. $200 if the basic pay in the quarter is $100.01-$200.00.
3. $300 if the basic pay in the quarter is over $200.

For active duty your credits for each month of active duty will generally amount to your basic pay plus $100. No additional deductions will be made from your pay for the extra $100 credits. You cannot, however, get Social Security credit for more than $7,800 in any year, including the extra credits.

For example, let us assume the case of an 0-1 with less than 2 years service. His monthly basic pay is less than $500 and less than 1/12 ($650) the maximum of $7800 annual basic pay on which Social Security payments are taxed. Thus, since his monthly basic pay is less than $650 per month, the 0-1 would receive a free $100 monthly additional Social Security credit. An officer earning $600 basic pay would receive only the difference up to $650 or $50 free credit. An officer making $650 or more per month would receive no free credit. Cadets in Service Academies are *not* eligible for the $100 free credit per month.

These credits will appear on your Social Security permanent earnings record. They should be counted automatically when you or a member of your family make a claim for benefits. It is in your interest to doublecheck this by requesting a statement of your earnings from Social Security. However, your Federal Income Withholding Statement, Form W-2 will not show these additional credits.

If you have any doubt about your eligibility for Social Security benefits, consult either the more detailed references in the bibliography or your nearest Social Security office.

Calculation of Cash Benefits. In most cases, benefits payable under the social insurance programs are based on the insured individual's *Worker's Benefit* (this is sometimes referred to as the PIA or Primary Insurance Amount). We will use the term Worker's Benefit (WB). The WB, in turn, is determined from his Average Monthly Wage (AMW)—also referred to as Average Monthly Earnings (AME).

The exact amount of your benefit cannot be figured until you apply for benefits. This is because all of your earnings covered by the law are considered. The Social Security Administration will, of course, figure your exact benefit but you may estimate the amount in the following manner:

1. Determine the "benefit computation years." Count the years beginning with 1951 or upon reaching age 21 (whichever is later) up to (but not including:

   a. The year of death.

   b. The year age 65 (62 for a woman).

2. Drop the 5 years of lowest earnings. However, at least 2 years of earnings must be used to figure survivors or disability benefits; 5 years for retirement benefits. It may be necessary to leave years in which the person had no earnings on the list.

3. Divide the total earnings of the remaining years by the number of years included times 12 (to derive AMW). Do not count more than:

   $3600 a year during 1951-1954;
   $4200 a year during 1955-1958;
   $4800 a year during 1959-1965;
   $6600 a year during 1966-1967; and
   $7800 a year during 1968 and after.

As an example, a man reaching age 65 in 1971, if he was paid at least the maximum amount of wages taxable for Social Security purposes during the years 1951-1971 would have earned benefits computed as follows:

1. Drop the 5 years of least earnings, 1951-1955.

2. Add the earnings of years 1956-1970. (3 x $7800) + (2 x $6600) + (7 x $4800) + (3 x $4200).

3. Divide $82,800 by 180 months (15 years x 12) and compute an AMW of $460.

4. The Worker's Benefit (WB or PIA) corresponding to any calculated AMW can be found in standard Social Security tables such as Table C-12, Appendix C. These tables also indicate the retirement and survivor benefits corresponding to any calculated AMW or WB.

There is one important option available to retirees between the ages of 62 and 65. Such a person, who is otherwise eligible for Social Security retirement benefits, can choose either to receive a reduced benefit or wait until age 65 to receive the full retirement benefit. If he elects to receive a reduced benefit, the amount received will continue for life. All Social Security retirement benefits end with the beneficiary's death. No retirement benefit can be paid for the month of death. However, survivor benefits may be payable to the insured person's qualified survivors beginning with the month of his death.

In order to receive Social Security retirement benefits, beneficiaries under age 72 must qualify under an annual-earnings test. Under the current law, a beneficiary can earn up to $1680 a year and receive full Social Security benefits each month. One who earns more than $1680 per year, however, gives up $1 of Social Security benefits for each $2 he earns between $1680 and $2880. For every $1 of earnings over $2880, he must give up a matching $1 of benefits.

There is one exception to this provision. No matter how much a beneficiary earns in a year, he can still be paid a full benefit for any month in which he does not earn wages of more than $140 and does not actively work in self-employment. Note that the earnings referred to under the annual-earnings test are wages resulting from employment or self-employment. Thus other income, such as that derived from savings and investments, is not included as "earnings."

This brief discussion of the Social Security system has been greatly simplified; it certainly does not have the effect of law. You are encouraged to study the more detailed sources listed in the bibliography below, especially if your situation deviates from that of the typical male officer discussed above. One final reminder: Social Security benefits must be applied for before they can be received. They are not paid automatically. You should therefore visit your local Social Security Office well in advance of the date you expect to become entitled to retirement benefits (allow for a "lag time" of 90 to 120 days).

COMPLETING THE RETIREMENT INCOME PLAN

Let us now return to the construction of the Retirement Income Plan displayed on Chart 11-1. Twenty years of active duty since 1957 would accumulate more than the 40 credits necessary for a fully-insured status. Thus the officer will be entitled to full retirement benefits based on his AMW when he reaches age 65. The AMW at that time will be greatly influenced by the employment of the retiree from the time he leaves the Service until reaching age 65. Let us assume, for the purposes of this example, an AMW which yields a WB (or Social Security retirement benefit) of $180 per month. This figure can be plotted on the Retirement Income Chart as indicated in Chart 11-1. His spouse may also be eligible for some Social Security payments.

Chart 11-1 presents the maximum Government retirement benefits to which our hypothetical officer would be entitled under the assumptions used. Any discrepancy between the amount of income desired and the amount provided by Government retirement benefits must be made up by savings and investments and/or additional employment. You should add the results of your present savings and investment program to your Retirement Income Chart to determine how well it suits your needs.

Often a commercial annuity bought with funds saved in the form of cash values in permanent life insurance policies or other savings media is used to close the gap between retirement income needs and government retirement benefits. An expert commercial insurance agent can provide valuable guidance in this matter.

After you have completed your Retirement Income Plan, including all sure income available, you can turn to the second plan necessary for the evaluation of your long-run financial situation—the Active Duty Survivorship Plan. This is the subject of the following chapter.

Appropriate portions of the publications listed in the bibliography for Chapter 3.

Commerce Clearing House, Inc., *Medicare and Social Security Explained.* New York: Commerce Clearing House, Inc., 1968.

Department of Defense, Armed Forces Information and Education. *Disability Separation.* DOD PA-IA. Washington: U.S. Government Printing Office, 1966

Department of Health, Education and Welfare, Social Security Administration. *Health Insurance Under Social Security.* Washington: U.S. Government Printing Office. October 1969.

——————. *Social Security Handbook.* 4th ed. Washington: U.S. Government Printing Office, February 1969.

——————. *Your Social Security Earnings Record.* Washington: U.S. Government Printing Office. May 1970.

Headquarters, Department of the Army. *The Army Personal Affairs Handbook.* DA Pamphlet 608-2. Washington: U.S. Government Printing Office, August 1969.

Office of the Surgeon General U.S. Army. *Uniformed Services Health Benefits Information.* Denver, 1968.

Veterans Administration. *Federal Benefits for Veterans and Dependents.* VA Fact Sheet IS-1. Washington: U.S. Government Printing Office, March 1970.

*He that hath a wife and children,
must not sit with his fingers in
his mouth.*

—Thomas Fuller

CHAPTER 12

ACTIVE DUTY
SURVIVOR BENEFITS

THE FAMILY'S loss of a loved one is tragic enough without being compounded with economic ruin. This can result from being underinsured. A few individuals, on the other hand, have been known to be so concerned with this risk that they become what is known as "insurance poor"— they burden their family budget with extraordinarily high insurance premiums, making family life a lot less comfortable and pleasant than it needs to be.

The need for proper planning to strike the best balance cannot be overemphasized. You cannot go strictly on rules of thumb. You would not buy a suit by picking the average size. Similarly, your life insurance programs must be tailored to the needs of your individual family.

PLANNING TECHNIQUES

The systematic approach advocated in this book is simply this:

1. Analyze the impact of the risk of your premature death on your family in light of the protection you already have from Government survivor programs, accumulated assets, and the earning power your family would still have should you die.

2. Determine what additional protection is required to meet your family's needs.

3. Examine the alternative methods of purchasing the necessary additional protection.

4. Integrate your choice of methods and their costs by the process of marginal analysis, so that each extra dollar you allocate to insurance protection buys about the same benefit for your family as that spent on food, housing, clothing, savings, etc.

In this chapter, government programs which protect your family against the risk of your premature death will be graphically portrayed, illustrating the situation that exists when an officer dies while on active duty. In the next chapter, we will deal with the situation in which an officer dies after retirement. Chapters 14 through 17 present information necessary for an understanding of the use of life insurance. Chapter 18 will complete the systematic planning process for treating the risk of premature death by adding to the government benefits described in this and the next chapter, the protection provided by other resources.

Active Duty Survivorship Chart. Now let us turn to the construction of a graphical presentation of an Active Duty Survivorship Plan (Chart 12-1). This plan, when added to your Retirement Income (Chart 11-1) and Retirement Survivorship Plans (Chart 13-1), will enable you to evaluate the adequacy with which your family's long-term financial needs will be met. Again, on the chart, monthly income is placed on the vertical axis and years are plotted on the horizontal axis. The ages of family members corresponding to selected years are also plotted. The year plotted at the origin is the assumed year of death.

The reason the Active Duty Survivorship Plan is keyed to the immediate death of the principal is because this represents the most conservative planning approach, an approach which identifies the smallest level of income the survivors can count on receiving for the longest conceivable period of need. Sometimes this is referred to as picking "the worst time to die," but unless this method is used, the adequacy of survivor income cannot be assured.

You want to be sure that your plan is adequate right now. Then, every time a significant change occurs in the family situation (new children, disabilities of family members, etc.), you should again review the adequacy of your plan. If possible, you should make such a review once each year.

One of the problems the planner faces is that of finding current data upon which to base his plan. This text includes data current at the time of writing. But pay tables, VA benefits and Social Security benefits are continually being revised. The bibliography at the end of this chapter contains VA and Social Security Administration publications that are updated periodically. Also, newspapers directed toward Servicemen (such as the *Army, Navy,* or *Air Force Times*) keep close tabs on legislation changing compensation and benefits. When you are constructing your own survivorship plans, use the most current data available.

The planning process, however, will remain the same. Since it is assumed that you are able to obtain data from appropriate pay and benefit tables, the figures we will use will not be derived from an actual table. Rather, we shall direct you to the proper table, and then assume figures for the purposes of illustration.

The first step in constructing a plan to treat the risk of premature death is to calculate those government benefits that provide at least partial protection. We will construct an Active Duty Survivorship Chart based upon three benefits which would be paid to survivors on a monthly basis, and three benefits which are paid to survivors in a lump-sum. The monthly survivor benefits are:

1. Dependency and Indemnity Compensation (DIC).
2. Social Security Survivor Benefits (SS).
3. War Orphans Educational Assistance (WOEA).

The three lump sum benefits are:

1. Lump-sum Death Gratuity.
2. Social Security Lump-sum Death Payment.
3. Pay for Accrued Leave.

In addition, Servicemen are eligible to participate in the Serviceman's Group Life Insurance Program (SGLI), to be discussed later.

We will use the case of a hypothetical officer who dies on active duty on 1 January 1972. On that date, the following data is assumed to apply:

1. The officer has 9½ years service, has just been promoted to O-4 and has a basic pay of $900 per month.

2. The age of the officer and his wife is 31; the ages of their two rchildren are 8 and 4.

3. The officer is a graduate of a Service Academy, reached age 21 in late 1961, and has never earned wages from civilian employment.

4. At the time of death, he has 30 days accrued leave.

5. He fully participates in the SGLI program.

The resultant calculations of government survivor benefits in the paragraphs below can be used as a model applicable to your Active Duty Survivorship Plan.

MONTHLY SURVIVOR BENEFITS

Dependency and Indemnity Compensation. DIC payments are payments payable to widows, unmarried children under 18 (as well as certain helpless children and those between 18 and 23 if attending a VA-approved school), and certain parents of Servicemen or veterans who die from:

1. a disease or injury incurred or aggravated in line of duty while on active duty or active duty for training; or

2. an injury incurred or aggravated in line of duty while on inactive duty training; or

3. a disability otherwise compensable under laws administered by the VA.

Although not applicable to our example, a limitation to note is that if a Serviceman or veteran dies of a service-connected cause with an In-Service waiver of premiums on GI life insurance in effect at the time of death, his survivors are eligible only for an older and almost always lower-paying death compensation.

Eligible widows, as defined by law, are entitled to a monthly DIC payment based upon the Serviceman's military pay grade. For officers, the amount varies upward from $211 per month for the widow of an 0-1 to $426 for the widow of an 0-10. Refer to Appendix Table C-9 for the amount pertinent to each pay grade. The amount payable to the widow of an 0-4 is $247 per month and can be plotted on the Active Duty Survivorship Chart as shown in Chart 12-1.

This DIC payment will continue for the life of the widow unless she remarries. Note that the amount of DIC paid does not increase concurrently with pay raises for active-duty personnel. DIC payments are fixed in amount and are not tied to military pay raises. Thus, no measure of protection against inflation is provided.

A widow who qualifies for DIC may be granted a special allowance for aid and attendance if she is: A patient in a nursing home; helpless or blind; or, so nearly helpless or blind as to need or require the regular aid and attendance of another person. The additional allowance is $50 monthly, which is payable in addition to the basic DIC rate for which the widow otherwise qualifies.

In addition to the above, DIC payments are increased by $20 per month to the widow for each child below age 18. Thus, in our example, the widow of the O-4 would receive an additional $20 per child besides her $247 widow's payment until the children reach age 18. Chart 12-1 reflects this increase.

A helpless child (one who has become incapable of self-support prior to age 18) entitles the widow to an additional $80 per month.

When no widow is entitled to DIC, payment for eligible children under age 18 is made as follows: $80 for one child; $115 for two children; $149 for three children; and $29 for each additional child. A helpless child (as defined above) is entitled to the rate payable for a child under age 18 plus $29.

Children 18 through 22 years of age and attending an approved school are eligible to receive the following DIC payments, provided they are not receiving payments under the War Orphans Educational Assistance Act:

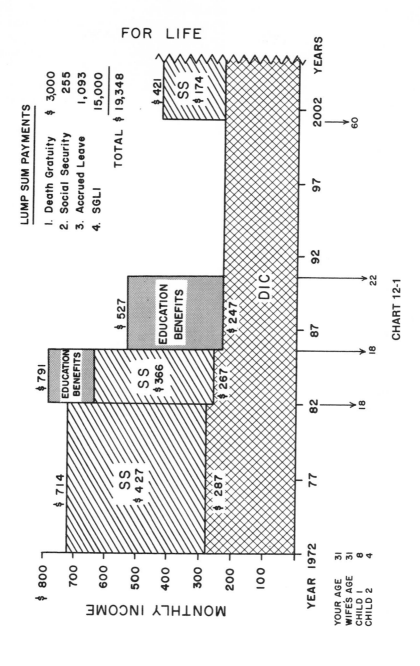

ACTIVE DUTY SURVIVORSHIP CHART

FOR LIFE

LUMP SUM PAYMENTS

1. Death Gratuity $ 3,000
2. Social Security   255
3. Accrued Leave   1,093
4. SGLI   15,000

TOTAL $ 19,348

MONTHLY INCOME

$ 800
700
600
500
400
300
200
100

YEAR 1972   77   82   87   92   97   2002   YEARS

$ 791   EDUCATION BENEFITS
$ 714
SS $427
$ 527   EDUCATION BENEFITS
SS $366
$ 267
$ 287
$ 247
DIC
$ 421
SS $174

18   18   22   60

YOUR AGE   31
WIFE'S AGE   31
CHILD 1   8
CHILD 2   4

CHART 12-1

1. If a widow is also entitled to DIC payments, $41 per month.

2. If a widow is not entitled, the rate payable for a child under age 18.

The benefits available under the War Orphans Educational Assistance Act (WOEA) are discussed below. You should note at this time, however, that if there is a choice between the educational benefits of DIC or WOEA, the WOEA benefit is higher. In a few instances, it may be desirable to continue receiving DIC payments for a limited time to preserve entitlement to WOEA for use later.

Once WOEA is selected, DIC benefits may not be claimed again. Caution should be exercised, however, to insure in this planning that the WOEA entitlement will be used prior to the child's 26th birthday or the later date provided in certain exceptional cases. This option can be particularly advantageous when the educational program of the child may be expected to be longer than the 36 months of WOEA entitlement.

DIC payments for dependent parents will vary according to the number of parents, the amount of their individual or combined income, and whether or not they live together (or, if remarried, live with a spouse). For a sole surviving parent living alone, rates range from $10 to $87. Rates for two parents range from $10 to $58 each per month.

No amount is payable if the income other than DIC of one parent or each of two parents not living together is more than $2000, or the total combined annual income other than DIC of two parents living together, or of a remarried parent living with a spouse, is more than $3200.

Social Security Survivor Benefits. Social Security survivor benefits are authorized for the widow of a fully-insured Serviceman when she reaches age 60. Note, however, that she has the option to wait and take increasingly larger benefits until she is eligible for full benefits at age 62. Her full benefit at 62 is equal to 82.5% of the Worker's Benefit (or PIA) of her deceased husband. The benefit that the widow becomes eligible for at age 60 is a reduced benefit which is computed by multiplying her full benefit by .866, the reduction factor found in Appendix Table C-11 for the number of months in the "reduction period." Thus with the passing of each month after the widow reaches age 60 (and postpones receiving benefits), the amount of the benefit to which she is entitled increases until she reaches age 62.

Although the decision actually made by a widow should depend upon her particular situation at the time, we shall assume the widow takes a reduced benefit at age 60.

Survivor benefits are also authorized for a widow caring for the deceased's child under age 18, or for his child either (1) under age 18, or (2) ages 18-21 and a full-time student, or (3) qualified under disability provisions, if the Serviceman was either fully or currently insured. The amount of any survivor benefit depends upon the Serviceman's Average

Monthly Wage (AMW). The calculation of the AMW was described in Chapter 11. See Table C-12, Appendix C which indicates approximate survivor benefits corresponding to various values for AMW. Be sure to use current tables when you construct your survivor plans.

Before adding Social Security benefits to the example shown in Chart 12-1, let us review how the AMW for our hypothetical officer would be computed.

Since the officer became 21 years of age in late 1961, the elapsed years are 1962 through 1971, or 10 in number. The number of benefit computation years would equal 10 - 5 = 5 (must not be less than 2 years in any event). To determine which years to use, we must find the years in which Social Security taxable wages were the highest.

In most cases, this would be the most recent years, since the base pay of an officer increases with time, and the taxable base for Social Security purposes has been increasing as shown in Appendix Table C-10. By referring to the appropriate pay tables for each of the years 1967 through 1971 (see Tables C-1 through C-3, Appendix), we find that the basic pay of an O-3 and O-4 would exceed the maximum taxable wage in each year.

Assuming the officer had been promoted at normal stages during his career, his AMW calculation would be (from Appendix Table C-10):

$$\frac{(1 \times \$6600) + (4 \times \$7800)}{5 \times 12} = \$630$$

Let us assume that standard Social Security tables showed the following:

AMW	WB	Widow Age 62	Widow + 1 Child	Family Maximum
$630	244	201	366	427

CALCULATION OF SURVIVOR BENEFITS

YEARS	SITUATION	BENEFITS DIC + SS
1972 - 82	Widow + 2 Children under age 18	$287 + 427 = $714
1982 - 86	Widow + 1 Child	267 + 366 = 633
1986 - 2001	Widow + 0 Children	247 + 0 = 247
2001 - Life	Widow Age 60	247 + 174 = 421

TABLE 12-1

These data permit us to calculate the monthly survivor income for which our hypothetical officer's family is eligible, exclusive of the children's education benefits discussed below. When the widow is age 60 she receives $174 (86.6% x $201) from Social Security. Table 12-1 indicates these calculations which have also been plotted on Chart 12-1.

Social Security Children's Education Benefits. Social Security benefits are available for eligible children under age 22 who are "full-time students" in an approved school. The amount of the benefit is equal to .75 of the Worker's Benefit (or PIA), provided the Maximum Family Benefit is not exceeded. A "full-time student" is defined as one who is in full-time attendance at an educational institution, in accordance with the standards and practices of the school involved. This definition provides for the payment of benefits for any period of four calendar months or less in which a person does not attend school, so long as he is still a full-time student. The calculation for our example is:

$$.75 \text{ PIA} = .75 \times \$244 = \$183$$

Thus each child is authorized $183 until the Maximum Family Benefit is reached. Then each benefit is reduced so that the family as a whole receives the Maximum Family Benefit.

War Orphans Educational Assistance. Children ages 18 through 25, of deceased veterans, or those living veterans who have total and permanent disabilities, are eligible for educational assistance for any month in which they actually attend an approved school. Each child can receive $130 per month of school for up to 36 months, if enrolled full time; $95 per month if enrolled three-quarters time, and $60 per month if enrolled half-time. Those enrolled in cooperative courses—alternating classroom study and related experience on the job—will receive $105 per month.

As stated above, a child cannot receive the WOEA benefit while receiving the $41 educational benefits under the DIC program. The benefits a family receives, therefore, will depend upon the manner in which they are applied for.

For the purposes of our example, let us assume that each child attends 9 months of college per year for four years and therefore receives $130 x 36 = $4680 over that period. This averages out to be a little over $97 per month for 4 years. This figure can be used for planning purposes. If we thus assume that no DIC educational benefits are applied for, and that each child attends college for four consecutive years (9 months per year) beginning at age 18, then we can summarize all monthly survivor benefits received in our example in Table 12-2.

LUMP-SUM BENEFITS

Death Gratuity. A lump-sum death gratuity is payable to the survivors of a Serviceman whose death occurred while on active duty, active duty for

SUMMARY CALCULATIONS OF SURVIVOR BENEFITS

YEARS	STUDENTS	CHILDREN'S EDUCATION BENEFITS			FAMILY BENEFITS		
		SS +	WOEA =	TOTAL	CHILD'S +	WIDOW'S =	TOTAL
1972 - 82	0	0 +	0 =	$ 0	0 +	714 =	$714
1982 - 86	1	61 +	97 =	158	158 +	633 =	791
1986 - 90	1	183 +	97 =	280	280 +	247 =	527
1990 - 2001	0	0 +	0 =	0	0 +	247 =	247
2001 - Life	0	0 +	0 =	0	0 +	421 =	421

NOTE: The benefits summarized in Table 12-2 are plotted on Chart 12-1.

TABLE 12-2

training, inactive-duty training, or as the result of a Service-connected cause within 120 days after discharge or release from active duty or active duty training under other than dishonorable conditions.

The amount of the benefit is equal to 6 months' pay of the deceased, including special incentive, hazardous duty, and basic pay, but not allowances. In no case, however, will the sum be less than $800 nor more than $3000. In the case of our example, the $3000 limit obviously applies.

Social Security Lump-Sum Death Payment. If a fully or currently-insured Serviceman dies, his survivors receive an amount equal to $255 or 3 times the deceased's Worker's Benefit (or PIA), whichever is smaller. In this case, the $255 maximum obviously applies.

Pay For Accrued Leave. The payment of pay (basic + quarters allowance + subsistence allowance) is authorized to dependents for earned but unused accrued leave up to 60 days. The assumed value for this case is $1093.

In summary, the lump-sum benefits payable to the widow of our hypothetical officer would be:

Death Gratuity:	$3000
SS Lump-sum:	255
Accrued Leave:	1093
	$4348

These values are listed as lump-sum payments on Chart 12-1.

GI LIFE INSURANCE

Except in a limited type of case GI life insurance can no longer be issued. Therefore the provisions of such policies will not be discussed. Only Servicemen separated with a Service-connected disability may apply to the VA for the special $10,000 nonparticipating National Service Life Insurance Policy (NSLI). Anyone in this category will be advised of this opportunity before separation.

Some individuals on active duty may yet be holders of GI life insurance (USGLI or NSLI). By now, all have probably exercised any conversion options appropriate to their case. If you are uncertain as to whether you hold a GI life insurance policy under the most favorable option, consult with a VA representative as soon as possible.

One point is worth emphasizing again. Those persons who elected the In-Service waiver of premiums may continue the waiver as long as they are on active duty and for 120 days thereafter. But if such a person should die with the waiver of premiums still in effect, his dependents would not be eligible for DIC benefits; they would be restricted to the old form of death compensation which, except under highly unusual circumstances, would mean lower benefits for his family.

SERVICEMAN'S GROUP LIFE INSURANCE PROGRAM

The Serviceman's Group Life Insurance Program (SGLI), established by Public Law 89-214 (1965), is a life insurance program for all members of the Uniformed Services who are on active duty. Coverage is automatic; the Serviceman must take positive action to refuse the insurance or to reduce his coverage from the maximum amount. If a Serviceman exempts himself from the program and then later applies for participation, he must fill out a questionnaire regarding his health.

Premium rates for SGLI are $3 per month for $15,000 coverage, $2 per month for $10,000 coverage, and $1 per month for $5000 coverage. In the future, the cost may be adjusted (hopefully downward) as experience dictates. The extra-hazard cost of insuring Servicemen is paid by the Government. Premiums are deducted from Service pay by the Department of Defense and remitted to the Veterans Administration. These premium deductions cover the administrative expenses of the VA.

The mode of settlement, to be determined by the beneficiary or beneficiaries in the absence of instructions from the Serviceman, is limited to a lump-sum payment or settlement over a 36-month period in equal monthly installments. The Serviceman may designate any person as a beneficiary. If an affirmative designation is not made, the insurance will be paid in the following order: (1) widow or widower; (2) child or children; and (3) parents. If none of these are living, the proceeds will be paid to the executor or administrator of the deceased's estate or to the next-of-kin under the laws of the domicile of the deceased.

Upon termination of active-duty, the individual is protected in the full amount of his policy for 120 days without further premium payment. On the 121st day (unless the individual has a total disability) he may convert his SGLI to a permanent policy offered by any participating insurance company. Any member leaving service with a total disability has one year rather than 120 days to convert SGLI to a commercial policy. If the totally disabled member dies within that year, SGLI proceeds will be paid to the beneficiary. Even if the individual is separated because of a Service-connected disability, he is eligible for this conversion without a medical examination.

Possession of USGLI or NSLI coverage is no bar to participation in the SGLI program. Since the net cost of SGLI coverage is less than any other protection available to the commissioned officer, any officer with the need for insurance protection should elect to participate in the program. Chart 12-1 indicates participation by our hypothetical officer and includes the $15,000 SGLI proceeds with the lump-sum benefits calculated above.

This completes our analysis of the government benefits available to the survivors of officers who die on active duty. The following chapter presents an analysis of the situation faced by the family of an officer retired from active duty.

Appropriate portions of the publications listed in the bibliography for Chapter 11.

Brinker, Paul A. *Economic Insecurity and Social Security*. New York: Appleton-Century-Crofts. 1968.

Commerce Clearing House, Inc., *Medicare and Social Security Explained*. New York: Commerce Clearing House, Inc., 1968.

Department of Defense, Armed Forces Information Institute. *Once A Veteran*. DOD Pamphlet PA-5A. Washington: U.S. Government Printing Office, 1969.

Department of Health, Education and Welfare, Social Security Administration. *Social Security Handbook*. 4th ed. Washington: U.S. Government Printing Office, 1969.

——————. *Your Medicare Handbook*. Washington: U.S. Government Printing Office, 1968.

Veterans Administration. *Federal Benefits for Veterans and Dependents*. VA Fact Sheet IS-1. Washington: U.S. Government Printing Office. March 1970.

Old Age isn't so bad when you
consider the alternative.
                              —Maurice Chevalier

CHAPTER **13**

RETIREMENT SURVIVOR BENEFITS

WE EXAMINED the financial situation of the officer living after retirement from active duty in Chapter 11. A Retirement Income Chart was constructed to present a graphical analysis of the income available to the retiree and his family. In Chapter 12, we illustrated the Active Duty Survivorship Plan which graphically indicates the income available to an officer's family if he dies while on active duty.

The risk of financial loss through the premature death of an officer continues for the family even after the officer retires. When the retired officer dies, his retirement pay, as well as any income derived from his civilian employment, ceases. Since there are significant differences between the government survivor benefits provided the family of an officer when he dies on active duty on the one hand, and when he dies in retired status on the other, the complete analysis of an officer's long-range financial situation requires a Retirement Survivorship Plan which will indicate the income available to the retiree's survivors. The purpose of this chapter is to illustrate the government programs designed to offer some protection to the retiree's family. First we will discuss the applicability of the survivor benefits discussed in Chapter 12; then we will discuss the Retired Serviceman's Family Protection Plan (RSFPP).

ELIGIBILITY FOR BENEFITS

Dependency and Indemnity Compensation (DIC) is not available to the survivors of a retired officer unless his death results from a disease or injury incurred or aggravated in line of duty while on active duty, active duty for training or inactive duty training, or from a disability otherwise compensable under laws administered by the V.A. Thus, for planning purposes, the healthy officer cannot include DIC in his Retirement Survivorship Plan.

Social Security Survivor Benefits are available as described in Chapter 12. The amounts of Social Security would be based on the deceased's AMW at the time of death.

War Orphans Educational Assistance is not available. It is available only to children, wives, and widows of veterans who have become totally and permanently disabled by reason of a Service-connected disability, and to children of veterans whose death was under one of the following conditions:

1. Death resulted from a Service-incurred or aggravated disability, disease or injury.

2. A Service-connected disability was a contributory cause of death.

3. The veteran was in receipt of or entitled to receive Service-connected disability compensation rated total and permanent at the time of his death. It should be pointed out, however, that if a deceased retiree had WWI, WWII or Korean Conflict service, his children might be eligible for certain pension benefits.

The *Lump-Sum Death Gratuity* is not payable to a retiree's survivors unless death resulted from a Service-connected cause within 120 days after retirement.

The *Social Security Lump-Sum Death Payment* of 3 times the Worker's Benefit (PIA) or $255 (whichever is smaller) is available. Payment for *accrued leave* should have already been made at the time of retirement.

In summary, then, the government programs to be included in the Retirement Survivorship Plan (unless a Service-Connected death or disability is involved) are:

1. Social Security Survivor Benefits.
2. The Social Security Lump-sum Death Payment.

Charting the Social Security Data. If we assume that the amounts of these benefits will be the same in 1982 as they are today, then we can plot the benefits applicable to the hypothetical officer described in Chapter 12 should he retire with 20 years service and a base pay of $1300 per month. Whether or not the officer converts his SGLI insurance to permanent insurance will be ignored in this chapter. Again, we will take the conservative approach and assume death in the year he retires. The calculation of his new AMW is as follows:

1. Elapsed years (1962 through 1981 = 20.
2. Benefit computation years = 20-5 (lowest 5) = 15.
3. Years included = 1967 through 1981 in which the maximum taxable amount was always earned (i.e., $6600 in 1967 and $7800 in the remainder. See Appendix Table C-10).
4. Therefore AMW = $\dfrac{(1 \times \$660) + (14 \times \$7800)}{15 \times 12}$ = $643.

Let us assume that standard Social Security tables such as Appendix Table C-12 showed the following:

AMW	WB	Widow Age 62	Widow + 1 Child	Family Maximum
$743	$248	$205	$372	$431

The total benefits to be plotted on the Retirement Survivorship Chart (Chart 13-1) are summarized in Table 13-1. Remember that the retirement of the widow at age 60 calls for the use of the reduction table factor in Appendix Table C-11. For simplicity the student's Social Security benefit of .75 the Worker's Benefit (or PIA) has been lowered so as not to exceed the family maximum allowed. In official computations both the widow's and children's benefits would be lowered proportionately down to the maximum family benefit.

A quick look at Chart 13-1 reveals that the above benefits cannot give a satisfactory level of income for the deceased's family. Indeed, there is an 11-year period when there is no income from government programs at all. The gap between the desired level of income and that already achieved must be made up with income from other sources such as accumulated assets, employment by members of the family, life insurance, or the Retired Serviceman's Family Protection Plan (RSFPP). Closing the gap with income from accumulated assets and life insurance is discussed in Chapter 18. The remainder of this chapter is concerned with RSFPP.

SUMMARY CALCULATION OF SURVIVOR BENEFITS

YEARS	CHILDREN'S SS BENEFITS STUDENT	BENEFIT	TOTAL BENEFITS CHILD'S		WIDOW'S		
1982 - 86	1	$ 59	$ 59	+	$372	=	$431
1986 - 90	1	186	186	+	0	=	186
1990 - 2001	0	0	0	+	0	=	0
2001 - Life	0	0	0	+	177	=	177

TABLE 13-1

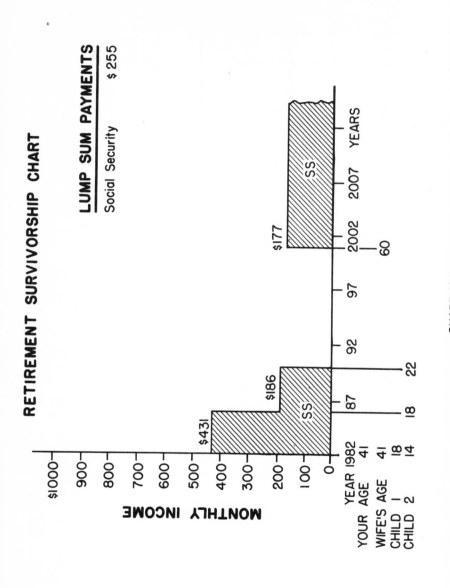

RETIREMENT SURVIVORSHIP CHART

LUMP SUM PAYMENTS

Social Security $ 255

MONTHLY INCOME

$1000
900
800
700
600
500
400
300
200
100
0

$431

$186

SS

$177

SS

92   97   2002   2007   YEARS

18   22   60

YEAR 1982   41
YOUR AGE   41
WIFE'S AGE
CHILD 1   18
CHILD 2   14

87

CHART 13-1

RETIRED SERVICEMAN'S FAMILY
PROTECTION PLAN

The purpose of the RSFPP is to make it possible for a Serviceman to purchase a survivorship annuity (monthly income for his widow for life or eligible children until age 18 or longer in certain circumstances) with payments automatically deducted from his retired pay. Officers desiring to participate in the RSFPP enroll in the plan by completing a form provided by their Service in which they select the amount of the annuity to be paid in the event of their death, and the beneficiaries to whom such annuities will be paid. RSFPP is geared primarily to the needs of the Serviceman voluntarily retiring after 20 years of service, but annuities calculated on the basis of separate cost factors are also available for Servicemen retired for physical disability with 19 but less than 20 years of service, and for those retired for physical disability with less than 19 years of service for pay purposes, if ineligible for DIC. This chapter will deal only with the first category—voluntary retirees having at least 20 years of service.

If an officer decides to participate in the RSFPP, he must enroll before completing 19 years of service for pay purposes or, if not then, at least 2 years before entitlement to retirement pay. Anyone who elects to participate after his 19th year of service must subsequently serve at least 2 years on active duty before his enrollment becomes valid.

Amount of Survivor Annuity. Annuities can be specified either in dollar amounts—such as $300 a month—or as a percentage of retired pay. (An annuity amount cannot be less than $25 a month in any case.) One advantage of specifying a percentage of retired pay is that no fixed dollar amount is set at enrollment. This allows the RSFPP annuity to increase at the same rate as the member's expected retired pay increases in the years between enrollment and retirement. If you do select a dollar amount, you can choose one somewhat higher than one-half of retired pay for your grade and service when you enroll. If this amount proves higher than the maximum one-half of the retired pay you are actually granted, it will be adjusted downward at your retirement.

The cost of the protection you select—as computed at the time you are granted retired pay—will not increase as your retired pay increases (now on the basis of rises in the cost of living index) during your years of retirement. Neither does the amount of the annuity you select change as your retired pay increases. Any annuity amount or percentage that would be paid at your death is tied directly to the amount of your retired pay at the time you retired, not at the time the annuity becomes payable to a survivor(s).

Beneficiary Options. Beneficiary selections are made by selecting one or a combination of three options under the plan. The "options" are as follows:

OPTION 1 provides a monthly annuity to your widow until her remarriage or death.

OPTION 2 provides a monthly survivor annuity for your eligible child (or children), including a stepchild or adopted child, until the child reaches age 18 or, as long as attending college or other training, age 23 or gets married, whichever occurs first. (In the case of a child who became disabled before reaching age 18, payments can continue without regard to age as long as the beneficiary remains unmarried and disabled.)

OPTION 3 provides a monthly annuity for your widow and eligible children. It is payable to the widow until her remarriage or death, and then continues to an eligible child or children as long as at least one child (including a disabled child) is eligible.

You may elect any one of the three options singly or Options 1 and 2 combined. You may not elect Options 1 and 3 combined or Options 2 and 3 combined.

Option 3 coverage possibly provides the greatest flexibility insofar as a maximum annuity (50 percent of the member's retired pay) continuing to be paid to one or more beneficiaries under conditions that cannot be predicted at the time of enrollment. However, because it is the most broadly inclusive protection, it also costs more.

One point you should know about electing Option 3 coverage is that its cost is computed at the time you retire on the basis of persons eligible at that time. Unless you later reduce the annuity amount, this cost remains the same as long as both you and your wife are living, regardless of how many years a child or children remain eligible for the annuity. When you no longer have an eligible child, your cost is not reduced. However, your wife is still protected to the maximum extent in that she can receive the full annuity amount until her remarriage or death. On the other hand, if your wife dies before you do, your full retired pay is restored, and any eligible children continue to be fully protected at no further cost to you.

When a combination of Option 1 and Option 2 is elected, the cost is about 3% less than Option 3, and the cost of Option 2 continues only as long as at least one child is an eligible beneficiary. Likewise, the cost of Option 1 continues only as long as there is an eligible wife. However, it is not possible with this method to provide the maximum annuity unless the wife and at least one child are both eligible, since a separate annuity is selected for each option, and the combined annuities cannot exceed 50 percent of your retired pay.

Limitations On Beneficiaries. An annuity to a widow can be provided only for the person who is the lawful spouse of the member on the date of retirement. Any spouse or dependent children acquired after retirement are not eligible for annuities under the RSFPP.

Limitations On Changes And Revocations. The last election, change or revocation on file on the date of the completion of 19 years of service for pay purposes will be your election unless you later modify or revoke it.

During the period between your enrollment and your retirement, you may modify your RSFPP protection or withdraw from the program. If occurring later than completion of your 19th year of service, any change of option or annuity amount or withdrawal will be valid only if the date of the change of revocation is at least 2 years prior to the first day for which you are granted retired pay.

A special provision protects you if, after your enrollment but before you are granted retired pay, a major change in marital or dependency status results from death, divorce, annulment, remarriage, or acquisition of a child. Following such an event, the enrollee has up to 2 years but before the first day for which he is granted retired pay to change his RSFPP election to fit the new family situation. The change cannot increase the protection originally provided. The member is also free to revoke, rather than modify, his election because of this family change if he desires.

When there is no family member eligible for a survivor annuity under RSFPP, monthly withholdings from your retired pay cease, and your full monthly retired pay is restored. (Formerly, this protection was known as Option 4 protection. Under the 1968 law this protection was made automatic for all enrollees who retire on or after August 13, 1968.)

After retirement you may reduce the size of an annuity you have chosen or you may withdraw from RSFPP at will. If you do either, the change in protection or the withdrawal will be effective after a 6-month waiting period. After your request, the proper portion (in the case of a reduction in annuity) or all (in the case of withdrawal) of your retired pay would be restored beginning with pay on the seventh month. Correspondingly, any reduced annuity or withdrawal would not be effective until the first day of the seventh month.

Cost Of Participation. The reductions in retirement pay required to pay for RSFPP annuities vary in amount depending upon:

1. The amount of retirement pay.

2. The number of years service for pay purposes at the time of retirement.

3. The amount (fraction of reduced retirement pay) of the annuity selected.

4. The option(s) elected.

5. The ages of the Serviceman and his beneficiaries at the time of his retirement.

The RSFPP is self-supporting on an "actuarial equivalent" basis, which means that participant's reductions must be large enough to defray the annuity payments. However, all administrative and overhead costs are paid by the government, thus making RSFPP usually less expensive than a commercial annuity contract purchased at retirement.

The calculation of the precise costs and amounts of annuities in each individual case is based upon a complete set of tables contained in the pamphlet the *Retired Serviceman's Family Protection Plan,* DOD PA-7B. The RSFPP Cost Tables in this DOD pamphlet (See Appendix Table C-13) state the monthly cost factor per $1.00 of the monthly annuity you wish to provide. Let us use Table C-13 to illustrate how this would be done for our hypothetical officer case.

Sample Calculation. Let us assume our hypothetical officer wants to evaluate the RSFPP as an alternative method for providing survivor benefits in the event of his death after retiring from 20 years active duty. He would probably pick a combination of Options 1 and 2—Option 1 to provide monthly income to his widow; Option 2 to provide monthly income to his eligible children (both of whom will be under age 23, the cutoff if they go to college). He has decided that Options 1 and 2 are more desirable (and less expensive) than Option 3. Let us also assume that he desires the amount of the annuity to be half his reduced retirement pay. He thus computes his retirement pay as 50% (for 20 years) of his basic pay at retirement ($1300) or $650. Of the $325 (1/2 his retirement pay) he decides to provide a $200 annuity for his wife and a $125 annuity for his children. His children will go on to college and are thus eligible until age 23.

To compute his reduction in retired pay you first compute his Option 1 costs from Table C-13. You find his age at retirement (41) in the left-hand vertical column and trace this horizontal line to the right until you reach the column for his wife's relative age (since she is 41, the zero column is used). The .17 figure at this location in the table is his monthly cost factor per $1.00 of the monthly annuity provided. Multiply the annuity amount ($200) by this factor and you obtain the approximate monthly cost of the RSFPP protection he selected. A $200 Option 1 annuity costs him a retirement pay reduction of $34.

Then we perform the same basic steps in Table C-13 (part 2) to compute the costs of Option 2. However, in this case the horizontal axis is based upon the age of the youngest child. His youngest child is 14 when he retires. It costs him one cent per dollar (or $1.25) for the $125 annuity he wishes to provide for his children. The combined cost for the 2 Options then is $35.25, reducing his $650 per month retirement pay to $614.75.

Note that if the officer decided to enroll in the RSFPP, he would then alter his Retirement Income Chart (Chart 11-1) by reducing his retirement pay from $650 to $614.75, and would add the $325 annuity to his Retirement Survivorship Chart (Chart 13-1) in the same way that DIC is indicated on his Active Duty Survivorship Chart (Chart 12-1).

Taxes. One more aspect of the RSFPP should be pointed out before we consider the factors underlying a decision to participate in the plan or not. Under Public Law 89-365, gross income from retirement pay is equal to the reduced amount (Net retirement pay after the RSFPP reduction.) Thus, in our example, if the officer received an annual non-disability retirement pay of $7,800 per year reduced by $423 for RSFPP, only $7,377 would represent taxable income. Note, however, that state income tax laws may or may not follow the Federal rule.

While the retiree pays no Federal income taxes on his RSFPP reduction, his survivors must report any RSFPP annuity payments as ordinary income, unless the deceased retired of a Service-connected disability and then died before reaching normal retirement age. In such a case, $5,000 RSFPP income may be excluded from gross income.

For further details on RSFPP tax questions, consult your Legal Assistance Officer or other competent tax authorities.

The Decision. Whether or not our hypothetical officer would elect to enroll in the RSFPP would depend upon several factors. He would have to consider the needs of his family during his retirement, the impact his death would have on the family, the other resources available to provide survivor benefits (such as his investments), the health of family members and the cost of alternative methods of providing survivor income. He would also have to consider the limitations on changes and beneficiaries and how the Plan's restrictions might apply to his situation. Recall that any dependents acquired in retirement cannot be beneficiaries under the plan.

Unfortunately, the question of whether or not enrollment in RSFPP is profitable or not can only be answered in retrospect. If a retiree died shortly after retirement and his widow lived unremarried to a "ripe old age," it would be obvious that his small investment in RSFPP had yielded large returns. On the other hand, consider the retiree and his wife who have sacrificed an RSFPP reduction from current income for many years only to have the wife predecease the retiree. Or consider the retiree who sacrifices current income to provide an income for a widow who chucks it all for a new husband shortly after he passes on.

As we pointed out in Chapter 9, decisions must be made amid uncertainty. The technique used to treat uncertainty is to most effectively and efficiently protect dependent families against risks of financial loss, without unjustly sacrificing current income. A balance must be struck so that the benefits per dollar spent on security and long-range needs equal the benefits per dollar spent on current consumption. The benefits derived from each are implicit in the value judgments made by individuals. To assist in making such judgments in the area of meeting long-range needs, we have initiated a planning technique using graphical presentations of the three fundamental situations each officer must plan for: living in retirement, dying while on active duty, and dying after retirement. How to most efficiently complete those three plans is discussed in Chapter 18, after the introduction to life insurance has been completed.

Department of Defense, Armed Forces Information Service. *Retired Serviceman's Family Protection Plan.* DOD Pamphlet PA-7B. Washington: U.S. Government Printing Office, 1969.

Headquarters, Department of the Army. *Retired Army Bulletin.* DA Pamphlet 600-1. Washington: Office of the Adjutant General, Published monthly.

——————. *Handbook on Retirement Services for Army Personnel and Their Families.* DA Pamphlet 600-5. Washington: U.S. Government Printing Office, 1969.

Veterans Administration. *Federal Benefits for Veterans and Dependents.* VA Fact Sheet IS-1. Washington: U.S. Government Printing Office, March 1970.

PART **THREE**

LIFE INSURANCE

Insurance is an ingenious modern game of chance in which the player is permitted to enjoy the comfortable conviction that he is beating the man who keeps the table....
—Ambrose Bierce

CHAPTER **14**

THE LIFE INSURANCE PRINCIPLE

IN PREVIOUS chapters, we described various government programs which help Armed Forces officers treat the risk of financial loss through premature death. Usually, such programs provide only a part of the financial resources survivors need to maintain their standard of living. The gap between projected needs and those satisfied by government programs can be filled with income from accumulated assets, employment or life insurance. This chapter introduces life insurance—its logic, sources, types, typical policy provisions and selection—so that you can better construct your own insurance program, and evaluate the advice of insurance salesmen and other advisors.

RISK SHARING APPLIED TO LIFE INSURANCE

Insurance is the most universal and probably the soundest scheme yet devised for avoiding or transferring risk. In general terms, insurance is a scheme of social cooperation whereby a hazard or risk, which is too great for any one person to bear, and to which a large group of persons is exposed, is spread over the entire group.

It is a common fallacy to think that because one does not "collect" on an insurance policy he has wasted his money or has somehow been cheated. Obviously, the peace of mind, the avoidance of the threat of great loss—in short, the insurance protection that each member of the entire group received—was more than ample compensation for the small expenditure.

The risk of premature death is one that is admirably suited to the insurance principle. Large groups of persons are continually seeking protection for their dependents against this risk, and whereas nothing is more uncertain than the length of a single life, few things are more stable than the number of deaths that will occur during a given period of time among a large group of persons. This fact has enabled statisticians to build tables that show for a given number of lives the average number of persons of any age that may be expected to die each year. These tables form the basis of most life insurance calculations.

Commissioners Standard Ordinary Table. The C.S.O. Table (1958) is the most recent mortality table. Most states now require that companies licensed to sell insurance within their borders use this table which is based on the experience of life insurance companies for the years 1950-54. This table (Table 14-1) is "padded" in favor of the companies in order to provide less risk to the companies from mortality fluctuations and other contingencies.

Basically, the table is "padded" in two ways. First, it assumes all persons die before or at age 99. Since not all die by then, some policyholders continue to pay beyond age 99 (or interest is earned on the policy reserves) and all rates are slightly higher on the assumption that all will be dead by a certain age.

Another way the table is "padded" is in its lack of currency. The 1958 C.S.O. Table is based upon the experience of companies during the years 1950-54. Thus, the data is almost 20 years old. Generally, the life span of the population is increasing due partially to technological and medical advances. Appendix Table C-14 compares the mortality rates of the 1958 C.S.O. Table with the 1959-1961 total population experience of the United States. Life expectations are definitely longer on the 1959-61 table which is not used by the companies. Thus, in general, the mortality experience of the life insurance companies should be lower than the C.S.O. Table upon which the companies base their premium calculations.

The 1958 C.S.O. Table starts with 10,000 male lives at Age 0. It follows the survivors through to Age 99. Each year the table shows how many of the original ten million will still be alive and how many of the remaining number will die that year. At age 23, 9,612,127 of the original 10,000,000 at Age 0 are still alive; of this number, 18,167 will die within the year. This means that the death rate for the year is 1.89 per 1000. (This rate is computed on the 9,612,127 alive at Age 23 rather than on the original 10,000,000.) The death rate is a determinant in the calculation of

COMMISSIONERS 1958 STANDARD ORDINARY
MORTALITY TABLE
(Basis: Period 1950-1954)

Age	Number Living	Number Dying	Death Rate per 1,000	Average Future Lifetime in Years and Hundredths	Age	Number Living	Number Dying	Death Rate per 1,000	Average Future Lifetime in Years and Hundredths
0	10,000,000	70,800	7.08	68.30	50	8,762,306	72,902	8.32	23.63
1	9,929,200	17,475	1.76	67.78	51	8,689,404	79,160	9.11	22.82
2	9,911,725	15,066	1 52	66.90	52	8,610,244	85,758	9.96	22.03
3	9,896,659	14,449	1.46	66.00	53	8,524,486	92,832	10.89	21.25
4	9,882,210	13,835	1.40	65.10	54	8,431,654	100,337	11.90	20.47
5	9,868,375	13,322	1.35	64.19	55	8,331,317	108,307	13.00	19.71
6	9,855,053	12,812	1.30	63.27	56	8,223,010	116,849	14.21	18.97
7	9,842,241	12,401	1.26	62.35	57	8,106,161	125,970	15.54	18.23
8	9,829,840	12,091	1.23	61.43	58	7,980,191	135,663	17.00	17.51
9	9,817,749	11,879	1.21	60.51	59	7,844,528	145,830	18.59	16.81
10	9,805,870	11,865	1.21	59.58	60	7,698,698	156,592	20.34	16.12
11	9,794,005	12,047	1.23	58.65	61	7,542,106	167,736	22.24	15.44
12	9,781,958	12,325	1.26	57.72	62	7,374,370	179,271	24.31	14.78
13	9,769,633	12,896	1.32	56.80	63	7,195,099	191,174	26.57	14.14
14	9,756,737	13,562	1.39	55.87	64	7,033,925	203,394	29.04	13.51
15	9,743,175	14,225	1.46	54.95	65	6,800,531	215,917	31.75	12.90
16	9,728,950	14,983	1.54	54.03	66	6,584,614	228,749	34.74	12.31
17	9,713,967	15,737	1.62	53.11	67	6,355,865	241,777	38.04	11.73
18	9,698,230	16,390	1.69	52.19	68	6,114,088	254,835	41.68	11.17
19	9,681,840	16,846	1.74	51.28	69	5,859,253	267,241	45.61	10.64
20	9,664,994	17,300	1.79	50.37	70	5,592,012	278,426	49.79	10.12
21	9,647,694	17,655	1.83	49.46	71	5,313,586	287,731	54.15	9.63
22	9,630,039	17,912	1.86	48.55	72	5,025,855	294,766	58.65	9.15
23	9,612,127	18,167	1.89	47.64	73	4,731,089	299,289	63.26	8.69
24	9,593,960	18,324	1.91	46.73	74	4,431,800	301,894	68.12	8.24
25	9,575,636	18,481	1.93	45.82	75	4,129,906	303,011	73.37	7.81
26	9,557,155	18,732	1.96	44.90	76	3,826,895	303,014	79.18	7.39
27	9,538,423	18,981	1.99	43.99	77	3,523,881	301,997	85.70	6.98
28	9,519,442	19,324	2.03	43.08	78	3,221,884	299,829	93.06	6.59
29	9,500,118	19,760	2.08	42.16	79	2,922,055	295,683	101.19	6.21
30	9,480,358	20,193	2.13	41.25	80	2,626,372	288,848	109.98	5.85
31	9,460,165	20,718	2.19	40.34	81	2,337,524	278,983	119.35	5.51
32	9,439,447	21,239	2.25	39.43	82	2,058,541	265,902	129.17	5.19
33	9,418,208	21,850	2.32	38.51	83	1,792,639	249,858	139.38	4.89
34	9,396,358	22,551	2.40	37.60	84	1,542,781	231,433	150.01	4.60
35	9,373,807	23,528	2.51	36.69	85	1,311,348	211,311	161.14	4.32
36	9,350,279	24,685	2.64	35.78	86	1,100,037	190,108	172.82	4.06
37	9,325,594	26,112	2.80	34.88	87	909,929	168,455	185.13	3.80
38	9,299,482	27,991	3.01	33.97	88	741,474	146,997	198.25	3.55
39	9,271,491	30,132	3.25	33.07	89	594,477	126,303	212.46	3.31
40	9,241,359	32,622	3.53	32.18	90	468,174	106,809	228.14	3.06
41	9,208,737	35,362	3.84	31.29	91	361,365	88,813	245.77	2.82
42	9,173,375	38,253	4.17	30.41	92	272,552	72,480	265.93	2.58
43	9,135,122	41,382	4.53	29.54	93	200,072	57,881	289.30	2.33
44	9,093,740	44,741	4.92	28.67	94	142,191	45,026	316.66	2.07
45	9,048,999	48,412	5.35	27.81	95	97,165	34,128	351.25	1.80
46	9,000,587	52,473	5.83	26.95	96	63,037	25,250	400.56	1.51
47	8,948,114	56,910	6.36	26.11	97	37,787	18,456	488.42	1.18
48	8,891,204	61,794	6.95	25.27	98	19,331	12,916	668.15	.88
49	8,829,410	67,104	7.60	24.45	99	6,415	6,415	1,000.00	.50

TABLE 14-1

premiums and tells the insurance company how much it should charge to insure all the group at Age 23 for one year.

YEARLY RENEWABLE TERM LIFE INSURANCE

The simplest illustration of the application of the insurance principle as protection against the threat of death is the yearly renewable term life insurance plan. Based on the expected number of deaths in a given group of persons, each member of the group contributes his share of the total sum that will be needed to pay the insurance benefits of those who die during the year.

Let us develop an example based on the 1958 C.S.O. Table. Of 10,000,000 males alive at Age 0—9,612,127 would still be living at Age 23. The Table also indicates that 18,167 would die during the next year. Suppose that each one of the entire group at Age 23 wishes to insure his life for $1,000 for one year. A fund of $18,167,000 will have to be raised and each participant, therefore, will have to contribute $18,167,000/9,612,127 or $1.89. As a matter of fact, assuming that the claims would be paid at the end of the policy year, this is more than would have to be collected since insurance is normally paid for in advance and consequently all payments start earning interest at once.

If this interest rate is assumed at 3%, a common interest base, the actual amount collected would be $189 x .9709 or $1.84 when rounded to the next higher cent. $.9709 is the present worth, figuring interest at 3%, or $1.00 due one year from now. If the 9,593,960 survivors desire to continue the plan for another year, each of them will have to contribute $1.91 (the result of $18,324,000/9,593,960) x .9709, or $1.86 when rounded to the next higher cent.

Note that the cost for the second year is greater than for the first year. This is true since there are fewer persons alive to participate and a greater number of deaths in the second year. Similar calculations can be carried on until all the members of the original group are assumed to be dead. Chart 14-1 shows the cost relationship between level premium and yearly renewable term insurance.

Comparable Costs. As might be expected, the cost curve of yearly renewable term insurance from Age 23 until about Age 55 is relatively low. Death in that age span is relatively improbable, and insurance protection for any given year is consequently cheap. After Age 50, however, death claims its toll with accelerating speed and annual insurance protection becomes very expensive.

If it did not become evident to the insured earlier, it would soon be painfully clear to the rapidly decreasing group who lived beyond 55, 60 or 70 years of age that they could not afford to continue the payments for—to jump to the ridiculous limit—the few hundred who lived beyond 97 years

COMPARISON OF NET LEVEL PREMIUMS FOR $1,000 INSURANCE

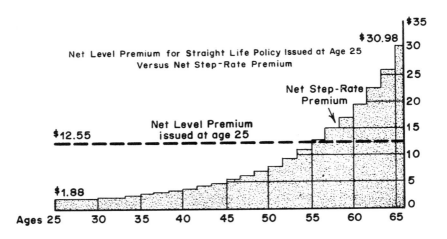

Net Level Premium for Straight Life Policy Issued at Age 25
Versus Net Step-Rate Premium

$30.98

Net Step-Rate Premium

Net Level Premium
$12.55 issued at age 25

$1.88

Ages 25 30 35 40 45 50 55 60 65

SOURCE: Institute of Life Insurance.

CHART 14-1

of age, despite the fact that they had paid into this scheme for over 70 years, for each would have to pay over $470 for $1000 of insurance protection for the next year! Normally, however, term insurance is not sold to individuals after age 65. Obviously, insurance needs after such an age can only be met through permanent type policies.

Assessment Insurance. Despite the weakness of the yearly renewable life insurance plan, many attempts have been made to use it as the basis for insurance organizations. The usual plan was for each member to pay, or be assessed, an equal share of the death claims at the end of each year. This type of insurance, therefore, came to be known as assessment insurance. Although fraternal spirit has enabled many of these organizations to continue, they have been unsuccessful in most cases.

There have been many modifications of the basic plan. In some instances an effort was made to link the amount of the annual assessment with the age of the particular group within the total membership, but these calculations were generally inaccurate. If the assessment were calculated strictly in accordance with the death rate for particular age groups this plan would resolve itself into the yearly renewable life insurance plan. Unless there is a steady influx of young persons into the organization, it is obvious that the death rate for the group is bound to increase as the years go by.

This will necessarily cause the assessments to be increased. This in turn tends to aggravate the situation, for observing the higher costs, fewer and fewer new persons join, and more and more of the members become aware of the future sky-rocketing premiums and drop out. Rates soon become prohibitive for the older members and the plan falls.

The assessment organizations, measured in terms of their consequences to the older members, have proven tragic failures. Not only have these older members paid most heavily for their insurance protection, but they have seen the scheme break down just when their need for protection was greatest.

There is no practical system of individual life insurance that can provide insurance for the whole of a lifetime and be payable on a year-by-year, pay-as-you-go basis. Instead, the principle of the *reserve* has been developed.

PRINCIPLE OF THE RESERVE

Under the plan of reserve insurance, each participant, during the early years, contributes more than his share of the anticipated death claims for his particular age group. These payments in excess of amounts necessary to meet death claims, make up the reserve which is kept invested with interest compounding.

In later years, when the death rate for this particular age group starts to increase sharply, the survivors need not contribute ever-increasing amounts, for the reserve can now be called upon to make up the difference between the premiums of the policyholders and the mounting death claims. Upon the basis of experience recorded in the mortality table and an assumed interest rate, it is possible to make exact mathematical calculations of the cost of any particular kind of insurance. All discussion of life insurance below assumes that the reserve principle is employed.

THE LEVEL PREMIUM PLAN

The actual calculations of the cost of reserve life insurance are somewhat involved. It is necessary, however, to discuss the general nature of these calculations so that you can fully comprehend the makeup of the premiums on the standard life insurance policies to be discussed.

Reference to the Mortality Table (Table 12-1) will show that of the original group of 10,000,000 males, 9,612,127 will reach Age 23 and over 88% of these will be alive 30 years later. Suppose now that each of the 9,612,127 persons wanted to have his life insured for $1,000 and was prepared to purchase that insurance by paying a net single premium.

Remembering that (1) all excess money in the hands of the insurance company is invested and that any accrued interest is promptly reinvested,

(2) the company, from experience, can predict how many of this group will die each year, and (3) most of these people will live a great many years—it is obvious that the insurer will give each of these persons a $1,000 life insurance policy upon receipt of a net single premium that is far less than $1,000.

Computing interest at 3%, which is a common insurance company rate, and disregarding expenses, this net single premium would actually be $265.75. But few people could afford to pay such a sum in one payment for a $1,000 insurance policy.

Most people prefer to buy their insurance on the installment plan just as they buy their homes or pay their rent (i.e., year by year or month by month, as they live). It makes no difference to the insurer whether the prospective buyer, age 23, pays him $265.75 in a single payment or whether the insured agrees to pay him a level premium every year that he lives. If the insured lives to be fairly old, the sum of these payments will total far more than $265.75, but his financial burden during these many years will have been relatively light. This net level annual premium, Age 23, is actually $10.54.

The relationship between the net step-rate premium (one year renewable term premium) and the net level premium is shown in Chart 14-1, where the curves show the net step-rate premium and the net level premium at Age 25. Below Age 55, the yearly renewable insurance plan is obviously the cheaper of the two. The odds of a male Age 25 living beyond Age 55 are almost 6 to 1. The general conclusions regarding the yearly renewable insurance plan that were drawn previously, therefore, remain valid.

The Reserve and the Level Premium Plan. For a basic understanding of the principles involved in the computation of premiums a simplified illustration should suffice. Let us consider a group of 10,000 individuals all age 20. Assume that each member of this group desires to insure his life for $1000. Each member of the group desires to pay an annual level premium rather than a single lump sum or an ever-increasing premium. What then must the annual level premium be in order to meet present and future death claims?

Reference to Chart 14-2 shows that the insurance company insuring the group must be prepared to pay $191,000 to the beneficiaries of the 191 of the group that die during the first ten-year period. During this period the insurance company has been collecting premiums and investing the money which is not needed to pay current death claims. We are assuming for simplicity that there are no expenses connected with the operation of this insurance company, obviously an untenable assumption in actual practice. During the first year 10,000 premiums will be collected; the second year only 9,982 premiums will be collected due to deaths in the group, and so

HISTORY OF 10,000 LIFE INSURANCE POLICY HOLDERS

ALL THE SAME AGE; EACH PURCHASED $1,000 OF ORDINARY LIFE AT AGE 20

MORTALITY TABLE USED: COMMISSIONERS 1958 STANDARD ORDINARY; 3% INTEREST; NET ANNUAL PREMIUM $9.56

10 YEAR PERIODS	Age 20-29	Age 30-39	Age 40-49	Age 50-59	Age 60-69	Age 70-79	Age 80-89	Age 90-100
Number Living at Beginning of Period	10,000	9,809	9,562	9,066	7,966	5,786	2,717	484
Total Premiums Paid During Period	$947,989	$927,960	$895,868	$825,965	$677,842	$422,552	$148,524	$16,501
Total Interest Earned During Period	$144,026	$444,253	$798,236	$1,122,276	$1,245,480	$953,592	$382,890	$46,046
Number of Persons Dying During Period	191	247	496	1,100	2,180	3,069	2,233	484
Total of Death Benefits Paid During Period	$191,000	$247,000	$496,000	$1,100,000	$2,180,000	$3,069,000	$2,233,000	$484,000
Fund at End of Period After Benefit Payments	$901,015	$2,026,228	$3,224,332	$4,072,573	$3,815,895	$2,123,039	$421,453	0

Source: Institute of Life Insurance.

CHART 14-2

on. The total number of premiums collected from the group from the start of the insurance until the last man has died will be 508,732.

Throughout this period of time, 508,732 premiums are collected and a total of $10,000,000 in death claims must be paid; therefore, the insurance company must also receive $10,000,000 in order to meet these claims. If the insurance company acted merely as an agent or repository, the liability for the $10,000,000 it must collect would be apportioned among the members of the group. The annual level premium each member would thus have to pay would be $10,000/508,732 or about $19.66. We have previously said, however, that under the level premium plan of life insurance an excess of funds above the sums actually needed to meet current death claims is accumulated in the early years.

This excess or reserve fund will be invested by the insurance company and earn interest. If we assume a rate of interest of 3%, then the premium for each member of the group needs to be only $9.56 rather than $19.66. The investment of the reserve, therefore, reduces the premium each member of our group must pay, since the group as a whole now need pay only approximately $4,863,201 instead of a total of $10,000,000 to the insurance company. The difference of $5,136,799 results from the investment of the reserve.

Reference to Chart 14-2 shows that during the first 30 years the premium payments have been more than sufficient to cover the death claims. The excess or reserve has been invested and the fund has been steadily increasing. When the surviving members of the group reach Age 53, however, the premiums are no longer sufficient in themselves to meet the increasing death claims. If the insurance company is not to increase its premium rates, the additional funds must be drawn from some other source. From the reserve fund the additional sums needed to meet death claims will be drawn. In the final period, the reserve fund plus the premiums received and the interest earned will be just sufficient to allow the insurance company to meet its obligations.

The premiums for the many various kinds of insurance contracts such as endowments, limited payment life insurance policies, etc., are computed in a similar fashion. For instance, the 30-payment life insurance policy has the same considerations as brought out in our illustration with the exception that under this plan the funds necessary to meet the death claims of the group must be collected over a period of 30 premium years. Obviously, the premiums for this form of insurance must therefore be higher than those for a whole life policy.

LOADING

The premiums referred to thus far are net premiums (premiums just sufficient to meet death claims and build up the reserve) and include no allowance for expenses and contingencies. It is evident that an insurance company could not do business on this basis, for with each insured paying only a net discounted premium, the total taken in as premiums would exactly equal or approximate the amount paid out as benefits over the life span of that age group.

The insurance company must own or rent offices and maintain an office force to transact its business. Agents' commissions for new business, examiners' fees, expenses of issuing policies and making investments and settlements, taxes, losses from unfavorable investments, losses when investments fail to earn the discounted 3% compound interest, and unexpected mortality above C.S.O. expectations are business expenses that must be met. To meet these expenses and contingencies, an additional sum is added to the net premium described above to form what is known as the gross premium.

Table 14-2 illustrates the net annual premiums as compared to the gross annual premiums charged by several large insurance companies. The difference between them represents the loading. Lower loading will generally reflect a more efficient company when comparing policies of identical types.

A composite report of the life insurance companies in the United States showed that during a typical year, for each dollar the companies received as income, 54.4 cents were paid out in benefits, 23.1 cents went into policy and special reserves, 17 cents constituted operating expenses, one cent was used for dividends, and the remaining 4.5 cents paid in taxes.

SAMPLE LOADING CHARGES

(COMMISSIONERS 1958 STANDARD ORDINARY TABLE)

3 PERCENT $1000 POLICY - AGE 23 - MALE

Policy Type	Net Annual Premium	Gross Annual Premium	Loading
Ordinary Life	$ 11.17	$ 15.84	$ 4.67
20 Payment Life	18.32	26.10	7.78
20 Year Endowment	38.01	46.27	8.26

TABLE 14-2

PLANS OF PREMIUM PAYMENTS

Life insurance premiums are paid in advance. Under a level premium plan it is immaterial, generally speaking, to the insurance company whether the insured pays the gross premium for an entire year or whether he pays his insurance in semi-annual, quarterly, or monthly payments. Premium payments other than annual are usually subject to an extra charge because of the consequent loss of interest by the company, the extra overhead involved in mailing bills and receipts, and in accounting. Waiving the balance of the year's premiums in case of death before an entire year's premium has been paid entails an extra cost to the company. Additional charges for payment other than by annual premium vary considerably with the different insurance companies, but generally fall within the following range:

Semi-annual..................... 2-4%
Quarterly....................... 4-6%
Monthly......................... 5-8%

Thus, to determine the monthly premium payment for a policy whose annual premium is $120 and whose extra charge for monthly payment is 6%, add 6% of $120 ($7.20) to the $120 = $127.20 and divide by 12 = $10.60. Inasmuch as the insured is paying his premiums by monthly installments the actual rate paid approximates 12%. In the purchase of insurance with premiums payable on a monthly basis one must consider the extra charges as part of the cost of insurance when comparing insurance costs of the various companies.

Payments by Allotment. A convenient method for a Serviceman to pay his life insurance premium is by monthly allotment, made by the Finance Center with the amount of the premium deducted from his pay. However, it is the individual's responsibility to see that the insurance company receives the payment.

The allotment or monthly method of payment should be used only when the extra charges are within a reasonable limit. For the individual who can do so, it is financially advantageous to pay premiums annually. This, however, necessitates a definite savings plan for the accumulation of the money to pay the premiums. For any individual who finds saving a difficult process, the payment of premiums by monthly allotment is advisable rather than hazard the possibility of lapse of his insurance through inability to pay the annual premiums when they fall due.

A few companies permit the payment of premiums in advance on a monthly basis which equals one-twelfth of the annual premium, although at the outset the insured may be required to pay one annual premium in a lump sum. Some companies, however, merely require that an allotment be made out for one-twelfth of the annual premium. This plan allows the insured the savings of the single annual premium payment method while at the same time allowing payment in monthly increments.

Bickelhaupt, David L. and John H. Magee. *General Insurance*. 8th ed. Homewood, Illinois: Richard D. Irwin, Inc., 1970.

Cohen, Jerome B. *Decade of Decision*. New York: Institute of Life Insurance, 1969.

Hammond, J. D. and Arthur L. Williams. *Essentials of Life Insurance*. Glenview, Illinois: Scott, Foresman and Company, 1968.

Institute of Life Insurance. *Handbook of Life Insurance*. New York: Institute of Life Insurance, 1969.

Institute of Life Insurance. *Life Insurance Fact Book*. New York: Institute of Life Insurance, Published annually.

McGill, Dan M. *Life Insurance*. rev. ed. Homewood, Illinois: Richard D. Irwin, Inc., 1968.

*A verbal contract isn't
worth the paper it's
written on.*
  —Samuel Goldwyn

CHAPTER 15

ANALYSIS OF
POLICY CONTRACTS

WHEN PURCHASING a life insurance policy, there are two primary considerations in which the purchaser should be interested. He will want to know first, how much he has to pay and, secondly, what the company promises in return. Both will depend on the nature of the policy, for many variations exist.

POLICY DIFFERENCES

These differences have been introduced to meet the needs and the circumstances of many different cases, with the result that a person desiring insurance protection can secure a policy which meets his requirements and fits his pocketbook. It should not be assumed that any one policy is "cheaper" than another except, perhaps, for a particular purpose. The question, "What is the cheapest type of insurance for me to buy at my age?" can be answered only if you can furnish the date of your death.

A certain amount of money may purchase varying amounts of protection combined with various other features. A sacrifice in the amount of protection secured may be offset through the enhancement of other features. While no one particular policy is universally better than another, there is usually one policy that is more nearly adapted to individual needs than any other. As is true of other commodities, prices, styles, and sizes vary to meet the desires and requirements of the buyer.

PROTECTION VS. SAVINGS

The basic function of life insurance is to protect dependents against the risk of financial loss through the premature death of an individual. But life insurance policies often do more than provide such protection. Some policies, called permanent (or cash-value type) policies, also provide a systematic savings program. Part of your premium buys protection while part of the premium constitutes a deposit into a savings fund held for you by the insurance company.

When you analyze insurance contracts, you must always keep the concepts of protection and savings separate. To compare policies and judge them properly you should determine the cost of protection and the rate of return earned on the savings portion of the policy. Then you can rationally choose among alternative uses of your premium dollars.

Although insurance companies have developed a great variety of insurance contracts, there are only three basic types: (1) term: (2) whole life; and (3) endowment. All contracts having the protection and savings functions will be made up of one or a combination of these three types. A fourth kind of contract, the annuity, has a function fundamentally different from that of the above contracts.

While permanent life insurance (whole life and endowment) provides for the accumulation of a savings fund, an annuity provides for the amortization (depletion or paying out) of a savings fund. Thus a savings fund accumulated through a permanent insurance policy could later be used to provide an annuity (a fund which would provide income payments for a selected length of time). Your analysis of insurance contracts will be sound if you can break them down into their three basic types, distinguish between the protection and savings features, and determine the cost of each benefit provided.

Keep this in mind as we now focus our attention on the principal life insurance contracts normally sold by insurance companies. Term insurance, ordinary life insurance, limited payment life insurance, endowment insurance, and several other modified forms of life insurance will be considered. The following points for each type of insurance will be covered: (1) an explanation of the contract; (2) the fundamental purpose of that particular type of insurance; (3) the advantages and disadvantages of that particular type of insurance: and (4) any other pertinent information or data of interest or value.

TERM INSURANCE

Term insurance is the closest thing to pure life insurance available, since it incorporates no savings plan at all. It gives protection for a limited period only. The company guarantees to pay a sum of money to the beneficiary if the insured dies within the specified period or term covered by the policy. Term insurance is based upon the principles that were discussed under yearly renewable term life insurance. It is not, therefore, an insurance scheme that can be continued throughout life. It meets the needs of an individual who wants maximum protection for minimum cost for a limited period.

Term policies are written for varying periods, the five, ten, or twenty-year term policies, or level premium to some specified age, sixty-five being the most common. Term insurance policies usually do not protect the insured beyond age sixty-four. The premium paid during the term of the policy is a level premium that is equivalent to the present worth of the net annual premiums, plus the necessary loading.

Although a small reserve may build up, there are usually no cash-surrender, loan, or other non-forfeiture values guaranteed by the company since the insured has purchased pure insurance for a stipulated period and nothing else. All individual policies except term contain nonforfeiture values. Under these provisions the policyholder may borrow money from his life insurance company, using his policy as collateral, or he may stop paying premiums and (1) continue the insurance protection on a modified basis or (2) receive a cash or income settlement and drop the insurance.

If the insured dies during the term of the policy, his beneficiary receives the sum insured. On the other hand, if he outlives the term of the policy, he has paid for and received his money's worth in protection and has no equity left in the policy.

Term policies usually contain guarantees of convertibility. They are generally convertible into a permanent form of insurance at some time during the term of the policy, upon payment of the appropriate premium. Conversion usually can be accomplished without further medical examination. The conversion provisions of a term policy merit close study, particularly in regard to physical examination requirements. If a physical examination is required the insured might not then be able to convert to a permanent type. Some term policies provide for renewal and are commonly called renewable term. Such policies may be renewed upon their expiration without physical examination upon the payment of the premium for the present age.

Term insurance serves certain definite purposes. In a sense these purposes may be classified in relation to three different temporary situations.

1. *Temporary Low Income — Large Insurance Need*. While the insured's income is relatively low but his insurance needs are great, a con-

vertible term contract gives him the required protection at the cheapest price with an option on permanent insurance which he may take up as his income increases. A renewal privilege extends the option of convertibility.

The value of renewable and convertible term contracts to young Service personnel is apparent from many examples. Take two officers, one a Captain and one a Major, each with a wife and four children. Both families have essentially the same insurance needs. Both families are entitled to nearly the same government survivor benefits that help meet these needs. Assume that for both families there is a gap that requires about $50,000 commercial life insurance to provide family security in the event of the breadwinner's death.

With a basic pay approximately $100 per month higher, the Major can better afford to buy this protection on a permanent basis. He may carry $50,000 ordinary life insurance for a premium outlay of approximately $97 per month. The Captain, on the other hand, can provide the same protection with term insurance that is both renewable and convertible for a monthly premium outlay of approximately $24 per month.

If the Captain purchases $50,000 coverage, he can gradually convert portions of the contract to ordinary life as his income increases. He should be aware of the fact, however, that the cost of converting term policies to one of the permanent forms will increase automatically each year. He should, therefore, convert each portion of the term policy at the earliest practicable time if permanent insurance is ultimately desired.

2. *Temporary Need.* The second situation in which term insurance serves a definite purpose is when the need rather than the insured's low income is a temporary situation. Depending on the duration of need, the contract may or may not require the privilege of renewal. Because of its purpose, it will not require the convertibility option.

There are many temporary needs that are best covered by term contracts. For instance, term insurance is recommended for the individual who has an obligation which must be paid over a period of years, such as a mortgage on a home. Most companies sell a decreasing term contract that fits this situation. It will provide an amount sufficient to guarantee the payment of the obligation should the insured die, and will leave his estate to his dependents unimpaired, which would not be the case otherwise.

A term policy might also be used in connection with educational requirements. Take the case of a man who, should he live, would expect to educate his children from current income. Term insurance on his life for a period of years sufficient to cover the education of his children would guarantee funds for this in the event his death occurred before their education was completed.

3. *Temporary Hazard.* The third situation is one in which the risk of death is unusual and temporary. Term insurance may be the "best buy" for a young Serviceman about to undergo a period of unusual risk, such as

serving in a combat zone. As he is about to embark on an extra hazardous assignment, a young married man, age 23, for example, might consider the alternatives of purchasing $25,000 of convertible term coverage at an annual premium of about $109 or of purchasing $10,000 of ordinary life coverage at an annual premium of about $167.

If he should die, the term contract is preferable. If he is seriously wounded and hence no longer insurable, a term contract that is convertible without further physical examination is certainly preferable. If he lives, is insurable, and ultimately desires $25,000 permanent protection, then he will come out of it cheaper to buy the $10,000 ordinary life at age 23 since on coversion of term coverage he will have to pay the slightly higher ordinary life premium for his age at the end of the period.

On balance, the $25,000 term coverage that provides greater protection of life and insurability for the period of risk appears to be the more prudent purchase. For this very reason term coverage is scarce during periods of national emergency, especially for military personnel. Only one major company, and incidentally the largest, wrote term insurance up to $10,000 on young officers during the Korean War.

One caution should be emphasized at this point. Insurance protection should be purchased to meet the family needs that would exist in the event of the insured's death. These needs would be the same regardless of the cause of the insured's death. Insurance should not be purchased merely because of variations in perils to which the insured might be exposed. It would be foolish to purchase insurance protection only when the officer heads for a combat zone. Such a program would leave the family dangerously exposed to financial loss should the breadwinner die some other time from one of the most routine causes.

The Agent's Commission. In summary, we can say that term insurance is very useful in one's insurance program for three general situations. First, term that is renewable and convertible serves the purpose of temporary protection for permanent needs when the officer's income is temporarily too low to pay premiums for permanent insurance coverage. Second, term that is renewable serves the purpose of temporary protection for temporary needs. Third, term insurance that is convertible serves the purpose of temporary protection for temporary risks.

Since so many officers seem to be in one or more of these three general situations, one might well ask why so few carry term insurance and why few agents recommend it. As to the first question, there are many reasons that probably go back to a lack of understanding of the principles of insurance. Too many are blinded by the feeling that term insurance is a "die to win" proposition. They forget that the basic purpose of true life insurance is to provide protection for the insured's dependents against the risk of his death. They fail to understand that in many circumstances term insurance provides the best means for fulfilling this basic purpose.

Many officers, on the other hand, purchase permanent insurance as a combination of protection plus savings. In other words, they depart from the basic purpose with their eyes wide open because they prefer the element of savings in insurance contracts to other forms of savings.

As to the second question, one must understand how the insurance agent gets paid to appreciate why he seldom recommends term insurance. The insurance agent is paid on a commission basis.

The commission schedule is graded according to size of premium—the highest being for the whole life policy. Term commissions are lower because their persistency is not good. Table 15-1 is illustrative of an agent's commissions for a company operating in New York State.

One might thus assume that the agent is hardly a disinterested party if he recommends a higher premium form of insurance than that best suited to your needs. Look at it this way. If an agent sells to each of 100 Second Lieutenants a $10,000 5-year renewable and convertible term contract in a given year, his commission that year for writing this $1,000,000 term coverage is less than the income of a Second Lieutenant. If, instead, he sells

SAMPLE AGENT'S COMMISSION SCHEDULE
(% of Annual Premium)

Policy	1st year	2nd thru 9th yrs.
One Year Term	25%	5% (2nd yr. only)
Two Year Term	25	5% (2nd yr. only)
Five Year Term	35	5 (2-5 yrs. only)
Ten Year Term	35	10, 8, 5 (3 yrs.) 2
Fifteen or Twenty Yr. Term	35	10, 8, 5 (3 yrs.) 2
Ordinary Life	55	5 (next 9 yrs.)
Twenty Pay Life	48	15 (2nd yr.) 10 (3d yr.) 5 (3 yrs.) 2 (4 yrs.)
Ten Pay Life	35	10, 8, 5, (3 yrs.) 2 (4 yrs.)
20 Year Endowment	35	2 1/2 (9 yrs.)
10 Year Endowment	20	2 1/2 (9 yrs.)

NOTES

Most companies pay about 2% commissions after the 9th year for the life of the contract.

Keep in mind that this table serves only as an example for a specific company and state. Perhaps it also reflects a particular commission option elected by a specific agent. Commission plans vary between different companies and they also vary within one company among its different agents, depending on which option the particular agent elects. Much higher first-year commissions than those here indicated and correspondingly lower following year commissions are not uncommon depending on the individual agent's election.

General Agents, as a rule, receive 5% override commissions on all business the first year and a reduced commission for subsequent years through the 10th year or longer.

TABLE 15-1

each a $10,000 ordinary life contract, his commissions that year are more than the income of most Majors. Moreover, if he sells convertible term contracts to Second Lieutenants, he stands a good chance of not making the second "sale" if and when the policies are converted.

If you purchase a term policy from one agent and convert it to ordinary life a few years later through another agent of the same company, the second agent usually gets credit for the "sale" and receives the higher commission on the ordinary life premium.

The disadvantages of term insurance are not all from the salesman's point of view, however. There are several that the buyer should bear in mind. First, if he needs permanent protection, then it may be cheaper to take out ordinary life insurance, depending upon how his insurance and investment programs are developed. Recall that the longer the insured lives past age 55, the steeper the rise in his term premiums. Furthermore, the renewal privilege on most term contracts expires around 64.

Second, term insurance provides no savings element. If the officer finds it difficult to save in other forms, a permanent policy paid for by allotment of premiums may be the best method of forced thrift for him. This is more a case of weakness of the individual than a disadvantage of term insurance.

Group Insurance. There is a type of coverage having characteristics similar to term insurance that is of particular interest to Armed Forces officers. Various associations (some of which are described in Appendix A) offer group insurance to Service personnel.

Group insurance is little more than term insurance written for groups rather than individuals. The association offering the coverage uses a master contract instead of individual policies, and does not use sales agents. This means lower business acquisition costs. Normally, no medical examination is required. If you require temporary protection, it is wise to compare group as well as term insurance alternatives.

WHOLE LIFE

In contrast with term insurance, which pays benefits only if death occurs within a specific time period, whole life insurance pays the face value upon the death of the insured whenever it occurs. Whole life protection can be purchased under either of two principal types of contracts, depending upon the method used to pay for it. One is known as ordinary life or straight life; the other is called limited payment life.

Ordinary Life. Ordinary or straight life insurance is the most popular and lowest cost form of permanent life insurance available. The policyholder agrees to pay a certain level premium throughout his lifetime in exchange for a guarantee that the face value of the policy will be paid to the beneficiary upon the insured's death. Thus ordinary life insurance provides the maximum amount of permanent insurance protection for a minimum cost.

Table 15-2 indicates what various policies in the amount of $10,000 cost at selected ages. The table also indicates the amount of protection an annual premium of $100 will purchase at age 22, and the cash value to which the savings will accumulate if the insured lives to age 65.

The ordinary life policy provides, in addition to protection, a savings component. Thus, after its first or second year, it has a cash value. The cash value is, in effect, a kind of savings account. It may be withdrawn by the policyholder by surrendering the policy, it can be used as collateral for a loan, it may be borrowed by the insured, himself, or it can be used in a number of other ways according to the terms of the contract.

If the insured dies, however, only the face amount of the policy less any borrowed amount still outstanding will be paid to the beneficiary. Thus, in effect, the ordinary life policy combines decreasing term insurance and increasing cash values in such a way that the total always equals the face value of the policy. If the insured dies, the beneficiary receives a death benefit composed of a return of accumulated savings plus an amount of insurance protection called the net amount at risk. Many persons do not understand this point. The beneficiary on a $10,000 policy receives only

SAMPLE COMPARISON OF THE
PROTECTION AND SAVINGS PROVIDED BY
VARIOUS TYPES OF POLICIES

TYPE OF POLICY	Approximate Annual Premiums for $10,000 of Insurance*			Amt of Ins. $100 a yr. Will Buy	Cash Value Per $100 Ann Prem
	AGE AT WHICH POLICY IS ISSUED				
	21	23	25	(Age 22)	(at Age 65)
Five Year Term (Renewable and Convertible)	$ 49.75	$ 50.25	$ 50.75	$20,000	None
Ordinary Life	136.00	144.00	152.00	7,100	$4,200
Life-Paid-Up-at-65	155.00	164.00	175.00	6,300	4,475
20-Payment Life	232.00	242.00	252.00	4,200	2,980
Retirement Income at 65	253.00	271.00	292.00	3,800	6,240
20-Year Endowment	453.50	454.50	455.50	2,200	Matured (Age 42)

*Rates shown are approximate premium rates for $10,000 of life insurance protection for men. Policies for women are at lower rates in recognition of somewhat lower mortality rates. Rates of "participating" policies would be slightly higher, but the cost would be lowered by annual dividends. "Non-participating" policy premium rates would be somewhat lower than those shown and no dividends would be paid. Premium rates for policies under $10,000 would be a little higher but lower for policies of $25,000 and over.

Source: Institute of Life Insurance

TABLE 15-2

$10,000, not the face value of $10,000 plus the amount of the savings or cash value.

Life insurance (other than term) as an investment has a number of similarities with the so-called "gilt-edged" security. The life insurance policy has a high rate of marketability, as the cash value or policy reserve is obtainable in most cases on demand. The investment diversification given the reserve by the life insurance company would be difficult if not impossible to achieve individually. Strict regulation by law guarantees high-quality investment of your funds. Safety of principal, an important feature to the small investor, is found in the insurance policy since the contract states the value that will be paid under any number of conditions.

The advantages of the ordinary life policy are many. A maximum amount of protection can be secured for the minimum amount in premiums (excepting term insurance which is not a cash-value type of contract). The policy combines protection with investment through the guarantee of certain non-forfeiture values such as loan value, cash value, paid-up and extended term insurance.

Ordinary life insurance can be utilized to provide almost any type of settlement either for the insured or the beneficiary. Ordinary life insurance can be made to serve the purpose of an endowment, an annuity, or almost any of the many forms life insurance policies take. The flexibility (adaptability) of ordinary life insurance should recommend it to anyone who desires to combine protection and investment in his life insurance program.

But since the rate of return earned on the savings portion of a life insurance policy is exceeded by many other kinds of investments, and since the savings portion becomes a part of the death benefit paid to the beneficiary in the event of the insured's death, some people have advocated a policy of buying insurance protection in the form of term insurance only, and investing the difference in higher-yielding investments. The factors involved in comparing this approach versus that of combining protection and investment in a life insurance program are discussed later in this chapter.

Limited Payment Life. Limited payment life is a type of whole life policy which merely uses higher premium payments to accelerate the growth of cash values so that the face value of the policy becomes paid up in a fixed period of time, such as 20 or 30 years. The purpose of this type of insurance is to satisfy those who want to buy permanent insurance protection, but who want to get it paid for in a limited period of time.

The outstanding advantage of this kind of insurance policy is that the insured's premium burden does not last indefinitely. It may therefore be planned to fall upon those years in which his earning power is greatest, provided, of course, that that period can be definitely determined. Thus, if a Serviceman could be sure that he would retire after a given number of years service, say thirty, and consequently face a sharp reduction in income, such a policy might meet his needs very nicely.

Note, however, that the periodic premium outlay required is considerably more than that required for the same amount of ordinary life insurance. Note also that if the officer purchases a limited payment life policy at the beginning of his career, he is buying it at a time when his Service pay is relatively small, and when he is most likely to take on other obligations and expense such as that of marriage and children. The latter situation usually requires a maximum of protection for the premium dollar.

It should be pointed out that the purchaser of a limited payment policy pays a higher premium to emphasize the savings portion of his insurance program, and to gain the privilege of terminating insurance premium payments at a fixed point. It would be unusual that the young officer would need these particular benefits. Also note that a participating ordinary life policy will provide approximately the same results if its dividends are used to pay up the policy.

Confusion between a limited payment policy and an endowment policy (described next) must be avoided. Sometimes insurance agents, either through carelessness or through unscrupulousness, have allowed policyholders to believe that their limited payment life policies will mature as endowments for the full amount at the end of the limited payment period. The limited payment life policies should always be purchased for exactly what they are—policies assuring life-long protection, but purchased with a limited number of premiums.

ENDOWMENT

Endowment insurance not only provides the same death benefit as that provided by term insurance but also pays its face amount if the insured survives to the end of the term period. It is written to mature at a definite time, usually twenty or thirty years or at a certain age such as 60 or 65.

At the end of the endowment period, the face value of the policy has accumulated in the savings fund and, in addition, term insurance in a decreasing amount is provided so that at any time during the period covered the savings fund plus the net amount at risk equals the face value of the policy. The policy calls for the payment of a level premium for the entire period of the contract. For convenience, the premium usually is calculated as the sum of the premium for term insurance and the premium for a pure endowment for the period. (A pure endowment is designed to pay the face amount of the policy to the insured if he lives to the maturity of the policy. No payment on a pure endowment is made if the insured dies prior to maturity of the policy.)

If the insured dies during the period covered by the policy the face value of the contract is paid to the beneficiary. If, however, the insured lives to the maturity of the policy the face value is paid to him. He has saved that much money at compound interest and in addition has paid for the protection offered by the decreasing amounts of term insurance involved. He has received just what he paid for.

Do You Really Need An Endowment Policy? There is widespread misunderstanding of insurance principles with regard to endowment insurance. It is only natural that the idea of buying the opportunity to receive a large sum in cash some twenty or thirty years hence should prove very attractive, especially to young persons. The emphasis which some agents place on this form of insurance is occasioned not only by the higher commissions, but also by the fact that the human weakness noted above causes such policies virtually to sell themselves.

The person who buys endowment insurance is wandering away from the basic purpose of true life insurance, which is to provide protection for the insured's dependents against the risk of his death. At the expiration of the term of years in the endowment policy the policyholder is no longer insured. If he still needs insurance protection, he may not be insurable. If he is, his premium rates have increased greatly.

For the average Servicemen, the purchase of an adequate amount of term or ordinary life protection is normally all that he can afford. He cannot afford the premium outlay required for added retirement income through endowment insurance unless he has an outside income.

Comparison of the premium outlay for a twenty year endowment and an ordinary life policy, illustrated in Table 15-2, emphasizes this point. Both policies provide the same amount of protection but one requires over 3 times the premium outlay as the other. It is obvious that it would be impossible for the average Serviceman to provide adequate protection for his family through the use of endowment insurance. The endowment policy is steadily losing favor and is not recommended for the Serviceman.

Endowment's Savings Appeal. Some Servicemen have purchased endowment insurance so that they themselves may secure the face value of the policy in middle or advanced age. Generally, the idea behind such a plan is that they will be able to invest the money, receive income for themselves, and still have the capital to leave to their families. Based on experience over many years, many Servicemen who programmed their insurance on this basis left their widows destitute. They lost their widows' security trading in the stock market or in other ways and no longer had the income or health to secure more life insurance.

It should be pointed out that the percentage of endowment policies that become lapsed for one reason or another far exceeds the percentage for other types of insurance. Many of these lapses have been due to individuals purchasing endowment insurance before acquiring dependents, then later finding that the premium outlay is more than they can afford with the added burden of dependents.

In defense of endowment insurance it must be noted that it offers a method of enforced savings. Few persons save regularly unless there is some compulsion, and the regular premium notices of endowment policies do provide such compulsion, since sober-minded persons scrimp and save on all other budget items before they fail to meet their insurance premiums.

Moreover, many persons would rather have their savings in the hands of a reliable insurance company than anywhere else, for they realize their own limitations as investors and know that the investment policy of insurance companies is, as required by law, very conservative.

MODIFIED FORMS

Commercial life insurance companies offer a variety of policies other than the standard types thus far discussed. In general, these contracts are modifications or combinations, in one form or another, of term, whole life, or endowment policies. A few of these modified forms will be considered.

Modified Life Policy. One popular type is known as the modified life contract. It is a combination of term insurance and ordinary life insurance, in that the premium changes after the first few years of the life of the policy. For the first few years, generally three or five, the premium is low, approximating the premium for term insurance. Thereafter, the premium rate goes up, generally approximating the premium for ordinary life insurance for the then-attained age.

Life insurance companies are not consistent in their methods of calculating these premium rates, but in every case it will be found that some sort of cost compromise has been worked out between the term and ordinary life insurance premiums. There are circumstances when these modified life policies may be very useful.

An officer can anticipate his pay increases with some degree of certainty. An officer with three years' service, for example, might have very pressing but temporary financial problems that would make it most difficult for him to pay for permanent life insurance. Knowing that he is due for a sizeable pay increase on promotion to Captain, however, he might well purchase a modified life policy.

The disadvantage of such a policy is that in many cases it is cheaper in the long run to take out ordinary life insurance.

Educational Policy. Another high premium form of insurance is the educational policy. Life insurance companies offer a wide variety of this type of contract. Many, however, are combinations of ordinary term insurance and savings. The fundamental purpose of these policies, as the name implies, is to provide insurance protection and at the same time build a fund that will be used to meet the costs of a college education for the Serviceman's children. These policies often provide for insurance protection against the death of the child, the parent, or both. In addition, they include a savings feature whereby an endowment is built up, to be available when the child is ready to go to college.

Attractive though such a policy may seem, the average person should consider the premium outlay required before he makes such a contract. These policies are essentially fifteen to twenty year endowment policies. The first consideration of the Serviceman in planning an insurance program should be to provide sufficient income to support his widow and raise his children in the event of his death.

While other savings are desirable, there is merit in trying to provide for education of children in the event of the death of the father, but only after adequate provision has been made for taking care of the family's more basic needs. Thus endowment educational insurance is not the solution for the Serviceman. For the Serviceman who wants to be secure in the knowledge that his children will receive the schooling he desires another plan is suggested. He might purchase term insurance and invest in other securities. As his holdings of securities increase he should decrease the term insurance. This plan may be cheaper than educational insurance but, of course, this depends on the officer's ability to carry out the savings program.

Income Endowment Policy. Another very popular type of insurance contract is the income endowment policy. These policies are invariably some sort of combination of endowment insurance and the life annuity. They generally provide that after the insured reaches a certain age, premium payments and insurance protection cease and the insured, or his beneficiary, is guaranteed an income of a specified amount for a specified period or for life. It is obvious that the possible variations under this type of contract are almost limitless.

Considering the retirement benefits with survivorship annuity options to which a Serviceman is entitled, this type of policy should not be particularly attractive to him. The thoughtful person should observe that such policies require a high premium outlay, since they offer a future privilege as well as insurance protection.

Family Income Policy. An increasingly popular form of insurance is the family income policy. Basically, this policy consists of a combination of decreasing term insurance and ordinary life. One of the more popular forms would provide that for a $10,000 policy:

1. If the policyholder dies within 20 years of the date of purchase, his beneficiary would receive $100 per month for the remainder of the 20-year period. At the end of the 20-year period, the beneficiary would receive $10,000 in cash or an income under one of the usual settlement options.

2. If the policyholder lives beyond the 20-year period, his premiums are reduced to those for an ordinary life policy at the age at which he originally purchased the policy. If he then dies, his beneficiary receives the proceeds for an ordinary $10,000 policy.

Variations may provide for 10 or 15 years' protection, or that if he dies within the term period, his beneficiary will receive $100 for 10, 15, or

20 years from date of death rather than for the expiration of the term period.

BUY TERM AND INVEST THE DIFFERENCE?

The advantages and disadvantages of each type of life insurance policy have been discussed. The technique for determining the amount of insurance protection required to meet your family's individual needs is described later in Chapter 18.

At this point we will consider some of the factors underlying a rather lively controversy over whether or not insurance policies should be used as part of a savings and investment program. Some advocate that permanent life insurance (including varieties of ordinary life, limited payment life, and endowment insurance) is the best medium for a savings and investment program, or at least should form a cornerstone for such a program. Others advocate an approach which has been labeled "buy term and invest the difference."

Under the latter approach, an individual purchases the protection he needs in some form of term or group insurance, and invests the premium difference between the cost of alternative permanent policies and the term coverage in an investment media which he believes will yield a higher return.

Those opposed to the "buy term and invest the difference" approach present several arguments against it. First of all, opponents point out that you are betting on continued inflation, which may or may not be a safe bet. Also, you subject yourself to the somewhat riskier venture of investing instead of the more certain return from the insurance company. They also point out that in a sense you are betting that you will die fairly early or that you will need less insurance (or none) after the children are grown. As we saw in Chapter 14, the premium for term insurance rises rather sharply as one reaches retirement age. Then to continue insurance protection may prove quite a drain on the reduced income of retirement years.

Finally, they will argue that it is a rare man who will faithfully invest the difference in premiums. There are competing demands upon the individual's income and it is easy to submit to demands other than periodic investment. Obviously, the whole scheme falls apart if the individual lacks the will to invest the difference in premiums faithfully.

Those who advocate the "buy term and invest the difference" approach point out that a successful investment program outside permanent insurance contracts will produce better results than an investment program incorporated in insurance contracts. Since no one will argue that term insurance satisfies protection needs that may exist after age 65, the controversy is restricted to alternative methods of combining protection and investment prior to about age 65. Protection needs beyond that point can be met only with permanent life insurance contracts.

It is not our purpose to settle the above controversy for you. Only you can decide which approach best suits your own individual situation, and ability to save and invest. We do suggest, however, that your decision rests primarily upon your evaluation of three factors:

1. Your ability to carry out a systematic savings and investment program.

2. The after-tax rate of return you can expect to earn on your investments.

3. The mathematics of the alternatives given your age, protection needs, cost of protection, etc.

Your ability to carry out a systematic investment program can be evaluated only by you. Young officers are very apt to overestimate their will power, especially in the face of the pleadings of "the little woman" who cannot understand why you can't get a new station wagon when all that money is just sitting there!

You must realize that the success of any long-range investment program depends upon your determination to carry it out. This is an easier task if savings are automatically allocated from your income, and a systematic investment program in equity-type media is maintained.

The rate of return your investment program will earn depends upon many factors. A choice of media is listed in Chapter 10. Keep in mind that short-term interest rates will vary, and that equity investments such as common stocks will have their "ups and downs." You must also keep in mind that if you deviate from a sound system of long-term equity investment (e.g., a dollar-cost-averaging program in high-quality growth stocks), you stand a good chance of destroying your program through unsuccessful speculation. A bad speculative investment can turn a good long-term after-tax return of 10% compounded annually into a loss!

The following analysis for a man aged 25 purchasing nonparticipating policies from one well-known stock company may provide some useful insights into the controversy. Chart 15-1 graphically compares alternative methods of purchasing protection and accumulating savings. (Only nonparticipating policies are used in the illustrations.) Note that the graphs indicate the amount of protection purchased by the premium as the *net amount at risk*. The *cash value* of a permanent life insurance policy constitutes its savings component. This is the "savings account" that you would receive if you surrendered the policy.

Note, however, only the face amount of the policy is paid to the beneficiary if the insured dies. This death benefit is composed of the net amount at risk at the time of death plus the accumulated cash value. In the case of a term policy coupled with an outside savings program, the accumulated

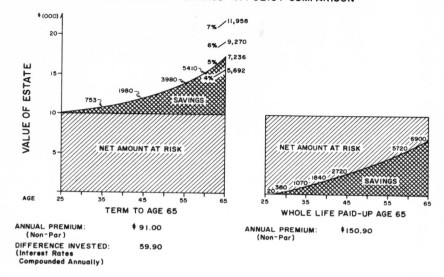

PROTECTION + SAVINGS - A POLICY COMPARISON

CHART 15-1

savings (which must be net of taxes) is graphically added to the face amount of the policy.

The rapidity with which the savings element increases depends upon the size of the periodic deposits into it and the rate of compound interest at which it accumulates. In permanent insurance policies, however, the cash value increases according to the table of nonforfeiture values contained in the policy. (See Chapter 17, Table 17-3 for an example.)

In Chart 15-1 we compare the results of purchasing either a "Whole Life Paid-Up at Age 65" policy to provide both protection and savings, or a level "Term to Age 65" policy at a lower premium to provide protection, with the difference in the amount of the premiums invested in other investment media at varying after-tax interest rates.

When a level term policy in the same face amount as the permanent policy is used, the total estate during the life of the policy is always greater for the term plus savings combination as long as an interest rate greater than zero is maintained.

This is because a permanent policy pays a death benefit in the face amount while the term plus savings combination will provide the same face amount plus any accumulated savings. Thus if the insured dies before age 65, it would obviously be better to have the term plus savings alternative. If the insured desires to surrender his policy at age 65, the whole life policy would accumulate a larger savings account for him unless he could obtain an after-tax yield on his savings program of almost 5% compounded annually or better.

If the insured does not want to maintain so much term insurance that the value of his estate continues to increase over that provided by his permanent insurance alternative, he could purchase either a decreasing term policy or successively smaller amounts of renewable and convertible term insurance. A decreasing term policy, the face value of which decreases during the life of the policy, can be purchased for a smaller premium that that required for a level term policy which maintains the initial face amount.

Chart 15-2 illustrates the use of successively smaller amounts of 5-year renewable and convertible term insurance. The amount of term insurance carried is adjusted so that the total value of the estate approximates the $10,000 estate provided by the ordinary life alternative illustrated. Note that in the case illustrated, the term plus savings alternative still provides a larger total estate for the beneficiary in all but two years during the life of the policy assuming an after-tax return on investments of 5%.

At age 60, the premium for $5000 term coverage exceeds that paid for the ordinary life policy. The illustration assumes that the insured withdraws $37.30 from his savings to pay the term premiums. Under this alternative, the value of his savings would still exceed the cash value of the ordinary life policy at age 65. If the insured decided he no longer required

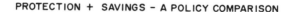

PROTECTION + SAVINGS - A POLICY COMPARISON

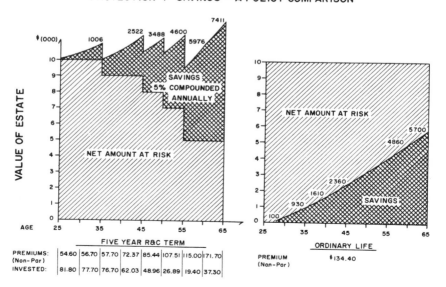

CHART 15-2

protection when he reached age 60, he could drop the term insurance and continue putting $134.40 per year into his investment program.

If he did so, at 5% compounded annually, his savings would accumulate to $8,368.69 by age 65. Note that if the insured's savings fund earned 4% compounded annually, it would accumulate to $5,574.68 by age 65 if he maintained insurance coverage. This is not quite as good as the $5,700 cash value of the ordinary life policy at age 65. Again we see a situation in which the savings fund must earn an after-tax yield of almost 5% or better to exceed the cash value of the permanent policy.

However, if the insured does not surrender the ordinary life policy at age 65, he will have to continue paying the $134.40 annual premium. Under the term plus savings alternative, if the insured put that amount into the savings fund accumulating at 5%, he would have $10,238.64 by age 70, which exceeds the face amount of the ordinary life policy.

Chart 15-3 illustrates a third comparison which is of particular interest to anyone who has been tempted to guarantee a child's education through the purchase of an endowment policy. Recall that the endowment policy guarantees the payment of the face amount of the policy if the insured dies during the endowment period or if he survives to the end of the endowment period. The policy, in effect, combines a rapidly decreasing term policy with a rapidly rising savings element in order to satisfy both promises under the contract.

Notice that two types of term insurance have been coupled with a savings program accumulating at 5% compounded annually in the illus-

PROTECTION + SAVINGS – A POLICY COMPARISON

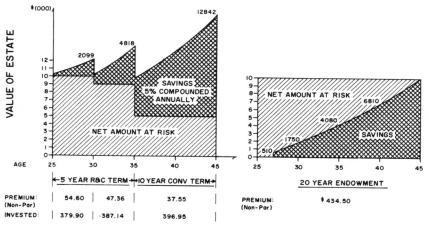

CHART 15-3

trated alternative to the endowment policy. Five-year renewable and convertible term was used for the first 10 years; a ten-year convertible term was used for the last ten years. Under the term plus savings alternative, the value of the estate always exceeds that provided by the endowment policy, and the amount of cash available at the end of the endowment period is almost $3,000 greater.

If an after-tax yield of only 4% is earned on investments, the estate is still always greater than that provided by the endowment policy, and the value of the savings at the end of the endowment period would be $1,574.93 higher than the endowment.

Again, you are cautioned against unwarranted generalizations from these three comparisons. Keep in mind that the savings components of permanent life insurance policies are guaranteed, whereas the after tax yield used in the above comparisons can easily not be attained if either you fail to carry out the investment program, or the investments fail to measure up to your expectations.

Because of these latter risks involved in the "buy term and invest the difference" approach, many officers attempt to construct a balanced life insurance program. Such a program would include enough ordinary life to guarantee any protection that you might need after age 65.

The savings component of such permanent life insurance would act as a hedge against the risks inherent in a "buy term and invest the difference" program. After sufficient ordinary insurance has been purchased, you can then buy term or group insurance to provide additional protection required. Concurrently, you must establish an investment program which should earn more than 5% annually after taxes, and thus protect you from the loss of purchasing power through inflation.

ANNUITIES

An annuity is a periodic payment made during a fixed period or for the duration of a designated life or lives. An annuity policy, therefore, is one under which the insurance company promises to pay a specified sum periodically (e.g. annually or monthly) for a given number of years or the lifetime of the annuitant. Thus, while permanent life insurance contracts provide for the accumulation of savings funds, annuity contracts provide for the amortization of existing funds.

Annuities can be classified according to six basic characteristics:
1. The number of annuitants.
2. The method of premium payment.
3. The time benefits begin.
4. The period over which benefits are paid.
5. The period, if any, that payments continue after the death of the annuitant.

6. The method by which the amount of each benefit payment is determined.

Every annuity can be identified by how each of these characteristics apply to it. Almost any combination is possible. The following paragraphs outline the major characteristics of annuities.

1. *Number of Annuitants.* Usually the annuitant is one individual. When there are two or more annuitants, the payments continue until both or all are dead. Such an annuity is called a joint-and-survivor annuity and is particularly useful to the married couple to protect them against the risk of superannuation.

2. *Method of Premium Payment.* Annuities may be purchased with either a single-premium or level periodic premiums. A single-premium annuity could be purchased with a lump sum accumulated through a systematic savings and investment program, inheritance, cash values from permanent life insurance policies or other media. On the other hand, the purchaser could systematically purchase an annuity through making periodic (e.g., annual) payments to a life insurance company.

3. *Time Benefits Begin.* Annuities are either immediate or deferred depending on whether the first benefit payment is due either one or more than one payment interval from the date of purchase. Thus a widow with life insurance proceeds or a man reaching retirement age could purchase an immediate annuity so that benefits would begin one payment interval (e.g., one month) from the date of purchase. A deferred annuity on the other hand, could be purchased with a single premium to begin at a future date (e.g., upon reaching age 65), or could be purchased with periodic premiums paid over the purchaser's working years.

4. *Period of Benefit Payments.* Annuity payments may be continued: (1) until the death of the annuitant (lifetime annuity); or (2) for merely a fixed number of years (annuity certain); or (3) for a fixed period of time or until the annuitant's death, whichever comes first (temporary annuity).

A lifetime annuity, as the name implies, is used to provide periodic income for life; benefit payments continue until the death of the annuitant, whenever it occurs.

An annuity certain is simply the systematic pay-out of an interest-bearing fund for a fixed or certain period of time. The "fixed period" or "fixed amount" settlement options in life insurance contracts are annuities certain.

A temporary life annuity is most useful in providing income until a future income is available. An example is the so-called "blackout" period in Social Security benefits, which is portrayed on the survivor charts used herein. Thus a temporary annuity could supplement a widow's income between the time her children reach age 18 until she elects to receive Social Security benefits at age 60 or 62.

5. *Payments After the Annuitant's Death.* Annuities can be either

straight-life annuities or guaranteed minimum annuities. The straight-life annuity pays a periodic income to the annuitant until he dies, which could be before any benefits are paid or until he lives well past 100 years old. This type of annuity yields the greatest annual return per dollar of premium.

Many people, however, object to the fact that it is possible to put their life's savings into a straight-life annuity and get only a small fraction of it back. To them it seems preferable to keep their savings in an interest-bearing fund and amortize it without getting involved with an insurance company. In this case, any residual in the fund at their death would go to their heirs. The only problem is the chance that they would continue living after the fund is exhausted.

These two conflicting interests are compromised in the "guaranteed-minimum" annuity, which employs either a refund feature or a guaranteed number of payments. Refund annuities are of two types: cash refund or installment refund. Both types guarantee that either the annuitant or his heirs will receive payments totaling the full amount of the premium paid for the annuity.

The cash refund type provides that any refund due will be paid at once in cash. The installment refund provides that, if the annuitant should die before receiving his purchase price back from the company, the annuity payments will continue until the total purchase price has been refunded.

A "life annuity period certain" guarantees a certain number of payments, whether the annuitant lives or not. After the number of guaranteed payments have been made, the annuity payments continue only as long as the annuitant lives. Thus a "life annuity, ten years certain" is an annuity which guarantees annuity payments for ten years or the lifetime of the annuitant, whichever is longer.

6. *Determination of Benefit Payments.* A variable annuity attempts to provide some compensation for inflation by basing annuity payments upon the earnings and asset value of an investment portfolio purchased with the premiums. Thus variable-annuity payments will fluctuate according to investment results. Generally, variable annuity systems have been very successful, and have provided higher benefits than conventional fixed-dollar annuities.

Selection of Annuities. Normally, an officer or his family would purchase an annuity through either the RSFPP, a single-premium payment after age 60 to provide retirement income, or as a settlement option under a life insurance policy. Before purchasing any annuity, you should compare the benefits of an annuity with a systematic withdrawal from your savings and investment program. Certainly, for example, it would be difficult to justify the purchase of an annuity when an income equal to the annuity benefit can be matched by the interest you earn on your investment program. While any choice must be made in light of individual family circumstances, it is generally economically unsound to purchase an annuity below age 60.

To assist you in making some rough judgments regarding annuities, Chart 15-4 shows the single premium required to purchase a lifetime annuity of $100 per month from one well-known company. These premiums may buy a slightly larger or smaller annuity depending upon the company issuing the contract.

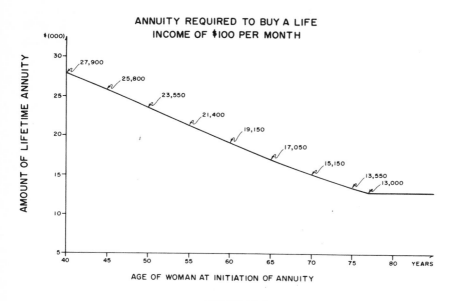

CHART 15-4

Bear in mind as you review the chart that $1,200 per year ($100 per month) is the equivalent to the interest yield on $30,000 at 4%, $26,667 at 4½%, $24,000 at 5%, $20,000 at 6% and $12,000 at 10%.

Appropriate portions of the publications listed in the bibliography for Chapter 14.

Dacey, Norman F. *What's Wrong With Your Life Insurance?* New York: Macmillan Company, 1969.

Gollin, James. *Pay Now, Die Later.* New York: Random House, 1969.

Reynolds, G. Scott. *The Mortality Merchants.* New York: David McKay Company, Inc., 1968.

If thou must deal,
be sure to deal with an honest man.
—John Ray

CHAPTER 16

SELECTING
THE COMPANY

TIME SPENT on selecting a company from which to purchase insurance undoubtedly saves you a good amount of money. Before assessing the quality of a particular company, it is useful to differentiate the three types of companies.

TYPES OF COMPANIES

Life insurance on the legal reserve plan is issued by three types of companies, namely, stock companies, mutual companies, and mixed companies. Inasmuch as mixed companies combine certain features of both other types they will not be further discussed.

Stock Companies. A stock company is organized for profit, the stockholders being entitled to any gain that may result from the operation of the business and sharing responsibility for any losses which may be incurred. Stock companies in practice frequently issue both *participating* (PAR) and *non-participating* (NON-PAR) policies. The stockholders participate in the profits of the non-participating policies while the policyholders participate through dividends in the profits of the participating policies. In the stock company all assets, other than policy reserves, belong to the stockholders.

Mutual Companies. A mutual company is one which has no capital stock and therefore no stockholders. It is composed of the policyholders who own all its assets and who control its management through some system of voting. Mutual companies issue policies commonly referred to as *participating* policies as the policyholder participates in any profits derived from the business. This profit, which is the result of savings in mortality, savings in expenses and excess earnings from investment, is distributed in the form of dividends.

Comparison of Stock and Mutual Companies. The gross premiums charged for participating policies by mutual companies include a loading which not only covers amply all expenses, but also includes an additional amount to safeguard the company against contingencies. Then, if the premium proves to be more than ample, as is nearly always the case, the over-charge is returned as dividends to the policyholders, thus giving them protection at approximately actual cost. Stock companies, likewise, usually load their net premium for non-participating policies, but the amount added is, as a rule, considerably less. In practice, therefore, the non-participating policy's gross premium is lower than that of the participating policy.

Table 16-1 indicates the annual premiums for $1000 insurance recently charged by a leading stock company and a leading mutual company. Note that the participating policy returns part of its premium in the form of dividends. The mutual company paid the indicated dividends on like policies issued 20 years earlier. Thus, the mutual company returned an amount more than sufficient to cover the difference in premiums.

PREMIUMS PER $1000 INSURANCE (Age 23)

(Based on 1941 Tables)*

Policy	Stock Company (NON-PAR Policy) Gross Premium	Mutual Company (PAR Policy) Gross	- Div	= Net
Ordinary Life	$ 15.73	19.76	5.50	14.26
20-Pay Life	27.33	31.62	7.30	24.32
20 year Endowment	47.05	50.52	8.50	42.02

*Premiums are based on the 1941 CSO tables in this example, since not enough time has elapsed for experience of 20 year dividends on the 1958 CSO tables.

TABLE 16-1

Past experience indicates that in most cases the net cost of participating policies has been less than that of non-participating policies, particularly when the policies have been carried ten years or longer. However, it must be noted that the original premium for non-participating policies is considerably less than that for participating policies and is a factor to be considered when insurance is secured by persons whose immediate outlay is limited.

Another factor to be considered is that when you pay a higher premium you are permitting the insurance company to earn interest which you could earn for yourself if you were to invest the annual difference in premiums. The insurance company may or may not pay you back in dividends more than you could earn by investing the difference. Competition between the companies offering the two basic types of policies should serve to keep the net costs of the policies relatively equal. Dividend histories are an important basis for consideration when comparing policies of various insurance companies.

DIVIDENDS—MEANING AND SOURCE

Dividends are a return of a portion of the premium not needed in the light of actual operating experience. This surplus is the sum which the company has on hand after deducting the reserves of its policies and after paying its current expenses and annual death claims. A life insurance company might derive a dividend from three principal sources: (1) a higher return on investments than the rate assumed in computing premium and reserve requirements; (2) a lower death rate than that indicated by the mortality table employed; and (3) a saving in the loading because total expenses are less than total loadings.

It should be noted that the last two are in the nature of salvage and that only the first—interest earnings on investments in excess of the assumed rate—may be truly characterized as a profit. Prudent and efficient management has enabled some insurance companies to reduce their annual expense to a figure less than their calculated allowance or loading for expenses and contingencies.

Hence, life insurance dividends are not dividends in the normal sense of the word, but are, for the most part, a return of that portion of the premium not needed to meet actual operating expenses. This is recognized by the Government in that life insurance dividends, as distinguished from interest earned by dividends left on deposit, need not be reported as income in the submission of Federal income tax returns.

APPRAISING THE COMPANY

In deciding on the company there are three basic considerations: (1)

the financial stability of the company, (2) the net cost record of policies issued, and (3) the specific contents of policies offered.

In the following chapter we will discuss the structure of the life insurance contract which is, in essence, a discussion of the third consideration. This chapter will include a discussion of the other basic considerations.

Financial Stability. The protection which an insurance policy gives is dependent upon the reserve; this is in turn dependent upon the financial stability of the company controlling the reserve. In the United States the regulation of insurance companies is a function of the various states. It therefore varies widely as to scope and effectiveness. However, most states require frequent publication of financial reports, subject the companies to frequent audits and inspections, regulate their investment policy, and require them to secure a license before doing business in the state. To be completely adequate, authorities feel that state insurance laws should regulate or provide for:

1. Regular and thorough examination of business, reserves, and assets.

2. The mortality tables to be used.

3. The rate of interest for valuation of policies.

4. Standard provisions for all policies as to surrender values, option settlements, loans, lapses, payment of premiums, etc.

5. Strict limitations as to investments in corporation stocks.

6. Prohibition or limitations of investment in real estate except for home office.

7. Stringent regulations of investment of reserves.

Notwithstanding such supervision, it should be noted that important variations occur in state standards for licensing insurance companies. Federal agencies such as the Securities and Exchange Commission and the Federal Deposit Insurance Corporation provide the investor or the depositor a nationwide protection. However, no similar agency exists for protecting the purchaser of life insurance.

The rule of "caveat emptor" (let the buyer beware) is evident in the insurance industry. By a study of the successive balance sheets and financial statements of an insurance company, an expert can determine its financial stability. The average Serviceman possesses neither the time, ability, nor access to the data needed for conducting such a study. He should, therefore, examine those prepared reports that are available for his use.

Best's Life Insurance Reports and *Flitcraft Compend* (both annuals) are two standard handbooks containing much valuable information. They are usually available in a public library. The prospective purchaser of insurance should note in *Best's Life Insurance Reports* the record of financial failures of life insurance companies since 1910, the states in which such failing companies were licensed; and the list of legal reserve companies receiving *Best's* recommendation.

Some of the indicators of financial stability upon which *Best's Reports* base their analysis are: (1) diversification of assets both as to kind and location (no single investment of relatively large size); (2) steadiness of earnings under adverse conditions, e.g., during depression years (cash yield on all assets); (3) liquidity of assets; (4) new policies written; (5) the ratio of the actual reserve to the required legal reserve; and (6) organization (e.g., management and expenses).

Occasionally companies do fail. The advantages of buying insurance from old, well-seasoned companies which are relatively large are many. They have many decades of proven success behind them. Furthermore, the mortality experience of a large company is less subject to fluctuations than that of a small company. Such companies have their risks well spread geographically, through all age groups, and through all occupations and professions. They are in a position to employ the most expert men in the various specialized fields necessary to safeguard and manage the policyholders' funds.

To the average person the record of a company's experience in which it has weathered the wars, panics, depressions, and epidemics that swept the country since its foundation is the safest assurance he can obtain. And this assurance of safety is of great importance. Buying insurance is in no sense a speculation. No head of a family can take a chance in this matter which vitally affects the welfare and happiness of his dependents.

Net Cost Record. The uninitiated is frequently led to believe that there is little or no difference in the net costs of identical types of policies issued by the various companies. This is far from being the case. The costs vary greatly between different companies. This difference may be attributed to variance in company expenses, mortality expense, and investment yield.

Difference in company expenses are due not only to efficiency of the management but also to the size and age of the company and the cost of acquiring new business. Mortality expense varies with the care with which new risks are selected. Investment yield is the net rate which has been earned on all assets, and will vary with the quality of company-owned assets.

In Chapter 5, we demonstrated a simple technique for comparing the cost of alternative credit contracts. In a few minutes, you could calculate which of several sources of credit is the least expensive. Unfortunately, comparing the costs of insurance contracts is not so easy. It is interesting to note that even some very expensive and sophisticated studies have been eminently unsuccessful in developing price comparisons of various companies' policies. Nevertheless, the great cost differentials that exist in the insurance market make shopping around a necessity.

Sometimes direct cost comparisons can be made. For example, the net cost per $1000 of protection for non-participating 5-year renewable and convertible term policies having the same key clauses, rights and settlement options, is easy to compare! But throw in varying dividend schedules under participating policies, or varied contract provisions and comparison begins to get more difficult.

To be able to approximate actual cost differences, it is almost a necessity to be comparing policies of the same kind. This is all the more reason to have a good idea of what kind of insurance you need before you begin shopping for policies. Then you can get prices, dividend projections and cash values for the policies you want. Having this information, you can estimate the cost difference by calculating a net surrendered cost by using the following widely-used formula.

20 year net surrendered cost per $1000 insurance = P - D - S, where
   P = gross premiums for 20 years for $1000 insurance.
   D = dividends for 20 years for $1000 insurance, and
   S = cash surrender value per $1000 insurance at the end of
twenty years.

To illustrate, let us apply the formula to Companies X and Y which have both issued a $1000 ordinary life policy at age 25 for many years. Company X is a stock (non-participating) company. Y is a mutual (participating) company. Many stock companies sell both participating and non-participating policies. A stock company of this type pays dividends only to the policy-holders of participating policies.

	P	D	S	20 Year Net Surrender Cost
Company X =	(20 x $13.45) -	$0.00 -	$233.00 =	$36.00
Company Y =	(20 x $17.37) -	$104.00 -	$255.00 =	$ + 11.60
				$47.60

The spread or difference, $47.60, is the added cost for carrying $1000 insurance for 20 years in Company X instead of Company Y. $20,000 insurance would increase the difference by 20 times. Note, however, that dividend projections are not guaranteed. If a company cannot pay as much in dividends as its projection assumes, the cost of the participating policy will increase.

Also note that the above formula does not take into account the opportunity cost of the extra dollars paid in gross premiums for the participating policy. If the $3.92 difference in gross premium in the illustration above were invested in a high-yield investment program, the non-participating policy could be the best alternative. Using standard interest tables we find that depositing $3.92 per year for 20 years into an investment fund would grow to $116.72 at 4% compounded annually, and $129.65 at 5%. Substituting these values for D in the above formula would reduce the net surrendered cost for Company X to minus $80.72 and minus $93.65 respectively.

This means that if the difference in premiums were invested at 4% compounded annually, the non-participating policy would actually be $69.12 per $1000 cheaper than the participating policy.

The best source of data on premiums, dividend performance and cash values is the *Flitcraft Compend*. It should be available in your library; certainly, any qualified insurance agent will have one. By using the above formula to compare the rates of common policies such as the 5-Year Term, Ordinary Life, Term to Age 65, and a 20 Payment Life, you can judge whether or not a company is using a comparatively high-cost loading formula.

If an agent will not allow you to examine his copy of the *Flitcraft Compend,* he either represents a high net cost company or is unwilling to give you the kind of service you should get from an agent you plan to do business with over the years. In either case, find another agent. A prospective buyer should not be "high-pressured" into purchasing insurance. He should investigate carefully and his investigation should be based on the financial stability of the companies and the net surrendered cost per $1000 of their comparable policies.

As previously discussed under methods of premium payment, one must compare the additional premium charges for making other than annual premium payments. Obviously a company that charges 8% for a monthly premium payment plan will have a much higher premium increase than a company charging 4% (an increase of P in the above formula). Be sure to use the premium you would actually have to pay when calculating cost differences.

Other Sources of Insurance. Most of the life insurance sold in the United States is sold by insurance agents. Yet, the best buys in life insurance are not available from agents of commercial companies, since their sales commissions plus sales promotion and advertising costs must be included in the premium load.

Whether or not you can buy a policy from a lower-cost source depends upon where you live, your job, and your rating status. For example, if you live in New York, Massachusetts or Connecticut, you may be able to buy *Savings Bank Life Insurance.* If you live in Wisconsin, you may be able to obtain $10,000 coverage from Wisconsin's *State Life Fund.* For more information, write to the State Life Fund, Department of Insurance, 4802 Sheboygan Avenue, Madison, Wisconsin 53702. If you are presently assigned to the staff and faculty of a college such as one of the Service Academies, you may be able to buy life insurance from the Teacher's Insurance and Annuity Association (TIAA). This non-profit organization, which pioneered the variable annuity is located at 730 Third Avenue, New York, N.Y. 10017.

Finally, no Armed Forces officer should overlook the insurance available from the associations listed in Appendix A.

DEALING WITH AN AGENT

Even if you satisfy many of your insurance needs with policies from the low-cost sources mentioned above, you will still find occasion to deal with a commercial life insurance agent. By observing a few commonsense procedures, you can avoid costly mistakes and obtain valuable service.

Keep in mind that all life insurance agents are trained salesmen who depend for their living on selling life insurance. Table 15-1 gives one example of the commissions that can be earned by an agent. When an agent sells you a policy, he increases his own income. He thus will have an interest in increasing the size of your insurance program.

The repute and technical competence of agents varies greatly. Some are highly qualified and dedicated professionals who look upon the prospective buyer as a client. Such an agent can give the officer valuable assistance in establishing a sound life insurance program tailored to his individual needs. He can also service your policies during your career, and recommend adjustments in your program as your situation changes over time. This is the kind of agent to look for.

Find an agent who is both professionally and personally qualified to handle your continuing insurance needs. Then work with him closely whenever you contemplate changing your insurance program.

In contrast to the dedicated professionals who attempt to service their clients, some agents are unscrupulous policy peddlers whose only interest is to put more cash in their own pockets. Such an agent will try to sell the Serviceman more coverage than he needs or can afford. He will try to sell high-premium policies in an effort to maximize his commission. He may even sell Servicemen policies which contain war clauses or aviation clauses which are more restrictive than those available elsewhere.

Every insurance agent knows that Service personnel fly voluntarily or involuntarily as passengers in military aircraft. Their families need no less income if they die in an air crash than if they die by some other means. If an insurance agent cannot sell a Serviceman a policy that gives full and unrestricted protection against such perils, and he knows that the Serviceman can obtain such coverage from another company, he is guilty of unscrupulous and unconscionable behavior if he makes the sale.

Avoid the solicitor; buy insurance, don't get sold insurance. Don't buy insurance just to help out a relative or family "friend." Too many families have burdened themselves for life by trying to help out Uncle Harry who spent a few months selling insurance before moving on to something else. If you really want to help Uncle Harry, make him go out and earn his living in the cold world right from the start.

When you talk with an agent, take the iniative in the interview. You don't need a sales pitch. Save his time and yours by getting right down to business. Make maximum use of your agent's expertise by coming to him armed with as many relevant facts as possible. Have some idea of your needs. Know what government benefits, accumulated assets and life insurance you already have. Have a tentative plan worked out based upon your best effort to meet your needs at minimum cost.

If you have the kind of agent you need, he will be able to analyze your programming effort and suggest alternatives for you to choose from. He can show you what plans his company can offer to better meet your needs. If he is honest, he will not attempt to sell you a policy when he knows you have a better alternative. Evaluate his recommendations and then make your own decision.

Appropriate portions of the publications listed in the bibliographies for Chapters 14 and 15.

Best's Flitcraft Compend. Morristown, N.J.: A.M. Best Company, Inc., Published annually.

Best's Insurance Reports. Morristown, N.J.: A.M. Best Company, Inc., Published annually.

Best's Review, Life/Health Insurance Edition. Morristown, N.J.: A.M. Best Company, Inc., Published monthly.

Best's Settlement Options Manual. Morristown, N.J.: A.M. Best Company, Inc., Published annually.

What the large print giveth,
the small print taketh away.

CHAPTER **17**

STRUCTURE
OF THE CONTRACT

NO TWO LIFE insurance companies issue identical contracts. The prospective buyer of insurance therefore must carefully study the terms and conditions of any policy he contemplates buying. This is particularly important in the case of Servicemen who all too often buy insurance under contracts which specifically exclude payment in the case of death occurring as the result of military hazards.

Certain of the provisions, or "clauses," that appear in most contracts will now be discussed. Because of their prior importance the provisions relating to military and aviation risks will be taken up first.

RESTRICTIONS AND EXCLUSIONS

War Clauses. Under these clauses the company describes the restriction, if any, on its liability if the insured enters the Armed Services in time of war. *A Serviceman should refuse to accept a policy containing a war clause.*

During the Korean War, some companies again included war clauses in contracts for military personnel. Some, anticipating all-out war, even included war clauses in policies for civilians. Others permitted military personnel to purchase up to a certain limit, usually $5,000 to $10,000 coverage, without a war clause. Thus, by shopping around, military personnel (except pilots; see below) had little trouble in building an insurance estate during this period.

Aviation Exclusion Clauses. Some policies carry provisions which limit the liability of the company if death occurs as the result of an aircraft accident. In such cases, the beneficiaries usually receive either the policy reserve or the premiums paid to date instead of the face value of the policy. Some companies assume full responsibility only when the insured is a passenger in a commercial airplane or on a regularly scheduled flight of the Military Airlift Command (MAC).

Such restrictions are unfavorable to a Serviceman because, even though he is not a pilot or crew member, the average Serviceman must travel in military aircraft from time to time. Many companies are loath to assume this risk at ordinary rates and usually include an aviation "rider" in the policy. An example of an aviation rider is as follows:

AVIATION PROVISIONS

Death of the insured under any of the following circumstances is a risk not assumed by the Company under this policy:

Death as a result of travel or flight in, or descent from or with, any kind of aircraft, unless the insured is being transported solely as a passenger in such aircraft without any duties whatsoever in connection with such travel, flight or descent.

In the event of such death the Company will pay to the beneficiary an amount equal to the premiums actually paid on this policy less any dividends returned, with compound interest thereon at the rate of three per centum per annum, less any indebtedness on the policy; provided however that the amount so paid shall not be more than would be payable in the absence of these provisions, nor less than the reserve on this policy and on any dividend additions plus the value of any dividends deposits and less any indebtedness on the policy. The reserve on the policy for the purposes of these provisions shall be computed on the basis of the Commissioners 1958 Standard Ordinary Mortality Table with interest at the rate of 3% per annum by the Commissioners Reserve Valuation Method.

These provisions shall also be included in any policy to which this policy or any supplemental agreement attached thereto may be changed or converted.

The incontestability provision of this policy shall not be construed to require payment by the Company of any amount in excess of that provided in these provisions if death of the insured occurs under any of the circumstances set forth herein.

A non-rated (not on flying status) Serviceman should make certain his contract contains no unfavorable aviation rider. Some major companies will omit the aviation rider for officers who are not or do not plan to become rated officers. It appears to be wiser for non-rated personnel, particularly paratroopers or those planning to take jump training, to limit their selection of contracts to those that have no aviation rider. The reader is challenged, for example, to peruse the sample aviation rider above and make a decision as to whether or not the death of a paratrooper whose parachute did not open would be fully covered with such a contract provision.

It is well to remember that it is not your interpretation nor what the agent says, but what is written in the contract that is binding. If other considerations lead you to select a company whose contract does contain an aviation rider, have an officer of the company who is authorized to endorse the policy confirm your interpretation in writing before you make the purchase. Many companies will cover paratroopers without extra charge. Others will charge an extra premium of $2.00 to $2.50 per year per $1000 coverage. If you are or plan to become a paratrooper it is best to determine precisely the practice of the company whose contract you are considering.

Do not rely on your own or your agent's interpretation if the aviation clause is at all ambiguous. Do not leave your widow destitute or faced with a lawsuit because you made a faulty interpretation of the "small print" in your insurance contract. You would not be fully covered if your contract contained the preceding sample rider. She would suffer and you will have wasted your money.

Aviation Coverage - General. Military aviators are not considered standard insurance risks. Moreover, as substandard risks they do not all fall in the same class. Pilots are considered poorer risks than bombardiers or navigators; jet pilots and SAC pilots are considered poorer risks than MAC pilots. Younger and inexperienced pilots are regarded as especially poor risks; many companies will not insure student pilots at all.

Some companies place a geographical restriction on pilot coverage; the policy will cover aviation hazards only within the United States, for instance. Company practices vary considerably in the selection and assessment of these risks. There is a general trend towards greater selectivity and increased "rate-ups." A young jet pilot, for example, has to do some shopping to find an insurance company that will sell him protection. The extra premium rates of one major company are given here in Table 17-1. The rates are the extra premiums per year per $10,000 insurance coverage.

A pilot shopping around for life insurance today will find it very difficult to buy term insurance (except group coverage). When he can purchase any kind of insurance, he can expect to find its cost more or less double that of the same policy purchased by a non-rated officer. Nevertheless, paying the higher premium is preferable to purchasing insurance with an aviation exclusion.

Incontestability Clause. Under this clause, the insurance company is given only a limited time, generally two years, for setting up a defense for error, concealment, or misstatements on the part of the insured. If the contract is not cancelled or contested by the company during that period, the company is barred from contesting its obligation, except for non-payment

EXTRA ANNUAL AVIATION PREMIUMS PER $10,000 POLICY

AGE	Fighter-Type Aircraft	Bombers, Helicopters, Utility & Patrol Aircraft	Multi-Engine Cargo, Transport, Tanker, & MAC Aircraft
Pilots*			
Under 30 (Navy & Marine)	$150.00	$55.20	$39.60
Under 30 (Others)	110.40	55.20	39.60
30-39	55.20	39.60	27.60
40 and over	27.60	27.60	27.60
Crew Members			
Under 30	55.20	55.20	39.60
30-39	55.20	39.60	27.60
40 and over	27.60	27.60	27.60

* Student Pilots (other than Army) fall under the fighter-type aircraft classification

TABLE 17-1

of premiums and misstatement of age and sometimes for other specified reasons.

Provisions for disability and double indemnity are usually excluded from the operation of the incontestability clause. For misstatement of age, there is usually a special clause to the effect that if the age has been misstated, the amount payable under the policy shall be as much as the premium paid would have purchased at the correct age.

The incontestability clause provides peace of mind since it assures the insured and his family that the payment of the proceeds will be without delay or protest.

Suicide Clause. All companies provide that if the insured commits suicide before the policy has been in force for a specified time, usually two years, the face value of the policy is not payable to the beneficiary. In this event, the company is liable only for the premiums already paid or the reserve of the policy. A suicide clause is, of course, a necessity. To omit it would be to invite the financially desperate man to insure his life and then kill himself.

Lapses, Reinstatement and Automatic Premium Loans. Servicemen move about the country and foreign service in their duties. It sometimes happens that during a transfer of pay records and bank accounts there is a delay in the payment of policy premiums. This being the case, the insured should take steps to make certain that his policies will not become void without reinstatement privileges. Most policies specify a grace period (usually 31 days) at the expiration of which the policy will lapse. If the policy lapses, extended or paid-up insurance goes into effect automatically.

After a policy has lapsed for non-payment of premiums, if it has not been surrendered for cash, or if its extended-term insurance has not expired, the reinstatement clause provides that the policyholder may reinstate the policy with full benefits and privileges, as of the original date of issue, provided certain conditions are met. Usually, these conditions are the payment of back premiums with interest, the payment or reinstatement of any loans outstanding on the policy, and the submission of evidence of insurability.

Some companies include the automatic premium loan clause in their policies which provides that if a premium is not paid upon the last day of the grace period the company will automatically loan the amount required to pay the premium at a specified rate of interest until the premiums are paid or until the cash value of the policy is exhausted.

Companies writing participating contracts usually apply dividend accumulations, if any, before applying the loan provision. Under this clause the policy is kept in full force as long as the cash value is great enough to pay the premium. The advantages of such a clause are obvious. *Servicemen should submit whatever written authorization is required by the companies to put these provisions in effect in all of their policies.*

Change of Plan Clause. Most companies include a contract clause specifying the terms under which the policyholder may change his policy from one plan to another for the same face amount, or less. If the change is from a lower premium to a higher-premium plan, the change can be made without medical examination. The usual practice is for the company to charge the difference between the two premiums for the number of years the policy has been in force, plus interest. If the change is from a higher to a lower-premium plan the company usually requires evidence of insurability and makes an adjustment on the basis of the difference between the reserves of the respective policies.

Entire Contract Clause. This clause usually states that the policy and the application for it constitute the entire contract between the policyholder and the company. The application is photographed and made a part of the contract so that every statement made by the applicant either to the medical examiner or to the agent, can be verified by either party. This part of the contract assures the company that its obligations are clearly defined and do not include any promises or special agreements, oral or written, made by the agent.

This clause usually provides further that statements made by the applicant with respect to matters not material to the risk need only be substantially true and not literally true. For example, if you said your father died at 75, whereas he actually died at 73, that would be a false statement not material to the risk. If you said that you had not been hospitalized within the last five years and you had, in fact, had a malignant tumor removed from your throat two years ago, that would be a fraudulent statement material to the risk. If the company found out the truth within the contestable period it could avoid liability under the policy.

ADDITIONAL BENEFITS

Waiver of Premium Disability. Most companies will add a provision for an extra premium, which exempts the insured from paying further premiums if he becomes "disabled" as defined in the policy. In essence, the waiver of premium provision is a small disability-income insurance policy and money spent for it should be considered allocated for that purpose and not for life insurance. Also, the provision usually contains a statement to the effect that premiums will not be waived if disability occurs as a result of an act of war while the insured is in the Armed Forces.

Quite often the provision will not be available to military personnel even with a war exclusion statement within the provision. Since these provisions do have a self-contained war rider, and since Servicemen who become disabled are normally hospitalized at public expense and are entitled to disability compensation from the Government, it appears that this type of protection is not as necessary for them as it might be for individuals in other walks of life.

Accidental Death Benefit (Double Indemnity). Many companies will, for an additional premium, pay double the face value of the policy in the event that death results from certain accidental causes. Excluded from these provisions are deaths as a result of war or of travel on, flight in, or descent from military aircraft while on a duty (as opposed to leave) status. These war and aviation exclusions are enough to make a double-indemnity clause unattractive to a Serviceman.

Over and above these objections, the clause is of questionable value in anyone's insurance program. The amount the insured's dependents will need in the event of his death is in no way related to the manner in which he dies. If he is killed in an automobile accident it will not take twice as much to support his dependents than if he had died of pneumonia.

DIVIDEND OPTIONS

In Chapter 16 we discussed the meaning and source of dividends. In this section we shall discuss the ways in which they can be used. Dividends are paid annually on the anniversary of the policy. The first dividend is generally paid upon the termination of the second or third policy year. Generally, the first dividend is conditioned upon the policyholder paying the premium for the next succeeding year.

It is customary for companies to allow the insured to use dividends in one of a number of ways. The policyholder may elect an option at the time of application, at a later date or he may change from one option to another on any policy anniversary. The following dividend options are generally allowed the policyholder.

Option 1. He may accept the dividend in cash. This he might do because he has better uses for this money than are open to him under any of the other options, i.e., he needs the cash for other expenditures, or he wants to invest it at a higher rate of return, and/or he doesn't need any more insurance protection.

Option 2. He may apply the dividends to reduce premium payments. If he finds full premium payment a hardship, this option is advantageous. In computing premium payments due for the succeeding year the company simply subtracts the dividends accrued during the past year. This option is incompatible with paying premiums by allotment since it necessitates changing the allotment each year. Individuals paying premiums by allotment should select Option I if they find full premium payment a hardship.

Option 3. He may leave the dividends with the company to accumulate at interest. On this plan the dividends grow as a savings fund, subject to withdrawal by the policyholder at any time. This option usually specifies a guaranteed minimum rate at which interest will be credited with allowances for excess interest as declared by the company. Both the guaranteed and the current rate vary considerably with different companies. This is indicated in the following sample selection from *Best's 1970 Flitcraft Compend,* a book which analyzes companies and policies:

Interest Paid On Dividend Accumulations

Company	Guaranteed Rate	Current Rate
Company A	2.5%	4.20%
Company B	2.5%	4.25%
Company C	3.0%	3.75%
Company D	3.0%	4.40%
Company E	3.0%	4.00%
Company F	3.5%	4.25%

Both the guaranteed rate and the current rate of interest paid on dividend accumulations sould be among the factors the policyholder should consider in selecting a company if he planned to make use of this option. Since a higher interest return can often be realized on other investments the policyholder might prefer Option 1.

Option 4. He may use the dividends to buy paid-up additions to his insurance. In such a case, when the dividend is declared the company uses it to buy for the policyholder additional insurance of the same type as the original insurance. The paid-up additions, *in effect,* increase the face value of the original policy as long as this option is in force. These additions may be surrendered for their cash value at any time.

In choosing between Options 3 and 4 one must weigh whether the accumulation of savings or the accumulation of insurance is most important to him. Moreover, one must determine if paid-up additions are subject to some "risk" qualification which may be included or denied in the regular policy. Table 17-2 illustrates the advantages of each option to an individual age 23 for a $10,000 ordinary life contract. As always, the dividends are illustrative and not guaranteed.

If Option 4 is selected and at the end of 10 years the policyholder decides to cash-surrender his $980.00 paid-up additions he will get somewhat less cash than $441.30. The reason for this is that when paid-up additions are purchased a part of the money is necessarily used to buy protection, whereas under Option 3 there is no mortality cost to be considered. This also accounts for the fact that under Option 3 a policy will become paid up or will mature a year sooner than if Option 4 is selected. The other side of the comparison is that if the insured dies at the end of 10 years,

RESULTS OF DIVIDEND OPTIONS

End of Policy Year	Option 3 Div. Accumulations	Option 4 Paid-Up Additions
5	$ 167.90	$ 410.00
10	441.30	980.00
15	832.50	1670.00
20	1347.50	2430.00
Age 55	3142.10	4420.00
Policy Pays Up	27 yrs	28 yrs
Policy Matures	39 yrs	40 yrs

TABLE 17-2

under Option 3 his widow will receive $10,441.30 whereas under Option 4 she will receive $10,980.00.

Option 5. Dividends may be applied to purchase a non-participating one-year term insurance addition. Not all companies offer this dividend option.

NONFORFEITURE PROVISIONS

All insurance contracts, except term policies, provide the policyholder with certain options should he exercise his right to cancel his contract and make no further premium payments. In Chapter 14 we noted that level premium policies build up a reserve. This reserve is the cash value of the policy. It is the policyholder's savings account. He may borrow this money at any time at a specified rate of interest (usually 5%), or he may let his policy lapse and exercise one of the following options:

1. he may demand and receive in cash the full amount of his cash value;

2. he may use his cash value to buy a single premium, paid-up policy, for a reduced amount of life insurance; or

3. he may use his cash value to buy term insurance in the face amount of his policy for a limited number of years.

If the policyholder allows his policy to lapse and has not authorized the company to put the automatic premium loan provision into effect, then usually the extended-term option becomes effective automatically unless the insured selects one of the other nonforfeiture options.

These options, including the loan provision are termed nonforfeiture values. They are guaranteed and are shown in a table of values in the contract. Table 17-3 is a sample table taken from a specimen ordinary life policy issued at age 25.

Cash Values. Cash values should be compared since they are one of the determinants of the investment values of the policy. They vary with different companies as the following sample taken from *Best's Flitcraft Compend* shows:

Cash Values On $1000 Ordinary Life Issued Age 25
Selected Companies

Company	End of 20th Year	Age 65
Company A	$269	$592
Company B	$283	606
Company C	$253	578
Company D	$281	608
Company E	$277	606
Company F	$256	586

On a $25,000 insurance program the difference between the highest and lowest in the above sample amounts to $500 at the end of the 20th year and $750 at age 65.

Loan Values. Loan values show how much the insured can borrow against the policy. He can borrow this amount from the company at a set rate of interest or, by assigning the contract to a bank, he can use it to secure a commercial bank loan for the amount of the loan value. Since bank and other commercial interest rates will fluctuate from time to time while the interest rate on loans guaranteed in a life insurance policy will not, the insured will thus have more flexibility in borrowing funds than the individual without life insurance assets. An ability to use a life insurance policy as collateral for a bank loan adds to an individual's means of securing funds swiftly in an emergency.

If the insured borrows from the company against his policy contract, he gets up to the exact amount of the loan value and pays a set rate of interest (about 5% for most companies). He may carry the loan for as long as he is able to pay the interest charges. There is no specified period within which the loan must be liquidated, nor must he make periodic payments. He is not obligated to repay the loan according to any set schedule.

However; one serious warning should be entered. Having either borrowed from the company or a bank (and assuming that consumption desires are usually greater than income capabilities), it becomes tempting to drop

TABLE OF CASH, LOAN AND NON-FORFEITURE VALUES

For each $1,000 of the face amount of the policy free from indebtedness and without dividend accumulations or paid-up additions. Paid-up insurance will be adjusted to the nearest dollar.

Premiums Paid to End of Policy Year	Paid-up Insurance (Participating)	Cash Value — Loan Values, Subject to the "Loans" Clause	Extended Term Insurance (Participating) Years	Days	Premiums Paid to End of Policy Year	Paid-up Insurance (Participating)	Cash Value — Loan Values, Subject to the "Loans" Clause	Extended Term Insurance (Participating) Years	Days
1	$0	$0	0	0	12	$345	$164	21	284
2	11	5	1	226	13	370	179	22	50
3	50	20	5	347	14	393	194	22	147
4	86	35	9	179	15	413	210	22	288
5	120	50	12	120	16	441	226	22	261
6	154	65	14	209	17	463	242	22	284
7	188	81	16	231	18	485	258	22	287
8	221	97	18	107	19	506	274	22	273
9	252	113	19	234	20	520	290	22	325
10	282	130	20	148	35†	769	542	18	316
11	316	147	21	115	40†	826	623	16	340

†Anniversaries Nearest Ages 60 and 65

TABLE 17-3

the policy, thus liquidating the loan instead of repaying it out of current income.

This is quite logical if the insurance was purchased with the intention of eventually dropping it. For example, one may buy an ordinary life policy to provide protection prior to retirement with the intent of cashing it in and buying a home after retirement. On the other hand, if the policy is part of a permanent program, dropping the policy reduces insurance protection by an amount which can be replaced on a permanent basis later only at higher cost and if still insurable. Thus, utilizing the loan values of a policy may require an exercise of will by the insured.

Extended-Term Insurance. Extended-term insurance is generally not available as an option on policies sold to flying officers, but other officers who do have this option in their contracts might use it to advantage in two ways. Referring back to Table 17-3, if an officer buys ordinary life instead of term insurance to cover the temporary need of a child up to age 20, he may pay premiums for 6 years, and then by exercising the extended-term option have full coverage for over 14 years. Or, if he should become afflicted with a dread disease and his life expectancy becomes less than the number of years that extended term insurance is available to him, there would be no point in his continuing to pay the premiums. Complicating individual decision, however, could be the consequential and irrevocable loss of such features as Disability Income protection, Guaranteed Insurability options, etc., depending on the particular policy.

Paid-up Insurance. A paid-up policy is advantageous for the officer who finds that after his children are grown up and married he no longer requires as much insurance as he formerly did. He may stop paying premiums on his insurance and take a reduced amount of paid-up insurance commensurate with his reduced needs.

CHANGE OF BENEFICIARY

The policyholder may specifically deny himself the right to change his beneficiary. This is often done when someone else is making the premium payments.

In purchasing family protection, the insured usually designates his wife as primary beneficiary and his children as contingent beneficiaries. He retains the right to make a change in the designation whenever and as often as he wishes. Furthermore, when the policyholder retains the right to change the beneficiary he retains every interest in the policy such as dividend, settlement and nonforfeiture option rights, change of plan and cash surrender; he may exercise these rights without the consent of the beneficiaries. Through the various settlement options, to be discussed below, arrangement can be made to pay each beneficiary's share according to his or her best interests and needs.

SETTLEMENT OPTIONS

In Chapter 18 we shall discuss insurance programming and offer some guidance in the selection of settlement options to plan the disposition of insurance proceeds. In this section we shall limit the discussion mainly to the modes of settlement available.

Lump-sum cash settlements serve a purpose where capital rather than income is needed. In the case where the beneficiary is able to invest and manage the money properly the insured may choose to have all proceeds paid in a lump sum. On the other hand, insurance proceeds can be paid off as assured income under one or more of the settlement options discussed below.

In order to determine the amount of insurance needed to produce a given income, one must understand the various options which companies offer for the settlement of death claims. Only the most common and most fundamental are discussed here. All others are derived from, or bear a relation to, these basic forms.

Proceeds from policies are usually payable in cash unless the insured selects one of the permitted options before his death or unless the beneficiary selects one after the insured's death. Proceeds from a given policy may be paid part in cash and part under one or more income options. The policyholder may give the beneficiary the right to select the options or to change any options he has selected. Also in some contracts the insured may give the beneficiary the right of withdrawal, with or without stipulating the amount even though proceeds are being paid under income options. Usually, however, the rate of interest paid by the company under the options is lower if the beneficiary has the right of withdrawal.

Income Options. The income options offered by one of the prominent mutual companies are shown in Table 17-4. The amounts payable under several of these options are shown in Tables 17-5 and 17-6.

Option A. This option provides for an income for a fixed number of years. The principal, plus interest, is used up in paying an agreed number of installments of a specified amount. For instance, $1000 proceeds will pay $17.70 per month for five years (Table 17-5). The amount of each installment necessarily varies with their number. If the beneficiary dies before the elected number of installments has been paid, the remaining installments are paid to his estate or to a designated beneficiary. When the elected number of installments has been paid, the proceeds from the policy are completely liquidated and the company has no further obligation.

The option is well adapted to provide for the care of children up to their maturity. As they approach that stage, the insured can gradually decrease the amount of insurance payable in this way.

Option B. This option provides for an income for twenty years certain and thereafter during the life of the beneficiary. This option is a type of refund annuity previously mentioned under annuities. Life income is

INCOME OPTIONS

The whole or any part of the Net Proceeds of this Policy, or of its Net Value payable in cash upon surrender, may be made payable in accordance with any one of the following Options, if written election is filed at the Home Office. The person entitled to receive payments under any Option is hereinafter designated "payee."

Option A   An income for a fixed period of years not exceeding thirty.

Option B   An income for twenty years certain and thereafter during the life of the payee.

Option C   An income for ten years certain and thereafter during the life of the payee.

Option D   An interest income on the Net Proceeds or Net Value, as the case may be, at the guaranteed rate of 2 per cent per annum, increased by dividend additions.

Option E   An income of a fixed amount until the Net Proceeds or Net Value, as the case may be, and interest to be added thereto (at the guaranteed rate of 2 1/2 per cent per annum), increased by dividend additions are exhausted--the final payment to be the balance then remaining with the company.

Option F   A Life Income Without Refund payable during the lifetime of the payee and terminating with the last payment preceding death.

Option FR A Refund Life Income payable during the lifetime of the payee and terminating with the last payment preceding death; provided, however, that if the payee dies before the total income paid equals the amount of the Net Proceeds or Net Value, as the case may be, applied under this Option, the Company will continue income payments until the total thereof shall equal said amount.

Option G   A Life Income payable during the joint lifetime of the two payees and the lifetime of the survivor and terminating with the last payment preceding the death of the survivor. This Option is not available if either payee is under age 50.

TABLE 17-4

TABLE OF INCOME

The income under Options A, B, C, F, FR, and G will be payable in accordance with the following tables, which state the monthly income provided by Net Proceeds or Net Value of $1000 and apply pro rata to this Policy. The first payment will be made upon maturity of this Policy or upon proper surrender. Under Options B, C, F, FR, and G, the income varies according to age and sex, and is based upon the age of the payee at his or her nearest birthday.

Option A

Number of Years	Monthly Income	Number of Years	Monthly Income	Number of Years	Monthly Income
1	$84.28	11	$8.64	21	$5.08
2	42.66	12	8.02	22	4.90
3	28.79	13	7.49	23	4.74
4	21.86	14	7.03	24	4.60
5	17.70	15	6.64	25	4.46
6	14.93	16	6.30	26	4.34
7	12.95	17	6.00	27	4.22
8	11.47	18	5.73	28	4.12
9	10.32	19	5.49	29	4.02
10	9.39	20	5.27	30	3.93

TABLE 17-5

INCOME FROM SETTLEMENT OPTIONS

Age of Beneficiary on Nearest Birthday	Option B 20 Years Certain		Option C 10 Years Certain		Option F Without Refund		Option FR Until Proceeds are Refunded	
	Monthly Male	Female	Monthly Male	Female	Monthly Male	Female	Monthly Male	Female
15 and under	$2.77	$2.68	$2.78	$2.69	$2.79	$2.69	$2.75	$2.66
16	2.79	2.70	2.81	2.71	2.81	2.71	2.77	2.67
17	2.81	2.71	2.83	2.73	2.83	2.73	2.79	2.69
18	2.84	2.73	2.85	2.74	2.86	2.75	2.81	2.71
19	2.86	2.75	2.88	2.76	2.88	2.77	2.83	2.73
20	2.88	2.77	2.90	2.78	2.91	2.79	2.85	2.75
21	2.91	2.79	2.93	2.81	2.93	2.81	2.88	2.77
22	2.93	2.81	2.95	2.83	2.96	2.83	2.90	2.79
23	2.96	2.84	2.98	2.85	2.99	2.86	2.93	2.81
24	2.99	2.86	3.01	2.88	3.02	2.88	2.95	2.83
25	3.02	2.88	3.04	2.90	3.05	2.91	2.98	2.85
26	3.05	2.91	3.08	2.93	3.08	2.93	3.01	2.88
27	3.08	2.93	3.11	2.95	3.12	2.96	3.04	2.90
28	3.11	2.96	3.14	2.98	3.15	2.99	3.07	2.93
29	3.15	2.99	3.18	3.01	3.19	3.02	3.10	2.95
30	3.18	3.02	3.22	3.04	3.23	3.05	3.13	2.98
31	3.22	3.05	3.26	3.08	3.27	3.08	3.17	3.01
32	3.25	3.08	3.30	3.11	3.31	3.12	3.20	3.04
33	3.29	3.11	3.34	3.14	3.36	3.15	3.24	3.07
34	3.33	3.15	3.39	3.18	3.41	3.19	3.28	3.10
35	3.37	3.18	3.43	3.22	3.45	3.23	3.32	3.13
36	3.41	3.22	3.48	3.26	3.50	3.27	3.36	3.17
37	3.45	3.25	3.53	3.30	3.56	3.31	3.40	3.20
38	3.50	3.29	3.59	3.34	3.61	3.36	3.44	3.24
39	3.54	3.33	3.64	3.39	3.67	3.41	3.49	3.28
40	3.59	3.37	3.70	3.43	3.73	3.45	3.53	3.32
41	3.64	3.41	3.76	3.48	3.79	3.50	3.58	3.36
42	3.69	3.45	3.82	3.53	3.86	3.56	3.63	3.40
43	3.74	3.50	3.88	3.59	3.93	3.61	3.68	3.44
44	3.79	3.54	3.95	3.64	4.00	3.67	3.74	3.49
45	3.84	3.59	4.02	3.70	4.08	3.73	3.80	3.53
46	3.90	3.64	4.09	3.76	4.15	3.79	3.85	3.58
47	3.95	3.69	4.17	3.82	4.24	3.86	3.91	3.63
48	4.01	3.74	4.25	3.88	4.33	3.93	3.98	3.68
49	4.07	3.79	4.33	3.95	4.42	4.00	4.04	3.74
50	4.12	3.84	4.42	4.02	4.51	4.08	4.11	3.80
51	4.18	3.90	4.50	4.09	4.61	4.15	4.18	3.85
52	4.24	3.95	4.60	4.17	4.72	4.24	4.26	3.91
53	4.30	4.01	4.69	4.25	4.83	4.33	4.33	3.98
54	4.36	4.07	4.79	4.33	4.95	4.42	4.42	4.04
55	4.41	4.12	4.90	4.42	5.07	4.51	4.50	4.11
56	4.47	4.18	5.01	4.50	5.20	4.61	4.59	4.18
57	4.53	4.24	5.12	4.60	5.34	4.72	4.68	4.26
58	4.59	4.30	5.23	4.69	5.48	4.83	4.77	4.33
59	4.64	4.36	5.35	4.79	5.64	4.95	4.87	4.42
60	4.70	4.41	5.48	4.90	5.80	5.07	4.98	4.50
61	4.75	4.47	5.61	5.01	5.97	5.20	5.08	4.59
62	4.80	4.53	5.74	5.12	6.15	5.34	5.20	4.68
63	4.85	4.59	5.87	5.23	6.34	5.48	5.31	4.77
64	4.90	4.64	6.01	5.35	6.54	5.64	5.44	4.87
65	4.94	4.70	6.16	5.48	6.75	5.80	5.57	4.98
66	4.94	4.75	6.30	5.61	6.97	5.97	5.70	5.08
67	4.94	4.80	6.45	5.74	7.21	6.15	5.84	5.20
68	4.94	4.85	6.60	5.87	7.46	6.34	5.99	5.31
69	4.94	4.90	6.76	6.01	7.73	6.54	6.15	5.44
70	4.94	4.94	6.91	6.16	8.02	6.75	6.31	5.57
71	4.94	4.94	7.07	6.30	8.32	6.97	6.48	5.70
72	4.94	4.94	7.23	6.45	8.64	7.21	6.66	5.84
73	4.94	4.94	7.38	6.60	8.98	7.46	6.84	5.99
74	4.94	4.94	7.54	6.76	9.34	7.73	7.04	6.15
75	4.94	4.94	7.69	6.91	9.72	8.02	7.25	6.31
76	4.94	4.94	7.84	7.07	10.13	8.32	7.46	6.48
77	4.94	4.94	7.98	7.23	10.57	8.64	7.69	6.66
78	4.94	4.94	8.13	7.38	11.03	8.98	7.93	6.84
79	4.94	4.94	8.26	7.54	11.53	9.34	8.18	7.04
80	4.94	4.94	8.39	7.69	12.06	9.72	8.45	7.25
81	4.94	4.94	8.51	7.84	12.62	10.13	8.73	7.46
82	4.94	4.94	8.63	7.98	13.22	10.57	9.02	7.69
83	4.94	4.94	8.73	8.13	13.86	11.03	9.34	7.93
84	4.94	4.94	8.83	8.26	14.55	11.53	9.66	8.18
85 and over	4.94	4.94	8.92	8.39	15.28	12.06	10.00	8.43

TABLE 17-6

provided for the beneficiary, and in the event the beneficiary dies before receiving twenty years of payments, the balance of the payments is made to a designated beneficiary or the commuted value is paid to the estate.

Under this option $1000 proceeds would provide a female age 50 a lifetime income of $3.84 per month, guaranteed for 20 years (Table 17-6). This option is particularly suitable when there are young children, for if the beneficiary—usually the wife—should die before having received the 20 years of payments the remaining payments may be continued to the children, thus assuring them of an income to maturity.

Option C. This option is the same as Option B except the guaranteed period of income is 10 years instead of 20 years. When the children reach the ages of 10-12, this option may then be selected in lieu of Option B since it provides a slightly larger income.

Option D. This option provides that the company retains the proceeds of the policy and pays interest to the beneficiary at a guaranteed rate of interest.

It should be noted that under Options A, B, and C both the principal and the interest are consumed in providing the income and hence no estate is left after the stipulated number of payments has been made. Under Option D only the interest is paid. This option is particularly useful to a Serviceman in programming his insurance. For the period while Social Security is payable he may put his commercial insurance on the interest option with the provision that as the children become of age (usually he must specify dates) and Social Security payments cease, one of the life income options will become effective. Or, he may leave it up to his widow to withdraw cash or select any income option when she wishes it to become effective.

Other Options. Other options are indicated in Table 17-4. Option E provides for an income of a fixed amount until the proceeds plus interest are exhausted. Option F is a life annuity. Option FR is a form of refund annuity. Option G is a joint and survivorship annuity. Most of these were described under annuities and will not be further discussed. Usually these options are available to the insured as well as to the beneficiary, if he should elect to use the proceeds or cash value of the policy.

As in the case of dividend options, the guaranteed and the current rates of interest paid on policy proceeds left with companies under income options vary considerably. In comparing contracts and companies with respect to settlement options the Serviceman should look further than a comparison of guaranteed and current rates of interest paid. For example, many companies will reduce both the guaranteed rates and the current rate of income options if the insured gives the beneficiary the right of withdrawal. The reduction varies from .25% to .75%.

Since the average Serviceman purchases insurance to provide his family with income rather than capital he should become thoroughly familiar with the various privileges and restrictions in the settlement options of the policies he has under consideration. A reference book that makes this comparative analysis on most insurance contracts is *Best's Settlement Options,* published annually. This reference book should be available in most public libraries along with a sister publication, *Best's Flitcraft Compend* which gives a short policy analysis, premium rates, dividend schedules, nonforfeiture values and other information, arranged by company. Both may be very valuable and time-saving in one's investigation before purchasing life insurance.

Amortization of Savings Fund. As an alternative to receiving the proceeds of an insurance policy in the form of an income option, a beneficiary could receive insurance proceeds in a lump sum, and place them into an investment program which yields a higher return than the income option on the amount of insurance involved.

Chart 17-1 indicates how long an original fund of $10,000 would last if specified monthly withdrawals were made when the fund is earning various interest rates (fixed amount annuity). It also shows how much can be withdrawn each month from a fund starting at $10,000, so that the fund would be exhausted in a specified number of years (fixed-period annuity).

Table 17-7 indicates the approximate amount of monthly income earned by a $10,000 fund at various interest rates. Thus the indicated

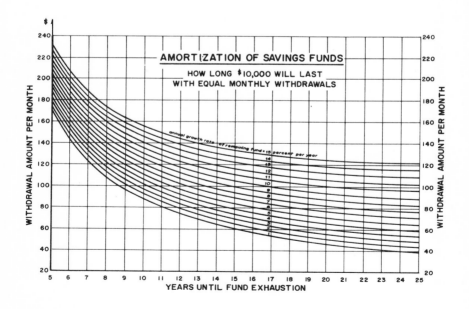

CHART 17-1

APPROXIMATE MONTHLY INCOME EARNED ON $10,000

Interest Rate	3%	4%	5%	6%	7%	8%	10%	12%	14%
Monthly Income	$24.65	$32.75	$40.75	$48.70	$56.55	$64.35	$79.75	$94.90	$109.80

TABLE 17-7

amounts could be withdrawn monthly without impairing the principal. The amounts available from any other size fund can be obtained by simple proportion.

The following chapter discusses the programming technique for determining your own life insurance requirements. The better your own programming efforts, the better your chance of satisfying your needs at minimum dollar cost.

Appropriate portions of the publications listed in the bibliographies for Chapter 14, 15, & 16.

Institute of Life Insurance. *Specimen Policy*. New York: Institute of Life Insurance, 1969.

It is not the crook ... that
we fear, but the honest man who
doesn't know what he is doing.
                    —Owen D. Young

CHAPTER 18

PROGRAMMING
LIFE INSURANCE

A FEW HOURS of planning can help you avoid the gaps in your financial resources that could mean economic disaster to a family unprepared for the financial risks it must face. Chapters 8 and 9 concluded with a checklist of minimum and recommended insurance coverages that are believed necessary to protect the typical officer against serious financial loss through property and liability risks. In Chapter 11 we began an analysis of personal risks and their treatment. The construction of a Retirement Income Chart was begun, and in Chapters 12 and 13 we initiated the Active Duty and Retirement Survivorship Charts by programming key government survivor benefits.

The purpose of this chapter is to illustrate how these graphical representations of your long-range financial plans can be completed using the results of a savings and investment program and various life insurance media. Again we should emphasize the important services qualified life insurance agents can provide. They can explain what their company can offer to efficiently complete your plans.

Each planning situation will have unique circumstances which qualified agents will be able to understand and make clear to you. But unless you approach the agent with a sound understanding of your basic financial problem and the kinds of alternatives you have to solve them, you cannot make maximum use of his expertise. Neither will you be able to evaluate insurance coverages which are not sold through agents, and which may provide the required benefits at a lower cost. If you are aware of such alternatives, you can at least ask an agent to explain why his company's product is better for you.

The more you know about insurance, the better your ability to evaluate advice you receive. Remember that if a mistake is made, you or your family are the ones who must pay for it.

AN APPROACH TO PLANNING

There are two fundamental approaches to determining the amount of life insurance a family should maintain on the life of the breadwinner. One is the *human life value* approach, which recognizes that the income-earner's life has an economic value to the dependent members of the family, and seeks to equate insurance coverage to that economic value. Thus the insured, using this approach, would purchase that amount of life insurance which, if invested at the current rate of interest, would yield an income equivalent to at least one-third to one-half of his lifetime earnings potential. If a man expected to earn $200,000 during his lifetime, he would purchase $66,000 to $100,000 worth of insurance, discounted at the current rate of interest (i.e., the present value of $66,000 to $100,000 earned over the years of employment).

The principal difficulty with this approach is that few can afford to pay the premiums involved. Just imagine the premiums that would have to be paid by an officer on flying status, who can expect to earn over $540,000 (not including the present value of his retirement benefits) during a thirty-year career! Thus the approach used in this book is the *needs approach,* which attempts to calculate the various financial needs that the family would have if the breadwinner should die. Once the needs have been determined, then the planner must determine how family resources can best be used to meet those needs.

In the remainder of this chapter, we will consider the long-range plans of the hypothetical officer introduced in Part Two of this book. It should not be inferred that the particular devices used to "close the gaps" in this illustration are optimum or best suited to your needs. The main purpose in selecting our methods is to illustrate a variety of means that could be used. Obviously, there are a number of ways in which the various needs can be satisfied.

EXAMINING NEEDS

There are two kinds of financial needs to provide for: cash needs and income needs. The amounts of each must be determined in light of your family's preferences and the information contained in your Family Income and Expenditure Chart (Chart 3-2) and your Family Balance Sheet (Chart 3-4).

Cash Needs. Let us assume that at the time of planning (1 January 1972), the following cash needs exist at the start of the officer's two survivorship plans.

CASH NEEDS	January 1972	June 1982
Clean-up Fund	$ 3,000	$ 3,000
Emergency Fund	3,000	3,000
Mortgage Retirement	18,000	6,000
Education Fund (for 2)	18,000	18,000
Tax Fund	NONE	NONE
Other Funds	NONE	NONE
	$41,000	$30,000

The above figures indicate that the officer intends to provide a reasonable amount of cash for "clean-up" of outstanding indebtedness not covered by life insurance. The Emergency Fund is established to provide a cushion for unforeseen emergencies. Regarding Mortgage Retirement, the officer evidently intends to pay off all but $6,000 of an outstanding mortgage by the time he could retire in 1982. If he occupies government quarters instead of his own home during his Service career, he could accumulate the equivalent of his equity in a mortgage through systematic investment in a savings medium.

The Tax Fund would be required if the officer's estate were to grow large enough to incur estate and inheritance taxes at his death. As the size of an estate grows, providing a source of liquid funds becomes more and more important. It is tragic when the need to pay such taxes forces survivors to sell securities, etc., at depressed market prices.

The Education Fund is really a multipurpose fund which has as its primary purpose the guaranteeing of a college education for the children. The funds may not be required for actual college expenses if, for example, a child goes to a Service Academy, earns a scholarship, receives a government or other grant, or goes to a school where the costs are low enough to be met out of income earned by the student and his parents. Such eventualities would release the Education Fund for other purposes, such as providing retirement income or buying a yacht.

Income Needs. Normally insurance programs are based on the assumption that the survivors will continue the standard of living existing before the breadwinner's death. The survivor's income necessary to achieve this can be estimated by examining the Family Income and Expenditure Chart, and subtracting out expenses that would not exist after the breadwinner's death.

Such expenses include Federal income tax, FICA, life insurance premiums, and savings that would be discontinued, any reduction in charitable gifts, mortgage payments on the home (assuming the mortgage is retired or a new house is purchased for cash), and the deceased's personal expenses for food, clothing, transportation, club dues, etc.

Let us assume that our hypothetical family decided it desires:

1. $600 per month until both children graduate from college.
2. $500 per month for life thereafter.

These income goals can be plotted on the survivorship charts as shown in Chart 18-1. The income goals thus established are designed to maintain the family at its current standard of living at current price levels. If we calculate needs on a current basis without padding them for possible inflation, the amount of insurance required will be less than if the needs were inflated. Thus we have the problem of including in our plans the effects of any inflation that may occur.

Inflation. No one can foretell with assurance the future rate of infla-

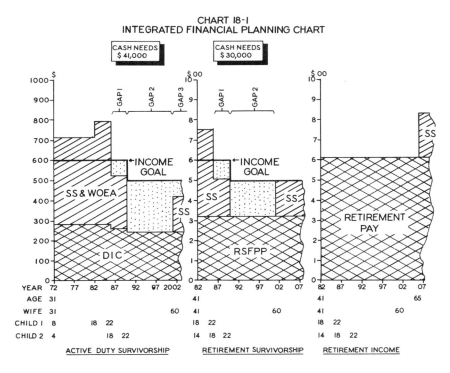

CHART 18-1
INTEGRATED FINANCIAL PLANNING CHART

CHART 18-1

tion. There are many ways to handle this problem in the planning process and the choice is up to you.

The method used here simply assumes that increases in government benefits will compensate for increases in the cost of living. Before you argue that increases in such benefits are not likely to be enough to fully compensate for inflation, let us look at the result of this assumption.

Insurance is a fixed-dollar contract which cannot increase in face value as the cost of living increases. By contrast, an investment program based upon equity investments does provide protection against inflation. For this reason, it is desirable to limit insurance protection to the amount you think is sufficient, maximizing the imput of dollars into your investment program. Dollars spent on over-insurance cannot be invested in a higher yielding investment program.

We do not mean to imply that you should underinsure. You should plan to fully satisfy your estimated insurance needs and express this in current dollar terms. But to provide more than this is to give your family a higher standard of living in case of your death, at the sacrifice of a potentially higher standard of living while you live. Also, as the analysis to follow illustrates, a successful investment program can soon go beyond meeting the needs insurance was once required to meet.

As stated before, your financial plans must be periodically reviewed. As time passes, if you find that the larger and larger amounts of government benefits you program are not sufficiently compensating for inflation or the rising standards of living desired by your family, and your investment program is not appreciating fast enough to keep pace with your family's needs, then you will be justified in increasing your insurance coverage.

RSFPP As A Factor. Another aspect of our approach is that we assume here that the officer will elect to participate in the RSFPP program and will choose Option 3 in the amount of one-half of his reduced retired pay. Based on the calculations made in Chapter 13, this would provide his widow and children under age 23 (assuming they continue their education beyond age 18) with a lifetime annuity of $325 per month, and would reduce his retirement pay to $613.75 per month. If Options 1 and 2 were selected instead, his retirement pay would only be raised approximately $1.00 per month.

The reason for assuming participation in RSFPP is that this assumption again reduces planned insurance needs and thus frees a larger amount of income for a high-yield investment program. If the investment program is sufficiently successful, participation in RSFPP, at least to the degree of one-half of reduced retired pay, will not be required. If you prefer to place a large amount of your savings into permanent life insurance anyway, you may want to buy sufficient permanent insurance early in life to provide for your retirement survivorship needs. Or you may prefer to plan on the basis of a smaller RSFPP annuity.

Your insurance agent will prefer your use of commercial insurance to close the gaps; your stock broker will prefer that you go light on insurance and heavy in the market. The decision is yours. Keep in mind, however, that a successful investment program can eliminate the necessity to participate in the RSFPP, and thus both retirement pay and the income available from investments will be higher.

Retirement Needs and Goals. The income goal established for your Retirement Income Plan will vary widely according to your expected retirement activities. Normally, officers will not withdraw from employment at age 41. If an officer retires from active duty after 20 years of service, he probably will assume civilian employment for a number of years. As pointed out, a 20-year retirement was selected because, from a financial planning viewpoint, it is the worst time to retire. Retirement pay then is at its lowest level and survivor needs are their highest.

Officers approaching 18 years service should base their financial plans on their best estimate of their own situation. In the case of our hypothetical officer, we assume he will earn enough in civilian employment to maintain his standard of living, educate his children, and save $100 per month until reaching age 65, at which time he may retire with aggregate income from his military retirement pay, Social Security and that available from accumulated assets.

CLOSING THE GAPS—A COMPLETE WALK-THROUGH

Before attempting to describe simple estimation techniques that will help you quickly gauge your insurance needs, a step-by-step development of the situation of our hypothetical officer will provide some useful insights into what the planning process is based upon.

Examination of the Active Duty and Retirement Survivorship Charts illustrated in Chart 18-1 indicates certain gaps between the desired income goal and the government survivor benefits. Gaps can be divided up into several combinations. The most useful way to identify gaps is to match them with the means used to close them. For example, any time a lifetime annuity is used to provide income, the gap it closes is drawn from the date it begins, with its height indicating the amount of the annuity. The diagram below shows two ways to look at the same income need.

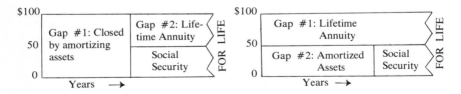

Chart 18-1 assumes that the widow plans to begin receiving reduced benefits at age 60 rather than wait for the full benefits available at age 62. Whether she actually does this or not must await her evaluation of the situation at the time of decision. Planning on the basis of age 60 benefits is the conservative approach since it requires the planner to provide a larger-size life income to meet the income goal.

A quick look at Chart 18-1 reveals that the income and cash needs for the Active Duty Survivorship Plan are larger than those required for the Retirement Survivorship Plan. Thus if the needs for the Active Duty Plan are met, the needs for the Retirement Survivorship Plan are also met, provided any protection counted upon continues long enough. For example, a group insurance plan which ceases when the officer leaves active duty without conversion to permanent insurance would provide no coverage for the retirement situation. Or, if participation in the RSFPP were reduced or eliminated, the case would also change.

For the purposes of our illustration, let us assume that on 1 January 1972 our hypothetical officer has a savings account of $2,000 which is earning interest at an annual rate of 4% compounded quarterly. His systematic investment plan is as follows. To his savings account he allots $50 per month which regularly accumulates interest. His common stock dividends are deposited automatically into his account. He periodically withdraws everything in his savings account over $2,000, and invests the funds in high-quality common stocks. He thus has a systematic investment program which provides for the investment of savings and the reinvestment of dividends in a high-yield medium.

As the size of his common stock portfolio increases, the dividends also increase. As they do, he makes his investments more frequently. (By investing at least $300 each time, he avoids the proportionately higher commission rates on small purchases.)

There is no way to forecast accurately what the value of his portfolio will be, or what the dividend yield will be at any selected point in the future, since stocks are constantly fluctuating in market value. For planning purposes, however, he assumes that his long-range dividend yield will be 4% of the market value of the portfolio, and that the portfolio will accumulate at an average annual rate equivalent to 10% compounded quarterly, when the dividends are automatically reinvested as planned. If at any time he decides to use the dividends for income instead of reinvesting them, he assumes the portfolio will accumulate at an annual rate of 6% compounded annually.

In addition to his $2,000 savings account, let us assume the officer's common stock portfolio is worth $8,000, and that he has a $15,000 group life insurance policy which may be continued or converted after retirement from active duty, and a $20,000 NON-PAR ordinary life insurance policy purchased at age 25. This is the same ordinary life policy shown in Chart

14-2, but in twice the amount. He also is eligible for the lump-sum survivor benefits shown on Chart 12-1. Now let us see how far his present assets go to meet his needs. Only after establishing the needs and applying present resources against them can he determine if more insurance protection is warranted.

For his *Active Duty Survivorship Plan,* the officer could allocate his resources to his cash needs as shown in Table 18-1. Notice that the survivor's income needs in Chart 18-1 are more than satisfied until 1986. If the widow places everything over $600 per month into her savings account earning interest at 4% compounded quarterly, by 1986 she would accumulate approximately $30,000. This figure can be approximated using Charts 10-1 and 10-2 and Tables 10-1 and 10-2, or by using standard interest tables for 4% compounded quarterly. The common stocks, if dividends were reinvested, would be worth about $32,000 if a 10% compounded quarterly rate were maintained (see Chart 10-2). The $14,000 remainder of the $20,000 NON-PAR ordinary life insurance policy, if left with the company to accumulate at 4% interest, would be worth approximately $24,000. (Most companies would be happy to agree to this procedure.) She could then apply her resources against the gaps defined in Table 18-2 as shown.

Now let us assume that the officer dies of a non-Service connected cause on the day after he retires. If his savings and investment program developed according to plan, at the time of death his savings account would contain about $2,000, and the value of his systematically built common stock portfolio would equal about $31,500.

For his *Retirement Survivorship Plan,* the resources could be applied as shown in Table 18-3. Let us assume that the officer converted his SGLI policy on the day he retired, but that he allowed his group insurance to lapse.

Note in Table 18-3 that the income needs can be met without reducing assets except during Gap #1. The planner could cover this deficiency by withdrawing the amount from his or his wife's excess income (income over $600/mo.) savings account.

For his *Retirement Income Plan,* we assumed the officer would earn enough income from his retirement pay and civilian employment to maintain his standard of living, educate his children, and save $100 per month until retirement at age 65. Assuming everything goes according to plan, the supplementary income available at age 65 will be as shown in Table 18-4.

The supplementary income, in the case illustrated, would amount to more than the officer's government retirement benefits.

In the preceding "walk-through"—the three basic long-range financial plans—we employed historically reasonable rates of return and appreciation on various types of assets. One might argue, however, that such a procedure is not sufficiently conservative—that you should not risk the

Programming Worksheet I
(Active Duty Survivorship)

CASH NEEDS

		RESOURCES USED TO COVER NEEDS	
Clean-Up Fund:	$ 3,000	Death Gratuity:	$ 3,000
Emergency Fund:	3,000	Social Security Lump Sum:	$ 255
		Accrued Leave:	1,093
		Savings Account:	2,000
			3,348
		Group Insurance:	
Mortgage on Home:	18,000	Portion of $20,000	15,000
		Ord. Life Policy:	3,000
			18,000
		SGLI:	15,000
Education Fund:	18,000	Portion of $20,000	
		Ord. Life Policy:	3,000
			$18,000

RESOURCES REMAINING FOR INCOME NEEDS:

Common Stocks:	$ 8,000
Leftover from Ord. Life Policy:	$14,000

Any funds in the savings account not actually used for clean-up expenses, emergencies, and education (considered to be zero here for planning purposes).

TABLE 18-1

PROGRAMMING WORKSHEET II
(ACTIVE DUTY SURVIVORSHIP)

INCOME NEEDS

GAP 1: 4 Years
$73/mo. = $876/yr.

GAP 2: 11 Years
$253/mo. = $3036/yr.

GAP 3: For Life
$79/mo. = $948/yr.

RESOURCES USED TO COVER NEEDS

Interest, Savings Account: $1,200

Interest, Savings Account: $1200
Dividends, Stocks (4% on $47,340):   1890   3,090

Interest, Savings Account: 1200
Dividends, Stocks: 3590
Lifetime Annuity: 2567   7,357

NOTES: By end of GAP 1 (4 years), common stocks appreciate at 10% compounded quarterly to $47,340.

During GAP 2 (11 years), common stocks appreciate at 6% compounded annually to $89,865.

On the $14,000 life insurance proceeds left with the company at 4% for 29 years she obtains a $43,660 lifetime annuity used in closing GAP 3. Using Settlement Option C, Annuity 10 Years Certain she receives $213.93 per month or $2,567 per year.

The excess income (above $600/mo.) in the early years is deposited in the Savings Account and accumulates to approximately $30,000 by 1986.

TABLE 18-2

(Retirement Survivorship)

CASH NEEDS

Clean-Up Fund:	$ 3,000	
Emergency Fund:	3,000	
Mortgage:	6,000	
Education Fund:	18,000	$30,000

RESOURCES USED TO COVER NEEDS

SGLI:	$15,000
Social Security Lump Sum:	255
3/4 Ord. Life Policy:	15,000
	$30,255

RESOURCES REMAINING FOR INCOME NEEDS

Common Stocks:	$31,500
Leftover from Ord. Life Policy:	5,000
Savings Account:	2,000
Approximate Addition to Savings Account from Income in Excess of $600/mo. ($156/mo. for 48 mos. compounded quarterly at 4%):	8,100

INCOME NEEDS

RESOURCES USED TO COVER NEEDS

Interest, Savings Accounts: ($8,100 + $2,000)	$ 410
Interest, Insurance:	200
Reduction of Savings Accounts (approximate drop of $2000 over 4 years, partially to make up for loss of interest income):	460

GAP 1: 4 Years
$89/mo. = $1068/yr.

Interest on $8,100 Savings Acct.:	325
Interest, Insurance:	175
Dividends, Common Stock (4% of $68,000):	2,720
	$1,070

GAP 2: 11 Years
$174/mo. = $2,100/yr.

Interest, Savings Account:	325
Interest, Insurance:	175
Dividends, Common Stock (4% of $129,000):	5,160
	3,220

For Life at Age 60 — 5,660

NOTES: Up to the beginning of GAP 2, common stocks grow at 10% compounded quarterly from $31,500 to about $68,000.
During GAP 2, common stocks grow at 6% compounded annually to about $129,000 ($68,000 x 1.898). The widow uses the stock dividends for income.
After GAP 2, the value of the portfolio grows at 6% compounded annually. Dividend income will continue to increase throughout the widow's lifetime.

TABLE 18-3

Programming Worksheet IV
(Retirement Income)

RESOURCES

Interest, Savings Account:	$ 80	
Interest, Insurance:	200	
Dividends, Stocks:	18,140	$<u>18,420</u>

NOTES: He still maintains $2000 in his Savings Account.

From 1982 to 2006 (24 years), his common stock portfolio should appreciate at 10% compounded quarterly from $31,500 to $453,500 (remember he saved $100/mo. even after military retirement).

TABLE 18-4

future security of your family by assuming high rates of return on accumulated assets. We shall therefore show the calculations for the Active Duty Survivorship Plan assuming different circumstances. The preceding "walk-through," however, should have pointed out the significance of the fact that assets do earn interest. It should also have emphasized the extraordinary results a sound, systematic, long-range stock market investment program can produce.

The results achieved can be expected from systematic investment in high-quality growth stocks—no speculation required. If the 10% figure is not conservative enough for your planning, use the 6% lines on Charts 10-1 and 10-2. This would assume only a 3% dividend yield and a 3% market appreciation.

Now let us look at the Active Duty Survivorship Plan using more conservative programming procedures. Let us assume that the widow sells her common stocks for $8,000 and places that sum in a savings account, which earns 4% compounded quarterly. Her cash needs would be satisfied as already indicated in Table 18-1. If she again allows her excess income from government benefits to accumulate in her savings account (along with the $8,000 proceeds from the stocks), it would grow to about $44,000 by 1986. Her ordinary insurance account would again grow to over $24,000 (using 4% interest). She could apply these resources against the gaps as shown in Table 18-5.

Again the original resources are adequate to meet the needs, but a great margin of safety and the ability to significantly raise the widow's standard of living was foregone since the high-yield potential of common stocks was not exploited.

The procedure we have just reviewed in detail can be summarized:

1. Determine case and income needs.

2. Apply the financial resources provided by government programs and accumulated assets to cash needs.

3. Apply financial resources provided by government programs to the income needs (as shown in Chart 18-1).

Programming Worksheet V
(Active Duty Survivorship - More Conservative Plan)

INCOME NEEDS

RESOURCES USED TO COVER NEEDS

GAP 1: 4 Years
$73/mo. = $876/yr.

Interest, Savings Account
($800 of Interest is Retained in the Account: $ 960

GAP 2: 11 Years
$253/mo. = $3,036/yr.

Interest, Savings Account: $1,900
Interest, Insurance: 1,123
Savings Account Withdrawal: 13   3,036

GAP 3: For Life
$79/mo. = $948/yr.

Interest, Savings Account: 1,820
Interest, Insurance: 1,120   2,940

NOTES: By GAP 2 the Savings Account has increased to about $47,500 due to the retention of some GAP 1 period interest. The $24,000 in the Insurance Account has increased to $28,080.

GAP 2 resources must partially fill GAP 2 by drawing down the Savings Account $13/mo. or $1716 during the 11-year period. As the amount in the Savings Account decreases, the interest payments will decrease slightly. Eventually about $1,900 will have to be withdrawn from the Savings Account principal, decreasing the Savings Account to $45,600 for GAP 3 computations.

TABLE 18-5

4. Identify the gaps.

5. Apply existing resources from insurance and accumulated assets to the gaps.

6. If existing resources cannot fully close the gaps, determine the additional amount of insurance needed to close the gaps.

AIDS FOR FINANCIAL PLANNING

If you have followed the above analysis, hopefully you can apply it to your own individual situation. For many people, however, interest tables are always somewhat ominous. Although we would like to encourage you to learn how to use such tables, we have included certain charts in this text which can help you quickly estimate some relationships vital to the planning process.

To assist you in determining your cash and income needs, the Family Balance Sheet (Chart 3-4), and Family Income and Expenditure Chart (Chart 3-2) are extremely useful.

Current Tables (Fall, 1970) are included in Appendix C. You should make sure you have the current tables whenever you construct your long-range financial programs.

To approximate how your assets and proposed investment programs would grow over time, Charts 10-1 and 10-2 can be used. These charts help you determine the results of various investment programs, and how much you must save out of income (assuming given interest rates) to reach a certain goal in a given number of years.

To determine how much interest income can be derived from a given principal, or to determine how much principal is required to produce a given income, apply the simple interest formula described in Chapter 4: $I = Prt$. Generally, close approximations are adequate in programming since many factors change continually.

Table 17-6 indicates representative figures for various kinds of life annuities. Charts 15-4 can be used to estimate the cost of annuities purchased by a widow at various ages.

Chart 17-1 shows how a $10,000 sum can be amortized at various interest rates. A simple proportion can be used to solve problems involving sums other than those upon which the chart is based. For example, if you want to know the monthly income available for 11 years from a $10,000 savings account earning 3% per year, you can enter the chart on the horizontal axis at 11 years, proceed vertically to the 3% curve, and read approximately $90 per month off the vertical axis. This means that if you were to withdraw $90 per month from a $10,000 fund accumulating at 3% per year, the fund would be exhausted in 11 years.

If you required more than $90 per month to close a gap in a survivorship or income plan, you could find the size of the fund needed by forming a simple proportion. Thus, if you needed $112.50 per month (or $1,350 per year) for 11 years, you could determine the size of the fund required by solving the following proportion for X:

$$\frac{\$112.50}{\$90} = \frac{X}{\$10,000}$$

In this case, X = about $12,500.

From the previous discussion you can see that the writer firmly believes that, when properly managed, the income of the Armed Forces officer is adequate to satisfy reasonable protection and savings needs without causing great burdens on current consumption. As a matter of fact, current consumption can be much more satisfying when the family has peace of mind through the knowledge that it is adequately guarded against financial disaster, and that it can look forward to greater economic opportunities as the years go by.

All sources listed in the bibliographies for Chapters 3 and 14.
Cissell, Robert and Helen Cissell. *Mathematics of Finance*. 3rd ed. Boston: Houghton Mifflin Company, 1969.

CHAPTER **19**

ESTATE PLANNING AND RELATED FINANCIAL MATTERS

THE PURPOSE of this chapter is to direct your attention to the most important administrative approaches to the execution of your financial plans. Thus, it will briefly touch on (1) some legal forms of ownership; (2) the use of a power of attorney; (3) some methods of transferring property; (4) the maintenance of valuable records; and (5) the necessity of using expert assistance. By attending to these matters property, you will be fully assured that your family will enjoy the most beneficial use of your property whether you live or die.

THE OWNERSHIP OF PROPERTY

During your lifetime you will accumulate property which is called your "estate." Such property can either be personal property (e.g., personal effects, household furnishings, automobiles, money, stocks, etc.), real property (i.e., land and associated buildings, or fixtures), or mixed property. You may hold complete title to such property, in which case it belongs to you alone. On the other hand, you may share ownership with another person (including various kinds of legal persons such as corporations). There are three variations of plural ownership in general use.

1. *Tenancy in Common* means that ownership is divided among the tenants and each has the right to sell, assign, or convey his share in the property.

2. *Joint Tenancy With Right Of Survivorship* means that each tenant owns all of the property, and in the event of one tenant's death, title to the property automatically passes to the surviving tenants.

3. *Tenancy by the Entirety* is a joint tenancy as in 2 above, except that the tenants must be husband and wife.

Joint Tenancy With Right of Survivorship. Quite often, an officer will hold property jointly with his wife or children in order to facilitate the use and control of property while he is living, and to reduce administrative problems and costs if one owner should die. Property held jointly passes outside of the will, and thus avoids some of the expenses and other problems associated with probate.

Real estate may be owned in Joint Tenancy With Right of Survivorship under proper deed. It is often recommended that a car and other personal property be titled either jointly or solely in the name of your spouse or next of kin. However, joint title to personal property may make your spouse subject to paying personal property taxes on half its value to the state in which you are temporarily living because of your military duty.

Another common use of joint ownership is for a husband and wife to open a bank account. Either party can draw funds from the account, even though only the officer's earnings go into it. One caution should be made, however. In some states, such accounts are frozen by the state when one of the tenants dies. Thus the account would not be available to the survivor until a tax release had been obtained.

Before creating a Joint Tenancy With Right of Survivorship, you should get legal advice regarding the advantages and disadvantages of holding your various kinds of property in such a way. Joint ownership can have economic and legal consequences which should be reviewed with your Legal Assistance Officer or other competent attorney.

POWER OF ATTORNEY

Numerous circumstances may arise, while an officer is absent or not immediately accessible, in which it may be necessary for someone to act for him. Under such circumstances his personal affairs can generally be conducted to best advantage by an agent or attorney acting for him and in his name and behalf. The authority so to act may be granted conveniently through a Power of Attorney to a member of his family, or to any other person of legal age and capacity, but it should be granted only to one in whom the grantor has complete trust and confidence.

The person executing the power of attorney is usually referred to as the grantor, and the person to whom the authority to act is given is usually referred to as the attorney-in-fact, or simply as the attorney for the grantor.

The requirements as to the form and content of a legally effective power of attorney designed to accomplish the intended purposes vary considerably under the laws and court decisions of the states. For this reason it is virtually impossible to draft a standardized form of power of attorney which will meet the legal requirements of all the jurisdictions throughout the United States. For example, the laws of the states vary as to the age at which a person ceases to be a minor and becomes capable of executing a valid power of attorney.

Because of the variations in the required legal formalities and in order to fulfill the needs and desires of the grantor, the power of attorney should be tailor-made for him under the advice of competent legal counsel familiar with the applicable state laws of its place of execution and of the probable place of its exercise of the powers granted, if known. Standardized forms should be avoided unless the need is urgent and counsel is not available, in which case the document should be regarded as a temporary expedient to be replaced as early as possible.

If you believe that a power of attorney is required in your situation, promptly seek the advice of your Legal Assistance officer. He can advise you whether you need a general power (one unlimited as to time and purpose), or whether the generally safer special power (one limited as to time and purpose) will best suit your needs. Whenever feasible, a special power of attorney should be used rather than a general power of attorney. This provides the Service member with a greater degree of control over his agent's activities on his behalf. It is sometimes highly desirable to provide in the power of attorney a certain date of termination, generally 2 to 3 years. Thus the power of attorney is automatically terminated as of that date. In the event it is desired to continue the power of attorney in operation, a new "power" should be executed.

Special Phrases. There are certain phrasing problems which may arise in connection with a power of attorney if the grantor is military. To help you avoid forgetting to consider such matters, the following paragraphs and clauses are listed for such use, adaptation, or modification as counsel deems desirable in your individual case.

1. The opening clause might properly state:

KNOW ALL MEN BY THESE PRESENTS: That I, ...
. . . . , a legal resident of the
(town, city, or county) of . . . ., State
of . . . ., United States of America, now in
the military service as a . . . . (Soc. Security No. . . . .)
in the (Army, Navy, Air Force, Marine Corps) of the United States, and anticipating that I may be required to go overseas in said military service have made, constituted and appointed and by these presents do make, constitute, and appoint . . . . whose address is . . . ., my true and lawful attorney to (insert the powers and authority granted to the attorney).

2. You may wish to grant the following powers:

a. to execute vouchers in my behalf for any and all allowances and reimbursements properly payable to me by the United States, including but not restricted to allowances and reimbursements for transportation of dependents or for shipment of household effects as authorized by law and .... Regulations, and to receive, indorse, and collect the proceeds of checks payable to the order of the undersigned drawn on the Treasurer of the United States.

(This clause may not be acceptable, and should not be relied upon to authorize the execution of Government vouchers by the attorney for the pay quarters, subsistence, and travel allowances of the grantor. The use of allotments is advisable if it is desired to have others directly receive any part of a Serviceman's pay.)

b. to take possession, and order the removal and shipment, of any of my property from any post, warehouse, depot, dock, or other place of storage or safekeeping, governmental or private; and to execute and deliver any release, voucher, receipt, shipping ticket, certificate, or other instrument necessary or convenient for such purpose.

3. The incorporation of the following declaration or parts thereof in a power of attorney may be beneficial, although its provisions may not prove effective in some jurisdictions:

And I hereby declare that any act or thing lawfully done hereunder by my said attorney shall be binding on myself, my heirs, legal and personal representatives, and assigns, whether the same shall have been done before or after my death or other revocation of this instrument, unless and until reliable intelligence or notice thereof shall have been received by my said attorney; and whether or not I, the grantor of this instrument, shall have been reported or listed, either officially or otherwise, as "missing in action" as that phrase is used in military parlance, it being the intendment hereof that such status designation shall not bar my attorney from fully and completely exercising and continuing to exercise any and all powers and rights herein granted, and that such report of "missing in action" shall neither constitute nor be interpreted as constituting notice of my death nor operate to revoke this instrument.

Acknowledgments And Recording. For many purposes, it is advisable to have three persons, in addition to a Notary Public or other official authorized to take acknowledgments, witness the execution by the grantor of the Power of Attorney. Such persons should have no personal interest in the affairs to be conducted under such powers.

The agent named in a power of attorney should have a sufficient number of executed copies (usually from 3 to 6) to meet prospective needs. One information copy should be retained by the maker. If additional copies are required by the agent and the maker is not available to execute them, the power can be recorded in a county or city office of record, and certified copies obtained from that office for use in place of executed copies. The requirements of the various pertinent state laws as to recording the instrument, in order to make it legally effective or for certain special purposes, such as the transfer of title to real property, will require special consideration.

ESTATE PLANNING

Estate planning may be viewed as the process of arranging your personal affairs to produce the most effective disposition of your estate. Estate planning involves not only many of the matters we have considered already, but it also incorporates the element of seeing that an estate is distributed most efficiently in light of the owner's desires. The tools of estate planning therefore include life insurance, annuities, amortization of assets, ownership arrangements that minimize tax liabilities, giving away property, establishing living and testamentary trusts, and wills.

The attention devoted to estate planning normally increases with the size of the estate. As your estate approaches a value of $60,000 (for tax purposes, your estate may include your life insurance and property held jointly), you should begin to be concerned about taking steps to insure that the estate you have built will go to your family instead of to the tax collector. But regardless of the size of your estate, you should certainly give careful consideration to the making of a will.

For guidance in arranging your affairs to minimize tax liabilities, refer to the sources listed in the bibliography and to a competent attorney specializing in such matters. In this chapter, our discussion is limited to a few brief comments regarding matters of importance to every Serviceman with a family.

Wills. It is difficult to imagine a situation in which having no will is better than having one which accurately expresses the desires of the maker. If you die having no will, you are said to have died "intestate." In such cases, state law determines the distribution of your property and the guardianship of your children. No matter how large or small your estate, not leaving a will results in some degree of hardship and inconvenience for your survivors. In some cases, it can result in an absurd disaster.

Consider the case as tragic as that involving a mother attempting to win custody of her own child in a judicial proceeding which can take years if there is competition from other relatives, or if the state law provides that the child should become a ward of the state. Normally, many of the tragic cases to be found in court records could have been avoided if the deceased had made a simple will.

By making a will, you can specify to whom your property should go, when it should go, in what amounts it should go, how it should be safeguarded, and by whom it should be handled. You can also settle the question of guardianship so that neither your wife nor your children have to endure the rigors of settling such a matter in the courts.

When making a will, there are certain matters of particular significance for Servicemen. Because the Serviceman often changes residence, it may be advisable to state in the will the maker's domicile, so that the will can be probated in the proper place. It may also be advisable to include in the will a statement that the individual is now in the active military or naval service of the United States, together with his grade and Service or Social Security number.

The use of standardized forms of will should be avoided unless the need is urgent and counsel is not available, in which case the executed document should be considered a temporary expedient to be replaced as soon as possible.

Events such as marriage, birth of children, divorce, or death of a named beneficiary or administrator often affect the provisions of a will. A will is not effective until death and can be replaced by a new will or changed by a codicil (amendment) at any time. Unless the will is extremely complicated, the use of codicils should be avoided. If the will is replaced by a new will, all copies of the previous will should be destroyed. Whenever his circumstances change, the Serviceman should review his will with the assistance of legal counsel.

Only the original will should be signed. If you make a will and wish to keep a copy with you for reference purposes or to deliver a copy to the principal beneficiary or executor named in the will, any copy so retained or delivered should be a "conformed" unsigned copy, i.e., it should bear no signature; but your name as the maker and the names of the witnesses should be printed or typed thereon for information purposes.

Letter Of Instructions. In addition to a will, you should draw up a set of instructions for use by the executor of your will and your survivors. Comprehending the planning process as outlined in Chapter 18 should lead one to fully appreciate the complexity of executing his plan. Recall that much of the planning in Chapter 18 was based upon filling specified gaps with certain resources. In some cases, it would be necessary for the widow to save some money out of the income provided her by government benefits. If she did not understand that future security depended upon such saving, she would probably not carry out the plan. This indeed, would be tragic.

To avoid this and other problems, a letter of last instructions should accompany your will and the financial charts described in this text. Such documents will enable the widow to avoid serious errors and other inconveniences. Also, since the construction of your long-range financial plans should involve a great deal of family consultation, you should take pains to insure that your wife (children, too, when practicable) understand both your plans and your letter of instruction. You must educate your wife to be a widow; when she becomes one, it may be too late.

A letter of last instruction (or documents attached thereto) should contain:

1. the location of all your valuable documents (to include birth certificates, Social Security cards, certificates of marriage and divorce, naturalization and citizenship papers, papers establishing your right to government benefits, Service records, insurance policies, lists of savings accounts, bank accounts, stocks, bonds, deeds, and other evidence of ownership or debt);

2. instructions as to funeral and burial or other distribution of your remains;

3. instructions concerning any business you may be involved in, in the event you wish the business to be continued;

4. a statement of reasons for actions taken in your will, such as disinheritances;

5. the location of your long-range planning charts to include instructions of how your assets can be used to satisfy the economic needs of the family.

A great amount of the information suggested here can be contained in some kind of personal affairs record form, such as the Annual Legal Check-up Form (DD Form 1543) or the Personal Affairs Record in Appendix D. A copy of your will and associated letter of last instructions should be left with your executor-to-be. A strongbox at home is probably a good place to keep these and other valuable documents.

A safe-deposit box is not a recommended place to keep a will because, when a person dies, his safe-deposit box may be sealed by the safe-deposit company or bank until a court order to open it is obtained. Of course, if your wife has a safe-deposit box in her own name, you can keep her will in your box, and yours in hers.

PROFESSIONAL ASSISTANCE

One of the philosophical tenets of this book has been that each officer should understand as much as possible concerning the management of his financial affairs. The better your understanding, the more chance you have of maximizing the satisfaction your family derives from your economic resources. If you do not take the few minutes required to base your economic decisions soundly (e.g., determining what your insurance needs are, properly preparing a will and letter of last instructions, etc.), you and your family will pay the costs involved. Thus this book advocates that you attempt to plan the development of your financial condition. The Appendix B Glossary may help clarify many of your questions.

But along with learning to do things yourself, stress the necessity of getting expert assistance. Whether it be your banker, your life insurance agent, or your legal advisor, you should go to him with a basic understanding of your problem and the kinds of solutions that might be used to solve it. The more knowledge you have, the easier it is for your advisor to explain the reasons for the advice he gives, the easier it is for you to evaluate his advice, and the surer you are that the decisions you make are good ones. But do not neglect to get help from a professional. It is his business to know the latest information upon which rational decisions must be based. He can check you out on the work that you have done, and point out any errors you have made. This is a vital step in the decision-making process.

It has been said that a man who is his own lawyer has a fool for a client. This sentiment can be extended into the many other areas where professionals practice. Get to know professionals in whom you can place your confidence and then use them.

Commerce Clearing House, *Federal Estate and Gift Taxes,* Chicago: Commerce Clearing House, Inc., 1969.

Dacey, Norman F., *How to Avoid Probate*. New York: Crown Publishers, Inc., 1969.

How Estates are Distributed if there is No Will, Answering Questions about Trust Funds, and other pamphlets available free from Manufacturers Hanover Trust, 350 Park Avenue, New York, N. Y. 10022.

Spinney, William R. *Estate Planning*. 13th ed. Chicago: Commerce Clearing House, Inc., 1968.

Stephenson, Gilbert T. *Estates and Trusts*. 4th ed. New York: Appleton-Century-Crofts.

PART FOUR

APPENDICES

APPENDIX A - ASSOCIATIONS

THE PURPOSE of this listing is to identify for readers the nonprofit associations which cater to the military. The reader is advised to make his own independent evaluation of the net cost of insurance from both profit and nonprofit companies. No endorsement of any or all of the companies is meant or implied.

AIR FORCE ASSOCIATION (AFA)
1750 Pennsylvania Avenue, N.W.
Washington, D.C. 20006
Phone: 202-298-9123. Incorporated 1946.
Coverages:
Accident Insurance
Extra Cash Income Hospital Insurance
Flight Pay Insurance
Group Term Life Insurance

THE ARMED FORCES COOPERATIVE
INSURING ASSOCIATION (AFCIA)
Fort Leavenworth, Kansas 66027
Phone: 913-684-4941. Organized in 1887.
Coverages:
All-Risk Personal Property and Household Effects Insurance (World-Wide)
Comprehensive Personal Liability Insurance
Credit Card Insurance
Homeowners Package Policy

ARMED FORCES RELIEF AND
BENEFIT ASSOCIATION (AFRBA)
1156 Fifteenth Street, N.W.
Washington, D.C. 20005
Phone: 202-659-5140. Founded 1947.
Coverage:
Group Term Life Insurance (Family Plan Rider available)

ARMED SERVICES MUTUAL BENEFIT
ASSOCIATION (ASMBA)
P. O. Box 4646
Nashville, Tennessee 37216
Phone: 615-895-3331. Organized 1963.
Coverage:
Group Term Survivor Income and Family Plan

THE ARMY MUTUAL AID ASSOCIATION (AMAA)
Fort Myer, Arlington
Virginia 22211
Phone: 703-522-3060. Formed 1879.
Coverages:
Ordinary Life Insurance
20 - Payment Life Insurance
30 - Payment Life Insurance

ASSOCIATION OF THE UNITED STATES ARMY (AUSA)
1529 18th St., N.W.
Washington, D.C. 20036
Phone: 202-483-1800. Organized 1950.
Coverages:
Extra Cash Income Hospital Insurance
Group Term Life Insurance
(Family Plan Rider available with either policy)

MILITARY BENEFIT ASSOCIATION (MBA)
Warner Building, 13th & E. Streets, N.W.
Washington, D.C. 20004
Phone: 202-393-0466. Formed 1956.
Coverages:
Active Duty Group Term Life Insurance
Group Permanent Paid-Up at 65 Life Insurance
Retired Group Term Life Insurance
(Family Plan Riders available on all policies)

(Additional Accidental Death and Dismemberment available while on active duty)
THE NAVY MUTUAL AID ASSOCIATION (NMAA)
Navy Department
Washington, D.C. 20370
Phone: 202-OX4-1638. Organized 1879.
Coverages:
Paid-Up Life at 50, 55, 60, or 65
Whole Life Insurance

OFFICERS BENEFIT ASSOCIATION (OBA)
Second Floor Stonewall Building
Birmingham, Alabama 35202
Phone: 205-322-6758. Organized 1956.
Coverage:
Group Term Life Insurance (Family Plan Rider Available)

UNIFORMED SERVICES BENEFIT
ASSOCIATION (USBA)
1221 Baltimore Avenue
Kansas City, Missouri 64105
Phone: 816-471-0797. Formed 1959.
Coverages:
Group Ordinary Life Insurance
Group Term Life Insurance with Accidental Death and Dismemberment Coverage Included
(Family Plan Riders and additional Accidental Death and Dismemberment coverages are available with either policy)

UNITED SERVICES AUTOMOBILE
ASSOCIATION (USAA)
USAA Building
San Antonio, Texas 78215

Phone: 512-824-9011. Organized 1922.

Coverages:

Automobile Insurance
Boatowners Insurance
Comprehensive Personal Liability Insurance
Fire and Homeowners Insurance
Household Goods and Personal Effects Floater (World-Wide)
Personal Articles Floater
*Life Insurance

---

* An assortment of life insurance policies is offered the membership through a capital stock company; however, all the stock of this subsidiary is owned and held by the parent non-profit association.

APPENDIX B - GLOSSARY

ACCELERATION CLAUSE: A clause in a consumer loan contract which provides that if one of the borrower's payments is delinquent, all remaining payments immediately become due.

ACCUMULATION PLAN: An arrangement which enables an investor to purchase mutual fund shares regularly, usually with provisions for the reinvestment of income dividends and the acceptance of capital gains distributions in additional shares. Plans are of two types, voluntary and contractual.

ACTUARY: Primarily a person who applies to life insurance the principles which underlie all of its computations, such as those of premiums, reserves, surrender values, apportionment of dividends and the like. The word has now acquired a broader meaning and might be defined as "one versed in the mathematics, bookkeeping, law, and finance of life insurance."

ADD-ON METHOD: A computational method where (1) the finance charge for an installment credit contract as a whole equals the add-on rate, times the principal amount of credit at the start of the contract, times the number of years in the credit contract; (2) the finance charge is added to the principal; (3) the credit user receives the principal and pays back the principal plus the finance charge in monthly (or other periodic) installments.

ADD-ON CLAUSE: A clause in a consumer loan contract which requires that an entire series of purchases is subject to repossession if payments become delinquent on any one of the items.

ADD-ON-PLUS: A computational method differing from add-on only in that an investigation or service charge is included in computing the finance charge.

ANNUAL REPORT: The formal financial statement issued yearly by a corporation to its shareowners. The annual report shows assets, liabilities, earnings—how the company stood at the close of the business year and how it fared profit-wise during the year.

ANNUITY: A stated sum of money, payable periodically at the end of fixed intervals.

ANNUITY, CERTAIN: One payable throughout a fixed (certain) period of time, irrespective of the happening of any contingency, such as the death of the annuitant.

ANNUITY, CONTINGENT: An annuity which is contingent upon the happening of an event which may or may not take place.

ANNUITY, DEFERRED: An annuity modified by the condition that the first payment will not be due for a fixed number of years. Thus, an annuity deferred for 20 years is one on which the first payment is made at the end of 21 years, provided the annuitant is then alive.

ANNUITY, IMMEDIATE: An annuity on which the first payment falls due at the end of the first specified period— if payable annually, at the end of one year after issue.

ANNUITY, LIFE: A fixed sum payable periodically so long as a given person's life continues.

ANNUITY, SURVIVORSHIP: One payable throughout the lifetime of one person after the death of another person or persons.

ASSETS: "Gross assets" of a company is a term used to represent the total monetary value of all property in the company's possession at a given time. Market values are used in arriving at such monetary value; but, in the case of real estate, "book value" is often treated as "market value."

ASSET VALUE PER SHARE: The market value of an investment company's total resources—securities, cash and any accrued earnings—after deduction of liabilities, divided by the number of its shares outstanding.

ASSIGNEE: One to whom property, a policy, or any interest therein stands "assigned."

AUTOMATIC EXTENDED INSURANCE: Under which, without further action by the Insured, upon failure to pay a premium when due, and provided no one of the other options allowed by the contract is exercised, the policy is continued in force for its full amount but for a stated period of time only.

AUTOMATIC PAID-UP INSURANCE: Under which, without further action by the Insured, upon failure to pay a premium when due, the policy is continued as paid-up insurance for a definite sum. (A lesser value than the original protection guaranteed by the policy.)

BALLOON PAYMENT: A final payment in an installment loan contract which is several times larger than the preceeding schedule of payments.

BEAR: A person who believes stock prices will go down; a "bear market" is a market of declining prices.

BENEFICIARY: A person named to receive the amount guaranteed by the policy.

BENEFICIARY, CONTINGENT: One whose benefit under a policy depends on the happening of an uncertain event, such as outliving the first named beneficiary.

BENEFICIARY, DIRECT: One named in the policy as the immediate beneficiary, as distinguished from a contingent beneficiary.

BID AND ASKED: The bid is the highest price anyone has declared that he wants to pay for a security at a given time, the asked is the lowest price anyone will take at the same time. In mutual fund shares, bid price means the net asset value per share, less a nominal redemption charge in a few instances. The asked price means the net asset value per share plus any sales charge. It is often called the "offering price."

BOND: A bond is basically an IOU. The person who invests his money in a bond is lending a company or government a sum of money for a specified time, with the understanding that the borrower will pay it back and pay interest for using it.

BULL: A person who believes stock prices will rise; a "bull market" is one with rising prices.

CALL LOAN: A loan which may be terminated or "called" at any time by the lender or borrower.

CASH SURRENDER VALUE: The amount available in cash upon voluntary termination of a policy before it becomes payable by death or maturity.

CLAIM: An insurance policy contract refers to a demand made under an insurance policy contract at maturity.

COLLATERAL: Property, or evidence of it, deposited with a creditor to guarantee the payment of a loan.

COMMISSION: With respect to insurance policies, usually means a percentage of the premium paid to an agent as remuneration for his services.

COMMUTATION: The substitution of a present sum for a sum that might otherwise become due in the future.

COMPUTATIONAL RATE: The monthly or annual percentage rate used to compute a finance charge. It is applied to the dollar amount of credit advanced or of credit outstanding.

CONVERTIBLE: A bond, debenture or preferred share which may be exchanged by the owner for common stock or another security, usually of the same company. In a mutual fund the conversion privilege enables a shareholder to transfer his investment from one fund to another within the same fund group as his needs or objectives change.

CONVERTIBLE TERM INSURANCE: Convertible Term Insurance can be exchanged, at the option of the policyholder and without evidence of insurability, for another plan of insurance.

COUPON INTEREST: Refers to the rate of interest on bonds implied by the annual dollar amount of interest paid and the bond's face value.

CREDITOR: A person, group or company which extends credit; one to whom a borrower owes money.

DECLINATION: The rejection of an application for life insurance, usually for reasons of the health or occupation of the applicant.

DEMAND DEPOSIT: An account in a commercial bank subject to withdrawal by check.

DISCOUNT METHOD: A computational method where (1) the finance charge for the installment contract as a whole equals the annual discount rate times the principal amount of credit at the start of the contract times the number of years in the credit contract; (2) the finance charge is deducted from the principal; (3) the credit user receives the difference between the principal and the finance charge and pays back the principal in monthly (or other periodic) installments.

DISCOUNT PLUS: A computational method differing from discount only in that the investigation or service charge is included in computing the finance charge.

DIVERSIFICATION: Spreading one's investments among the companies in different industries. A company producing various lines of products is also considered diversified.

DIVIDEND ADDITION: Paid-up insurance purchased with a policy dividend and added to the face amount of the policy.

DIVIDEND, CASH: Dividend payable in cash. Cash dividends on insurance are not always drawn when declared, but are sometimes left on deposit to accumulate at interest, in which case they are termed "accumulated dividends," or "accumulated cash dividends."

DIVIDEND, REVERSIONARY (REVERSIONARY ADDITION, PAID-UP ADDITION): Paid-up insurance purchased by a cash dividend and added to the sum insured. The dividend is used as a single premium, usually at "loaded" rates, to buy insurance at the then age of the insured, maturing at the same time and in the same manner as the original policy.

DIVIDEND: TO POLICYHOLDERS: A share of surplus earned by and apportioned to a policy. The dividend in a mutual company or on mutual premiums arises from the fact that a higher premium is collected than is necessary under normal conditions to cover the cost of the insurance contract. The excess is returned in the form of a dividend.

DIVIDEND: TO STOCKHOLDERS: A distribution of cash, securities, or other valuables made by a corporation to its stockholders in proportion to the respective number of shares owned by them. Capital stock is used to guarantee insurance contracts. The stockholder takes the risk of loss of his capital. Therefore he is entitled to receive a dividend sufficient to compensate him for such risk, as well as interest on his investment.

DOLLAR COST AVERAGING: Buying a fixed dollar amount of securities at regular intervals. Under this system the investor buys by the dollars' worth rather than by the number of shares.

EFFECTIVE RATE, ANNUAL OR MONTHLY: The finance charge as a percentage per unit of time of the average unpaid balance of the credit contract during its scheduled life. Also called actual rate; annual effective rate.

EXECUTOR: An individual or a trust institution named in a will and appointed by a court to settle an estate. If a woman, she is an executrix.

FINANCE CHARGE: The dollar charge or charges for consumer credit excluding (1) any filing and recording fees which financing agencies and sellers collect from credit users in connection with a credit transaction and (2) charges on insurance written in connection with a credit transaction. Also called carrying charge, credit service charge, interest charge, and time-price differential.

GRACE, DAYS OF: A period allowed within which a thing may be done which otherwise was required to be done before the commencement of such period. In insurance, generally the time within which a premium might be paid, with or without penalty conditions, after the premium due date.

GROWTH STOCK: Stock that is characterized by the prospect of its increase in market value rather than by the cash dividends it earns for the stockholder.

GUARANTEED STOCK: Usually preferred stock on which dividends are guaranteed by another company; under much the same circumstances as a bond is guaranteed.

HOME LOAN: A real estate loan for which the security is a residential property; in Federal Home Loan Bank Board statistics, a loan on a residential structure housing one to four families.

INCOME BOND: A corporate bond that only pays interest if corporate earnings reach a specified level.

INCONTESTABILITY: In insurance, a provision that the payment of the claim may not be disputed by the company for any cause whatsoever except for nonpayment of premium.

INSURANCE, FRATERNAL: Insurance conducted by an association or order, having a lodge system and representative form of government.

INSURANCE, INDUSTRIAL: Insurance, usually of less than $500 in amount, generally effected without medical examination, with premiums payable weekly or monthly. If premiums are payable at longer intervals, it is termed "ordinary insurance;" the frequency of payment of premiums being, therefore, one of the distinguishing features. Such insurance is popular among the low income groups, premiums being usually collected from door to door each week.

INSURANCE, OLD LINE: A term generally applied to insurance conducted on scientific principles, guaranteeing the payment of a fixed sum, charging a fixed, level premium, and accumulating an adequate reserve.

INSURANCE, PAID-UP: Insurance on which there remains no further premiums to be paid.

INTEREST: In practice, a payment for the use of money.

INTESTACY: The condition resulting from a person's dying without leaving a valid will.

INVESTOR: An individual whose principal concerns in the purchase of a security are regular dividend income, safety of the original investment, and, if possible, capital appreciation. (See: Speculator.)

LAPSE: The voidance of a policy, in whole or in part, by the non-payment of a premium or installment of premium date.

LISTED STOCK: The stock of a company traded on a securities exchange for which a listing application and a registration statement, giving detailed information about the company and its operations, have been filed with the Securities and Exchange Commission, unless otherwise exempted, and the Exchange itself.

LIQUIDITY: The cash position measured by the cash on hand and assets quickly convertible into cash.

LOAD: The portion of the offering price of shares of open-end investment companies which covers sales commissions and all other costs of distribution. The load is incurred only on purchase, there being, in most cases, no charge when the shares are sold or redeemed.

LOADING: That addition to the net insurance premium which is necessary (1) to cover the policy's proportionate share in the expense of operating the company and (2) to provide a fund deemed sufficient to cover contingencies.

LOAN VALUE: The amount of money that can be borrowed from the insurance company, using the policy cash value as collateral.

MATURITY: The time of the happening of the contingency which makes the policy due and payable.

MORTALITY RATE (DEATH RATE): The ratio of those who die at a stated age to the total number who are exposed to the risk of death at that age per year.

MORTALITY, SAVING IN: The excess of the tabular, or expected mortality over the actual mortality for the period under observation (usually the calendar year).

MUTUAL WILLS: Wills made by two or more persons (usually but not necessarily husband and wife) containing similar provisions in favor of each other or of the same beneficiary.

NET COST: The total gross premiums paid, less total dividends credited for a given period.

NET SURRENDERED COST: The total gross premiums paid, less the total dividends credited for the given period and the surrender or cash value of the policy, plus the surrender charge (if any).

NON-FORFEITURE PROVISIONS: Provisions whereby, after the payment of a given number of premiums, the contract may not be completely forfeited because of non-payment of a subsequent premium, but is held good for some value in cash, or in paid-up insurance or in extended term insurance. These values are usually stipulated in a table printed in the policy. One of the two latter options is usually effective automatically; any other option is generally available only upon surrender of the policy.

ODD LOT: An amount of stock less than the established 100-share unit or 10-share unit of trading: from 1 to 99 shares for the great majority of issues, 1 to 9 for so-called inactive stocks.

OPEN-END INVESTMENT COMPANY: A company, popularly known as a "Mutual Fund," issuing redeemable shares, i.e., shares which normally must be liquidated by the fund on demand of the shareholder. With some exceptions such companies continuously offer new shares to investors.

OPEN-END MORTGAGE: A mortgage under which the mortgaged property stands as security not only for the original loan but for future advances which the lender may be willing to make.

OPTIONS OF SETTLEMENT: Options for receiving payment granted at maturity of the contract, in lieu of payment in a single sum.

OVER-THE-COUNTER: A market for securities made up of securities dealers who may not be members of a securities exchange. Over-the-counter is mainly a market over the telephone. Thousands of companies have insufficient shares outstanding, stockholders, or earnings to warrant listing on a stock exchange. Others may simply prefer not to list their securities on a national exchange. Securities of these companies are traded in the over-the-counter market between dealers for customers. The over-the-counter market is the chief market for U.S. Government bonds, municipal bonds, and bank and insurance stocks.

PARTICIPATING PREFERRED STOCK: A preferred stock that shares with common stock in exceptionally large corporate earnings, thus getting a rate higher than the stated maximum rate.

POLICY, DOUBLE ENDOWMENT: One which stipulates payment, upon death within a stated period, of the sum insured or, if the Insured survives this period, of double the sum insured.

POLICY, ENDOWMENT INSURANCE, OR ENDOWMENT: A policy under which the insured himself receives the proceeds if he survives until the policy matures. His beneficiary receives the proceeds if the insured dies before the policy matures.

POLICY, INSTALLMENT: A contract under which the sum insured is payable in a given number of equal annual installments.

POLICY, JOINT LIFE: One under which the company agrees to pay the amount of insurance at the death of the first of two or more designated persons.

POLICY, LIMITED PAYMENT: One which stipulates that only a limited number of premiums are to be paid.

POLICY LOAN: A loan secured by the cash value of the policy as collateral.

POLICY, NON-PARTICIPATING: One which is not entitled to receive dividends. Such a policy is usually written at a lower rate of premium than a corresponding participating policy. Stock Policy, or Stock Rate Policy are terms sometimes applied, although it is not always the case that such policies are issued by stock companies only.

POLICY, PARTICIPATING: One which participates (i.e. receives dividends) in the surplus as determined and apportioned by the company.

POLICY YEAR: The year beginning with the due date of an annual premium.

PORTFOLIO: Holdings of securities by an individual or institution. A portfolio may contain bonds, preferred stocks and common stocks of various types of enterprises.

PREMIUM: A stated sum charged by a company in return for the insurance. It may be payable in a single sum or in a limited number of payments, or periodically throughout the duration of the policy.

PREMIUM, EXTRA: An additional payment intended to compensate for some special risk or danger, as in case of hazardous occupations, etc.

PREMIUM, GROSS: The premium named in the contract. It is made up of the net premium and an addition called the "loading," imposed to cover expenses and contingencies. The net premium on similar contracts is the same for different companies using the same mortality table and interest rate, as it depends wholly upon the table and rate. But the loading, and consequently the gross premium, varies according to the amount which the managers of the different companies may consider it necessary to levy for expenses, and to provide a margin for safety.

PREMIUM, LEVEL: A premium of a fixed and uniform amount, in lieu of a varying or increasing premium.

PREMIUM, NATURAL: Insurance issued on this plan is in practice equivalent to yearly renewable term insurance, as the premium paid for a given year is theoretically just sufficient to cover the cost to the company of carrying the risks for that year.

PREMIUM, NET: The precise mathematical equivalent of the benefit guaranteed under the contract, either in a single payment or in limited or annual payments as the case may be, according to the table of mortality and rate of interest used as the basis. A portion of the net premium provides the "cost of insurance" and the excess goes to build up the cash reserve.

PREMIUM RENEWAL: Any premium subsequent to the first annual premium, by the payment of which the policy is continued in force.

PREMIUM, TEMPORARY: That premium which is charged to continue a policy in force from the date of its issue to the due date of the first regular annual premium. This temporary insurance is of great practical value to men who wish to have insurance protection begin immediately but who find it more convenient to pay their premiums at some special date, annually.

PREPAYMENT CLAUSE: A clause in a consumer loan contract which provides for a refund to a debtor who chooses to repay an installment account early.

PROSPECTUS: The official circular which describes the shares of a company and offers them for sale. It contains definitive details concerning the company issuing the shares, the determination of the price at which the shares are offered to the public, etc., as required by the Securities and Exchange Commission's rules.

PURE ENDOWMENT: A sum payable only provided the person survives a stated term.

REAL ESTATE: The right, title, or interest that a person has in real property, as distinguished from the property itself.

REAL PROPERTY: Land, buildings, and other kinds of property that legally are classified as real; opposed to personal property.

REDUCED PAID-IP INSURANCE: A form of insurance available as a nonforfeiture option. It provides for continuation of the original insurance plan, but for a reduced amount.

RENEWABLE TERM INSURANCE: Term insurance which can be renewed at the end of the term, at the option of the policyholder and without evidence of insurability, for a limited number of successive terms. The rates increase at each renewal as the age of the insured increases.

RESERVE BASIS: The amount of reserve depends on the table of mortality and the rate of interest assumed. Hence these two factors are said to constitute the basis of reserve. Assuming the same mortality table, an increase in the rate of interest produces without exception smaller net premiums and reserves. But assuming the same interest rate, a variation in the table of mortality may or may not result in smaller reserves.

RESERVE, LEGAL: That required to be held by the laws of the states. The legal basis of reserves may differ in different states, and for the same state there are sometimes two basis, one below which a company may not fall and continue to write new business, and a lower basis below which its assets may not fall and the company continue solvent. This latter is termed "legal minimum reserve."

RESERVE (POLICY RESERVES): The amounts that an insurance company allocates specifically for the fulfillment of its policy obligations. Reserves are so calculated that, together with future premiums and interest earnings, they will enable the company to pay all future claims.

REVIVAL: The reinstatement of a lapsed policy by the company upon receipt of evidence of insurability and payment of past due premiums with interest.

REVOLVING CREDIT: A continuing credit arrangement between seller and buyer in which the buyer (1) agrees to make monthly payments equal to a stipulated percentage of the amount owed at the start of the month plus interest and (2) is permitted to make additional credit purchases as long as the total debt owed does not exceed an agreed upon limit.

RIDER: A schedule or endorsement annexed to a document and made a part thereof.

RIGHTS OR WARRANTS: When a company wants to raise more funds by issuing additional stock, it may give its stockholders the opportunity, ahead of others, to buy the new stock. The piece of paper evidencing this privilege is called a right or warrant. Because the additional stock is usually offered to stockholders below the market price, rights ordinarily have a market value of their own and are actively traded. Failure to exercise or sell rights may result in actual loss to the holder.

ROUND LOT: A unit of trading or a multiple thereof. On the NYSE the unit of trading is generally 100 shares in stocks and $1,000 par value in the case of bonds. In some inactive stocks, the unit of trading is 10 shares.

SALES CHARGE: The amount charged in connection with the distribution to the public of mutual fund shares. It is added to the net asset value per share in the determination of the offering price and is paid to the dealer and underwriter.

SAVINGS ACCOUNT: An interest-bearing liability of a bank, redeemable in money on demand or after due notice, not transferable by check.

SECURITIES: Literally, things given, deposited, or pledged to assure the fulfillment of an obligation. In this narrow sense a mortgage is security; but the term is now generally used in a broader sense to include stocks as well as bonds, notes, and other evidences of indebtedness.

SIMPLE INTEREST METHOD: A computation method where the finance charge for a given month of an installment contract equals the monthly rate applied to loan balances at the end of each month times the loan balance at the end of each month.

SPECULATOR: One willing to assume a relatively large risk in the hope of gain. His principal concern is to increase his capital rather than his dividend income. Safety of principal is a secondary factor. (See: Investor.)

STOCK DIVIDEND: A dividend payable in stock rather than cash.

SURRENDER VALUE: The value granted the Insured by an insurance company for surrender of all rights under this policy. It may usually be taken in one of the following forms: (1) cash, or (2) paid-up insurance.

TERM POLICY: One which provides that the amount of the policy shall be payable only in event of death within a specified term.

TESTATOR: A man who has made and left a valid will at his death.

TRUST: A fiduciary relationship in which one person (the trustee) is the holder of the legal title to property (the trust property) subject to an obligation to keep or use the property for the benefit of another person.

VALUATION: The process of ascertaining the required reserves, under certain assumptions, of an insurance company under its outstanding policies. The present value of the outstanding liabilities less the present value of future net premiums on the same policies is the "net premium valuation," which is the one usually employed by companies at the end of the year for statement purposes.

WAGE-ASSIGNMENT AGREEMENT: A clause in a consumer loan contract which authorizes the taking of a portion of the borrower's wages for the satisfaction of a debt, if payments become overdue.

WILL: A legally enforceable declaration of a person's wishes in writing regarding matters to be attended to after his death and inoperative until his death. A will usually relates to the testator's property, is revocable or amendable up to the time of his death, and is applicable to the situation which exists at the time of his death.

YIELD: The dividends or interest paid expressed as a percentage of the current price or, if you own the security, of the price you originally paid.

APPENDIX C—TABLES

TABLE C-1
(Insert here any pay tables made effective after 1 December, 1970.)

MONTHLY BASIC PAY TABLE EFFECTIVE 1 January 1970 (PL 90-207)

OFFICERS

Pay Grade	Under 2	Over 2	Over 3	Over 4	Over 6	Over 8	Over 10	Over 12	Over 14	Over 16	Over 18	Over 20	Over 22	Over 26
O-10	1,956.90	2,025.90	2,025.90	2,025.90	2,025.90	2,103.30	2,103.30	2,264.70	2,264.70	2,426.70	2,426.70	2,588.70	2,588.70	2,750.40
O-9	1,734.30	1,779.90	1,818.00	1,818.00	1,818.00	1,863.90	1,863.90	1,941.30	1,941.30	2,103.30	2,103.30	2,264.70	2,264.70	2,426.70
O-8	1,570.80	1,617.90	1,656.60	1,656.60	1,656.60	1,779.90	1,863.90	1,863.90	1,941.30	1,941.30	2,025.90	2,264.70	2,188.20	2,426.70
O-7	1,305.00	1,394.10	1,394.10	1,394.10	1,456.20	1,456.20	1,540.80	1,540.80	1,617.90	1,779.90	1,902.30	2,025.90		
O-6	967.20	1,063.20	1,132.50	1,132.50	1,132.50	1,132.50	1,132.50	1,132.50	1,170.90	1,356.00	1,425.30	1,456.20	1,540.80	1,671.30
O-5	773.40	909.00	971.10	971.10	971.10	971.10	1,001.10	1,054.50	1,125.00	1,209.40	1,278.60	1,317.00	1,363.50	
O-4	652.50	793.80	847.50	847.50	862.50	901.20	962.40	1,016.70	1,063.20	1,109.40	1,140.30			
O-3	606.30	677.70	723.90	801.60	839.70	870.00	916.80	962.40	985.80					
O-2	486.00	577.20	693.30	716.40	731.40									
O-1	417.60	462.60	577.20											

COMMISSIONED OFFICERS WITH OVER 4 YEARS EM SERVICE

Pay Grade	Over 4	Over 6	Over 8	Over 10	Over 12	Over 14
O-3	801.60	839.70	870.00	916.80	962.40	1,001.10
O-2	716.40	731.40	754.50	793.80	824.70	847.50
O-1	577.20	616.50	639.60	662.40	685.50	716.40

WARRANT OFFICERS

Pay Grade	Under 2	Over 2	Over 3	Over 4	Over 6	Over 8	Over 10	Over 12	Over 14	Over 16	Over 18	Over 20	Over 22	Over 26
W-4	617.40	662.40	662.40	677.70	708.30	739.50	770.10	824.70	862.50	893.40	916.90	947.40	978.60	1,054.50
W-3	561.30	609.00	609.00	616.50	624.00	669.60	708.30	731.40	754.50	777.30	801.60	832.20	862.50	893.40
W-2	491.70	531.60	531.60	547.20	577.20	609.00	632.10	654.90	677.70	701.10	723.90	747.00	777.30	
W-1	409.50	469.80	469.80	508.80	531.60	554.70	557.20	600.90	624.00	647.10	669.60	693.30		

ENLISTED

Pay Grade	Under 2	Over 2	Over 3	Over 4	Over 6	Over 8	Over 10	Over 12	Over 14	Over 16	Over 18	Over 20	Over 22	Over 26
E-9							701.40	717.60	734.10	750.30	767.10	782.10	823.50	903.60
E-8						588.60	605.10	621.00	637.50	653.70	669.30	685.80	726.30	807.00
E-7	369.90	443.40	459.90	476.10	492.30	507.90	524.10	540.90	564.90	580.80	597.00	605.10	645.60	726.30
E-6	318.90	387.30	403.20	419.70	435.90	451.80	468.30	492.30	507.90	524.10	532.50			
E-5	275.40	339.30	355.50	371.10	395.40	411.60	427.80	443.40	451.80					
E-4	231.60	290.10	306.60	330.60	347.10									
E-3	167.70	233.70	249.90	266.40										
E-2	138.30	193.50												
E-1	133.20	177.00												
E-1*	124.50													

(* Under 4 months)

TABLE C-2

MONTHLY BASIC PAY TABLE EFFECTIVE 1 JULY 1969

OFFICERS

Pay Grade	Under 2	Over 2	Over 3	Over 4	Over 6	Over 8	Over 10	Over 12	Over 14	Over 16	Over 18	Over 20	Over 22	Over 26
O-10	1,810.20	1,874.10	1,874.10	1,874.10	1,874.10	1,945.80	1,945.80	2,094.90	2,094.90	2,244.90	2,244.90	2,394.60	2,394.60	2,544.30
O-9	1,604.40	1,646.40	1,681.80	1,681.80	1,681.80	1,724.10	1,724.10	1,795.80	1,795.80	1,795.80	1,874.10	2,094.90	2,094.90	2,244.90
O-8	1,453.20	1,496.10	1,532.40	1,532.40	1,532.40	1,646.40	1,646.40	1,724.10	1,724.10	1,795.80	1,874.10	1,945.80	2,024.10	2,024.10
O-7	1,207.20	1,289.70	1,289.70	1,289.70	1,347.00	1,347.00	1,425.30	1,425.30	1,496.70	1,646.40	1,759.80	1,759.80	1,759.80	1,759.80
O-6	894.60	983.40	1,047.60	1,047.60	1,047.60	1,047.60	1,047.60	1,047.60	1,083.30	1,254.30	1,318.50	1,347.00	1,425.30	1,546.20
O-5	715.50	840.90	898.20	898.20	898.20	898.20	926.10	975.60	1,040.70	1,118.70	1,182.90	1,218.30	1,261.20	1,261.20
O-4	603.60	734.40	783.90	783.90	798.00	833.70	890.40	940.50	983.40	1,026.30	1,054.80	1,054.80	1,054.80	1,054.80
O-3	561.00	627.00	669.60	741.60	776.70	804.90	848.10	890.40	912.00	912.00	912.00	912.00	912.00	912.00
O-2	449.70	534.00	641.40	662.70	676.50	676.50	676.50	676.50	676.50	676.50	676.50	676.50	676.50	676.50
O-1	386.40	427.80	534.00	534.00	534.00	534.00	534.00	534.00	534.00	534.00	534.00	534.00	534.00	534.00

COMMISSIONED OFFICERS WITH OVER 4 YEARS EM SERVICE

Pay Grade	Over 4	Over 6	Over 8	Over 10	Over 12	Over 14	Over 16	Over 18	Over 20	Over 22	Over 26
O-3	741.60	776.70	804.90	848.10	890.40	926.10	926.10	926.10	926.10	926.10	926.10
O-2	662.70	676.50	698.10	734.40	762.90	783.90	783.90	783.90	783.90	783.90	783.90
O-1	534.00	570.30	591.60	612.90	634.20	662.70	662.70	662.70	662.70	662.70	662.70

WARRANT OFFICERS

Pay Grade	Under 2	Over 2	Over 3	Over 4	Over 6	Over 8	Over 10	Over 12	Over 14	Over 16	Over 18	Over 20	Over 22	Over 26
W-4	571.20	612.90	612.90	627.00	655.20	684.00	712.50	762.90	798.00	826.50	848.10	876.30	905.40	975.60
W-3	519.30	563.40	563.40	570.30	577.20	619.50	655.20	676.50	698.10	719.10	741.60	769.80	798.00	826.50
W-2	454.80	491.70	491.70	506.10	534.00	563.40	584.70	605.70	627.00	648.60	669.60	690.90	719.10	719.10
W-1	378.90	434.70	434.70	470.70	491.70	513.00	534.00	555.90	577.20	598.50	619.50	641.40	641.40	641.40

ENLISTED

Pay Grade	Under 2	Over 2	Over 3	Over 4	Over 6	Over 8	Over 10	Over 12	Over 14	Over 16	Over 18	Over 20	Over 22	Over 26
E-9	----	----	----	----	----	----	648.90	663.90	679.20	694.20	709.50	723.60	761.70	835.80
E-8	----	----	----	----	----	544.50	559.80	574.50	589.80	604.80	619.29	634.50	672.00	746.40
E-7	342.30	410.10	425.40	440.40	455.60	469.80	484.80	500.40	522.60	537.30	552.30	559.80	597.30	672.00
E-6	294.90	358.20	372.90	388.20	403.20	417.90	433.20	455.40	469.80	484.80	492.60	492.60	492.60	492.60
E-5	254.70	313.80	328.80	343.20	365.70	380.70	395.70	410.10	417.90	417.90	417.90	417.90	417.90	417.90
E-4	214.20	268.50	283.50	305.70	321.00	321.00	321.00	321.00	321.00	321.00	321.00	321.00	321.00	321.00
E-3	155.10	216.30	231.30	246.30	246.30	246.30	246.30	246.30	246.30	246.30	246.30	246.30	246.30	246.30
E-2	127.80	179.10	179.10	179.10	179.10	179.10	179.10	179.10	179.10	179.10	179.10	179.10	179.10	179.10
E-1	123.30	163.80	163.80	163.80	163.80	163.80	163.80	163.80	163.80	163.80	163.80	163.80	163.80	163.80
E-1*	115.20	----	----	----	----	----	----	----	----	----	----	----	----	----

(*Under 4 months)

TABLE C-3

MONTHLY RATES OF BAQ EFFECTIVE 1 OCT 1967

Pay Grade	Title	Without Dependents	With Dependents
0-10	General	$160.20	$201.00
0-9	Lt. General	160.20	201.00
0-8	Major General	160.20	201.00
0-7	Brig. General	160.20	201.00
0-6	Colonel	140.10	170.10
0-5	Lt. Colonel	130.20	157.50
0-4	Major	120.00	145.05
0-3	Captain	105.00	130.05
0-2	First Lt.	95.10	120.00
0-1	Second Lt.	85.20	110.10
W-4	Chief Warrant Officer	120.00	145.05
W-3	Chief Warrant Officer	105.00	130.05
W-2	Chief Warrant Officer	95.10	120.00
W-1	Warrant Officer	85.20	110.10
E-9	Enlisted Members	85.20	120.00
E-8	Enlisted Members	85.20	120.00
E-7	Enlisted Members	75.00	114.90
E-6	Enlisted Members	70.20	110.10
E-5	Enlisted Members	70.00	105.00
E-4 (Over 4 years)	Enlisted Members	70.20	105.00

Pay Grade	Title	Without Dependents	1 Dep.	2 Dep.	3 or more Dependents
E-4 (4 years or less)	Corp, Specl. 4	$60.00	$90.60	$90.60	$105.00
E-3	Private 1st Cl	60.00	60.00	90.60	105.00
E-2	Private	60.00	60.00	90.60	105.00
E-1	Private	60.00	60.00	90.60	105.00

TABLE C-4

HAZARDOUS DUTY INCENTIVE PAY

FLYING CREW MEMBER AND SUBMARINE INCENTIVE PAY RATES

Pay Grade	Years of Service										
	Under 2	Over 2	Over 3	Over 4	Over 6	Over 8	Over 10	Over 12	Over 14	Over 16	Over 18
O-10	165.00	--	--	--	--	--	--	--	--	--	--
O-9	165.00	--	--	--	--	--	--	--	--	--	--
O-8	155.00	155.00	165.00	--	--	--	--	--	--	--	--
O-7	150.00	150.00	160.00	--	--	--	--	--	--	--	--
O-6	200.00	200.00	215.00	215.00	215.00	215.00	215.00	215.00	215.00	220.00	245.00
O-5	190.00	190.00	205.00	205.00	205.00	205.00	205.00	210.00	225.00	230.00	245.00
O-4	170.00	170.00	185.00	185.00	185.00	195.00	210.00	215.00	220.00	230.00	240.00
O-3	145.00	145.00	155.00	165.00	180.00	185.00	190.00	200.00	205.00	--	--
O-2	115.00	125.00	150.00	150.00	160.00	165.00	170.00	180.00	185.00	--	--
O-1	100.00	105.00	135.00	135.00	140.00	145.00	155.00	160.00	170.00	--	--
W-4	115.00	115.00	115.00	115.00	120.00	125.00	135.00	145.00	155.00	160.00	165.00
W-3	110.00	115.00	115.00	115.00	120.00	120.00	125.00	135.00	140.00	--	--
W-2	105.00	110.00	110.00	110.00	115.00	120.00	125.00	130.00	135.00	--	--
W-1	100.00	105.00	105.00	105.00	110.00	120.00	125.00	130.00	--	--	--
E-9	105.00	--	--	--	--	--	--	--	--	--	--
E-8	105.00	--	--	--	--	--	--	--	--	--	--
E-7	80.00	85.00	85.00	85.00	90.00	95.00	100.00	105.00	--	--	--
E-6	70.00	75.00	75.00	80.00	85.00	90.00	95.00	95.00	100.00	--	--
E-5	60.00	70.00	70.00	80.00	80.00	85.00	90.00	95.00	--	--	--
E-4	55.00	65.00	65.00	70.00	75.00	80.00	--	--	--	--	--
E-3	55.00	60.00	--	--	--	--	--	--	--	--	--
E-2	50.00	60.00	--	--	--	--	--	--	--	--	--
E-1	50.00	55.00	--	--	--	--	--	--	--	--	--
E-1 (Under 4 months)	50.00	--	--	--	--	--	--	--	--	--	--
Aviation cadets	50.00	--	--	--	--	--	--	--	--	--	--

If no amount is shown for a pay grade under cumulative year of service, the amount immediately to the left applies

TABLE C-5

Special Pay (Physicians And Dentists)

Years Service	Monthly Pay
0-2	$100
2-6	150
6-10	250
Over 10	350

SPECIAL PAY FOR DOCTORS

COMPUTATION OF CONTINUATION PAY FOR DOCTORS		
A	B	C
R U L E When an officer eligible for continuation pay is serving in pay grade		for each additional year of active duty, the continuation pay payable is
1 0-9		1 month basic pay
2 0-8		2 months basic pay
3 0-7		3 months basic pay
4 0-4, 0-5, or 0-6	and he has 5 years active duty (Notes 1 and 2)	4 months basic pay

NOTES: 1. This is based on total active duty and may include active duty as other than a medical officer.

        2. Time spent in civilian specialty training before entering service counts in calculating continuation pay eligibility if volunteering to serve at **least** one year beyond the two years of obligated service.

TABLE C-6

Weight Allowances For Shipment Of Household Goods
(Pounds)

Service and Grade[1,4]			
Army, Air Force and Marine Corps	Navy and Coast Guard	Temporary change of station weight allowance	Permanent change of station weight allowance[3]
General and General of the Army	Admiral ------------	2,000[2]	24,000
Lieutenant general ------------	Vice admiral --------	1,500	18,000
Major general ----------------	Rear admiral (upper half)	1,000	14,500
Brigadier general -------------	Rear admiral (lower half) and Commodore	1,000	13,500
Colonel ----------------------	Captain -------------	800	13,500
Lieutenant colonel ------------	Commander -----------	800	13,000
Major and warrant officer (W-4 pay grade).	Lieutenant commander and warrant officer (W-4 pay grade).	800	12,000
Captain and warrant officer (W-3 pay grade).	Lieutenant and warrant officer (W-3 pay grade).	600	11,000
First lieutenant contract surgeon warrant officer (W-2 pay grade).	Lieutenant (junior grade) and warrant officer (W-2 pay grade).	600	10,000
Second lieutenant, officer graduate of USMA and USAFA, and warrant officer (W-1 pay grade).	Ensign, officer graduate of USNA and Coast Guard Academy, and warrant officer (W-1 pay grade).	600	9,500
Aviation cadet ----------------	Aviation cadet ----------	400	400

[1] Members of reserve components of the Uniformed Services concerned and officers holding temporary commissions in the Army and Air Force of the United States are entitled to weight allowances for corresponding relative grades listed. The weight allowance of a member will be based on the grade or rating held by him on the date his orders authorizing shipment of household goods become effective.

[2] Exception to this limitation may be authorized by the respective Secretaries for the Chiefs of Staff, U.S. Air Force and Army, the Chief of Naval Operations in such additional amounts, not exceeding 2,000 pounds, as they may consider appropriate. (Applicable to all shipments made under orders which are effective on or about 15 October 1966.)

[3] Annual Department of Defense Appropriation Acts limit the weight of household goods which may be shipped at Government expense incident to a single change of station. Accordingly, the permanent change of station weight allowance for general officers in grade 0-8, 0-9, and 0-10 is limited to 13,500 pounds.

[4] Members of the regular components of the Uniformed Services concerned who are appointed from either an enlisted or warrant officer grade or rating to a commissioned officer grade will thereafter be entitled to the weight allowances of the grade or rating from which appointed or the grade to which appointed, whichever weight allowances are the greater, until such time as they are next promoted to a grade for which a greater weight allowance is authorized.

TABLE C-7

SINGLE Persons — MONTHLY Payroll Period

And the wages are—		And the number of withholding exemptions claimed is—										
At least	But less than	0	1	2	3	4	5	6	7	8	9	10 or more
		The amount of income tax to be withheld shall be—										
400	420	63.90	53.60	44.40	35.20	23.40	10.00	0	0	0	0	0
420	440	68.10	57.00	47.80	38.60	28.40	14.90	2.80	0	0	0	0
$440	$460	$72.30	$60.90	$51.20	$42.00	$32.80	$19.90	$7.00	$0	$0	$0	$0
460	480	76.50	65.10	54.60	45.40	36.20	24.90	11.30	0	0	0	0
480	500	80.70	69.30	58.00	48.80	39.60	29.90	16.30	4.00	0	0	0
500	520	84.90	73.50	62.10	52.20	43.00	33.70	21.30	8.20	0	0	0
520	540	89.10	77.70	66.30	55.60	46.40	37.10	26.30	12.80	1.10	0	0
540	560	93.30	81.90	70.50	59.10	49.80	40.50	31.30	17.80	5.30	0	0
560	580	97.50	86.10	74.70	63.30	53.20	43.90	34.70	22.80	9.50	0	0
580	600	101.70	90.30	78.90	67.50	56.60	47.30	38.10	27.80	14.30	2.30	0
600	640	108.00	96.60	85.20	73.80	62.50	52.40	43.20	34.00	21.80	8.60	0
640	680	116.40	105.00	93.60	82.20	70.90	59.50	50.00	40.80	31.60	18.20	5.60
680	720	124.80	113.40	102.00	90.60	79.30	67.90	56.80	47.60	38.40	28.20	14.70
720	760	133.20	121.80	110.40	99.00	87.70	76.30	64.90	54.40	45.20	36.00	24.70
760	800	142.10	130.20	118.80	107.40	96.10	84.70	73.30	61.90	52.00	42.80	33.60
800	840	152.10	138.60	127.20	115.80	104.50	93.10	81.70	70.30	59.00	49.60	40.40
840	880	162.10	148.50	135.60	124.20	112.90	101.50	90.10	78.70	67.40	56.40	47.20
880	920	172.10	158.50	145.00	132.60	121.30	109.90	98.50	87.10	75.80	64.40	54.00
920	960	183.30	168.50	155.00	141.50	129.70	118.30	106.90	95.50	84.20	72.80	61.40
960	1,000	195.30	179.00	165.00	151.50	138.10	126.70	115.30	103.90	92.60	81.20	69.80
1,000	1,040	207.30	191.00	175.00	161.50	147.90	135.10	123.70	112.30	101.00	89.60	78.20
1,040	1,080	219.30	203.00	186.80	171.50	157.90	144.40	132.10	120.70	109.40	98.00	86.60
1,080	1,120	231.30	215.00	198.80	182.50	167.90	154.40	140.80	129.10	117.80	106.40	95.00
1,120	1,160	243.30	227.00	210.80	194.50	178.30	164.40	150.80	137.50	126.20	114.80	103.40
1,160	1,200	255.30	239.00	222.80	206.50	190.30	174.40	160.80	147.30	134.60	123.20	111.80
1,200	1,240	267.30	251.00	234.80	218.50	202.30	186.00	170.80	157.30	143.80	131.60	120.20
1,240	1,280	279.30	263.00	246.80	230.50	214.30	198.00	181.80	167.30	153.80	140.20	128.60
1,280	1,320	291.30	275.00	258.80	242.50	226.30	210.00	193.80	177.50	163.80	150.20	137.00
1,320	1,360	303.30	287.00	270.80	254.50	238.30	222.00	205.80	189.50	173.80	160.20	146.70
1,360	1,400	315.30	299.00	282.80	266.50	250.30	234.00	217.80	201.50	185.30	170.20	156.70
1,400	1,440	327.30	311.00	294.80	278.50	262.30	246.00	229.80	213.50	197.30	181.00	166.70
1,440	1,480	339.30	323.00	306.80	290.50	274.30	258.00	241.80	225.50	209.30	193.00	176.80
1,480	1,520	351.30	335.00	318.80	302.50	286.30	270.00	253.80	237.50	221.30	205.00	188.80
		30 percent of the excess over $1,520 plus—										
$1,520 and over		357.30	341.00	324.80	308.50	292.30	276.00	259.80	243.50	227.30	211.00	194.80

Effective 1 July 1970

TABLE C-8

MARRIED Persons — MONTHLY Payroll Period

And the wages are—		And the number of withholding exemptions claimed is—										
At least	But less than	0	1	2	3	4	5	6	7	8	9	10 or more
		The amount of income tax to be withheld shall be—										
400	420	55.30	46.60	38.50	30.40	21.40	10.00	0	0	0	0	0
420	440	58.70	49.60	41.50	33.40	25.30	14.20	2.80	0	0	0	0
$440	$460	$62.10	$52.90	$44.50	$36.40	$28.30	$18.40	$7.00	$0	$0	$0	$0
460	480	65.50	56.30	47.50	39.40	31.30	22.60	11.20	0	0	0	0
480	500	68.90	59.70	50.50	42.40	34.30	26.10	15.40	4.00	0	0	0
500	520	72.30	63.10	53.90	45.40	37.30	29.10	19.60	8.20	0	0	0
520	540	75.70	66.50	57.30	48.40	40.30	32.10	23.80	12.40	1.10	0	0
540	560	79.10	69.90	60.70	51.50	43.30	35.10	27.00	16.60	5.30	0	0
560	580	82.50	73.30	64.10	54.90	46.30	38.10	30.00	20.80	9.50	0	0
580	600	85.90	76.70	67.50	58.30	49.30	41.10	33.00	24.90	13.70	2.30	0
600	640	91.00	81.80	72.60	63.40	54.20	45.60	37.50	29.40	20.00	8.60	0
640	680	97.80	88.60	79.40	70.20	61.00	51.70	43.50	35.40	27.30	17.00	5.60
680	720	104.60	95.40	86.20	77.00	67.80	58.50	49.50	41.40	33.30	25.10	14.00
720	760	111.40	102.20	93.00	83.80	74.60	65.30	56.10	47.40	39.30	31.10	22.40
760	800	118.60	109.00	99.80	90.60	81.40	72.10	62.90	53.70	45.30	37.10	29.00
800	840	126.60	115.80	106.60	97.40	88.20	78.90	69.70	60.50	51.30	43.10	35.00
840	880	134.60	123.80	113.40	104.20	95.00	85.70	76.50	67.30	58.10	49.10	41.00
880	920	142.60	131.80	120.90	111.00	101.80	92.50	83.30	74.10	64.90	55.70	47.00
920	960	150.60	139.80	128.90	118.10	108.60	99.30	90.10	80.90	71.70	62.50	53.30
960	1,000	158.60	147.80	136.90	126.10	115.40	106.10	96.90	87.70	78.50	69.30	60.10
1,000	1,040	166.60	155.80	144.90	134.10	123.30	112.90	103.70	94.50	85.30	76.10	66.90
1,040	1,080	174.60	163.80	152.90	142.10	131.30	120.40	110.50	101.30	92.10	82.90	73.70
1,080	1,120	182.60	171.80	160.90	150.10	139.30	128.40	117.60	108.10	98.90	89.70	80.50
1,120	1,160	190.60	179.80	168.90	158.10	147.30	136.40	125.60	114.90	105.70	96.50	87.30
1,160	1,200	198.60	187.80	176.90	166.10	155.30	144.40	133.60	122.80	112.50	103.30	94.10
1,200	1,240	206.60	195.80	184.90	174.10	163.30	152.40	141.60	130.80	119.90	110.10	100.90
1,240	1,280	214.60	203.80	192.90	182.10	171.30	160.40	149.60	138.80	127.90	117.10	107.70
1,280	1,320	222.60	211.80	200.90	190.10	179.30	168.40	157.60	146.80	135.90	125.10	114.50
1,320	1,360	230.60	219.80	208.90	198.10	187.30	176.40	165.60	154.80	143.90	133.10	122.30
1,360	1,400	238.60	227.80	216.90	206.10	195.30	184.40	173.60	162.80	151.90	141.10	130.30
1,400	1,440	246.60	235.80	224.90	214.10	203.30	192.40	181.60	170.80	159.90	149.10	138.30
1,440	1,480	254.60	243.80	232.90	222.10	211.30	200.40	189.60	178.80	167.90	157.10	146.30
1,480	1,520	262.60	251.80	240.90	230.10	219.30	208.40	197.60	186.80	175.90	165.10	154.30
1,520	1,560	272.60	259.80	248.90	238.10	227.30	216.40	205.60	194.80	183.90	173.10	162.30
1,560	1,600	282.60	269.00	256.90	246.10	235.30	224.40	213.60	202.80	191.90	181.10	170.30
1,600	1,640	292.60	279.00	265.50	254.10	243.30	232.40	221.60	210.80	199.90	189.10	178.30
1,640	1,680	302.60	289.00	275.50	262.10	251.30	240.40	229.60	218.80	207.90	197.10	186.30
1,680	1,720	312.60	299.00	285.50	272.00	259.30	248.40	237.60	226.80	215.90	205.10	194.30
1,720	1,760	322.60	309.00	295.50	282.00	268.40	256.40	245.60	234.80	223.90	213.10	202.30
1,760	1,800	332.60	319.00	305.50	292.00	278.40	264.90	253.60	242.80	231.90	221.10	210.30
1,800	1,840	342.60	329.00	315.50	302.00	288.40	274.90	261.60	250.80	239.90	229.10	218.30
1,840	1,880	353.90	339.00	325.50	312.00	298.40	284.90	271.30	258.80	247.90	237.10	226.30
1,880	1,920	365.90	349.70	335.50	322.00	308.40	294.90	281.30	267.80	255.90	245.10	234.30
1,920	1,960	377.90	361.70	345.50	332.00	318.40	304.90	291.30	277.80	264.30	253.10	242.30
1,960	2,000	389.90	373.70	357.40	342.00	328.40	314.90	301.30	287.80	274.30	261.10	250.30
2,000	2,040	401.90	385.70	369.40	353.20	338.40	324.90	311.30	297.80	284.30	270.70	258.30
2,040	2,080	413.90	397.70	381.40	365.20	348.90	334.90	321.30	307.80	294.30	280.70	267.20
2,080	2,120	425.90	409.70	393.40	377.20	360.90	344.90	331.30	317.80	304.30	290.70	277.20
2,120	2,160	437.90	421.70	405.40	389.20	372.90	356.70	341.30	327.80	314.30	300.70	287.20
2,160	2,200	449.90	433.70	417.40	401.20	384.90	368.70	352.40	337.80	324.30	310.70	297.20
2,200	2,240	461.90	445.70	429.40	413.20	396.90	380.70	364.40	348.20	334.30	320.70	307.20
2,240	2,280	473.90	457.70	441.40	425.20	408.90	392.70	376.40	360.20	344.30	330.70	317.20
2,280	2,320	485.90	469.70	453.40	437.20	420.90	404.70	388.40	372.20	355.90	340.70	327.20
2,320	2,360	497.90	481.70	465.40	449.20	432.90	416.70	400.40	384.20	367.90	351.70	337.20
2,360	2,400	509.90	493.70	477.40	461.20	444.90	428.70	412.40	396.20	379.90	363.70	347.40
2,400	2,440	521.90	505.70	489.40	473.20	456.90	440.70	424.40	408.20	391.90	375.70	359.40
		30 percent of the excess over $2,440 plus—										
$2,440 and over		527.90	511.70	495.40	479.20	462.90	446.70	430.40	414.20	397.90	381.70	365.40

Effective 1 July 1970

TABLE C-8 (Continued)

DEPENDENCY AND INDEMNITY COMPENSATION (DIC)

DIC is a monthly Veterans Administration benefit payable to widows, children, and parents, for war or peacetime service - connected deaths of servicemen and veterans.

Effective 1 December 1969, Public Law 91-96 introduced a new standard table of widow's DIC rates, related to the pay grade held by the deceased serviceman or veteran at the time of death or release from active duty. Where the deceased had previously served satisfactorily in a higher grade for at least six months during active service, DIC may be computed in the higher grade (if it provides a higher payment). The widow's income is not a factor in determining entitlement. The following monthly rates are applicable:

GRADE	AMOUNT	GRADE	AMOUNT
0-10	$426	W-4	$238
0-9	390	W-3	226
0-8	363	W-2	219
0-7	332	W-1	211
0-6	306	E-9	228
0-5	272	E-8	218
0-4	247	E-7	206
0-3	234	E-6	197
0-2	218	E-5	193
0-1	211	E-4	187
		E-3	177
		E-2	172
		E-1	167

In addition to the above, DIC payments are increased by $20 per month to the widow, for each child below age 18. Public Law 91-96 also provides payments to children, where there is no widow, and to parents under certain conditions (dependent upon their income). Payments to disabled widows may be increased by $50 per month under the disability provisions of the law if she is a patient in a nursing home or helpless or blind, or so nearly helpless or blind as to need or require the regular aid and attendance of another person.

TABLE C-9

SOCIAL SECURITY AND HOSPITAL INSURANCE RATES

Rate and Percentage Changes. The percentage rate of tax deduction and the total maximum tax by calendar years are:

Calendar Year	Basic FICA	+ = HI	FICA Total	Taxable Base	Maximum Base
1967	3.80%	.60%	4.40%	6600	290.40
1968	3.80%	.60%	4.40%	7800	343.20
1969-70	4.20%	.60%	4.80%	7800	374.40
1971-72	4.60%	.60%	5.20%	7800	405.60
1973-75	5.00%	.65%	5.65%	7800	440.70
1976-79	5.00%	.70%	5.70%	7800	444.60
1980-86	5.00%	.80%	5.80%	7800	452.40
1987 and after	5.00%	.90%	5.90%	7800	460.20

The employer's FICA tax is equal to the amount of FICA tax withheld from the member.

Indebtedness at Discharge. FICA taxes previously withheld may not be used to offset any indebtedness of a member on discharge, death, or release from active duty.

TABLE C-10

TABLE OF SOCIAL SECURITY REDUCTION FACTORS

This table of reduction factors can be used to find the reduced retirement benefit for the worker and/or wife under 65, or for the widow or disabled widower between 60 and 62. In most cases, the amount of the benefit can be figured exactly by this short-cut method. In some cases, the actual amount may be 10 cents higher.

Here's how it works: In Column "A" find the number of months for which benefits will be payable before 65 or before 62 for widow's or disabled widower's benefits. Multiply the appropriate factor in Column "B" or "C" by the amount of the unreduced benefit from Column 2, 3, or 5 of the preceding table, whichever is applicable. If the result is not a multiple of 10 cents, round upward to the next higher multiple of 10 cents. For example, $98.7042 (a benefit of $99.30 reduced 1 month) is rounded to $98.80.

NOTE: This table cannot be used to figure benefits for a disabled widow or disabled widower 50 to 60. The reduction factor for disabled widows and disabled widowers is 43/198 of one percent for each month of entitlement before 60.

(A) REDUCTION MONTHS	(B) FOR RETIREMENT, WIDOW'S, OR DISABLED WIDOWER'S BENEFITS	(C) FOR SPOUSE'S BENEFIT	(A) REDUCTION MONTHS	(B) FOR RETIREMENT, WIDOW'S, OR DISABLED WIDOWER'S BENEFITS	(C) FOR SPOUSE'S BENEFIT
1	.994	.993	19	.894	.868
2	.988	.986	20	.888	.861
3	.983	.979	21	.883	.854
4	.977	.972	22	.877	.847
5	.972	.965	23	.872	.840
6	.966	.958	24	.866	.833
7	.961	.951	25	.861	.826
8	.955	.944	26	.855	.819
9	.950	.937	27	.850	.812
10	.944	.930	28	.844	.805
11	.938	.923	29	.838	.798
12	.933	.916	30	.833	.791
13	.927	.909	31	.827	.784
14	.922	.902	32	.822	.777
15	.916	.895	33	.816	.770
16	.911	.888	34	.811	.763
17	.905	.881	35	.805	.756
18	.900	.875	36	.800	.750

TABLE C-11

TABLE FOR COMPUTING RETIREMENT, SURVIVORS, AND DISABILITY INSURANCE BENEFITS

(NOTE: Not all earnings levels are shown; for average monthly earnings levels between those shown, benefit amounts may be estimated.)

1 AVERAGE MONTHLY EARNINGS NOT MORE THAN	2 WORKER'S* BENEFIT	3 SPOUSE'S* BENEFIT	4 ONE SURVIVING CHILD	5 AGED** WIDOW'S OR WIDOWER'S BENEFIT	6 WIDOW UNDER 62 AND ONE CHILD	7 FAMILY MAXIMUM
$ 76	$ 64.00	$ 32.00	$ 64.00	$ 64.00	$ 96.00	$ 96.00
80	66.40	33.20	64.00	64.00	99.60	99.60
85	70.30	35.20	64.00	64.00	105.60	105.50
90	74.20	37.10	64.00	64.00	111.40	111.30
96	78.00	39.00	64.00	64.40	117.00	117.00
101	82.30	41.20	64.00	67.90	123.60	123.50
106	86.40	43.20	64.80	71.30	129.60	129.60
109	89.20	44.60	66.90	73.60	133.80	133.80
118	91.90	46.00	69.00	75.90	138.00	137.90
127	94.70	47.40	71.10	78.20	142.20	142.10
136	97.50	48.80	73.20	80.50	146.40	146.30
146	100.30	50.20	75.30	82.80	150.60	150.50
155	103.00	51.50	77.30	85.00	154.60	154.50
164	105.80	52.90	79.40	87.30	158.80	158.70
174	108.60	54.30	81.50	89.60	163.00	162.90
183	111.40	55.70	83.60	92.00	167.20	167.10
193	114.20	57.10	85.70	94.30	171.40	171.30
202	116.90	58.50	87.70	96.50	175.40	175.40
211	119.80	59.90	89.90	98.90	179.80	179.70
221	122.50	61.30	91.90	101.10	183.80	183.80
230	125.30	62.70	94.00	103.40	188.00	188.00
239	128.20	64.10	96.20	105.80	192.40	192.30
249	130.80	65.40	98.10	108.00	196.20	199.20
258	133.70	66.90	100.30	110.40	200.60	206.40
267	136.40	68.20	102.30	112.60	204.60	213.60
277	139.20	69.60	104.40	114.90	208.80	221.60
286	142.00	71.00	106.50	117.20	213.00	228.80
295	144.70	72.40	108.60	119.40	217.20	236.00
305	147.60	73.80	110.70	121.80	221.40	244.00
314	150.40	75.20	112.80	124.10	225.60	251.20
323	153.00	76.50	114.80	126.30	229.60	258.40
333	155.90	78.00	117.00	128.70	234.00	266.40
342	158.60	79.30	119.00	130.90	238.00	273.60
351	161.50	80.80	121.20	133.30	242.40	280.80
361	164.30	82.20	123.30	135.60	246.60	288.80
370	166.90	83.50	125.20	137.70	250.40	296.00
379	169.80	84.90	127.40	140.10	254.80	303.20
389	172.50	86.30	129.40	142.40	258.80	311.20
398	175.40	87.70	131.60	144.80	263.20	318.40
407	178.20	89.10	133.70	147.10	267.40	325.60
417	180.70	90.40	135.60	149.10	271.20	333.60
426	183.40	91.70	137.60	151.40	275.20	340.80
436	185.90	93.00	139.50	153.40	279.00	348.80
445	188.50	94.30	141.40	155.60	282.80	352.40
454	191.20	95.60	143.40	157.80	286.80	356.00
464	193.70	96.90	145.30	159.90	290.60	360.00
473	196.40	98.20	147.30	162.10	294.60	363.60
482	198.90	99.50	149.20	164.10	298.40	367.20
492	201.50	100.80	151.20	166.30	302.40	371.20
501	204.20	102.10	153.20	168.50	306.40	374.80
510	206.70	103.40	155.10	170.60	310.20	378.40
520	209.30	104.70	157.00	172.70	314.00	382.40
529	211.90	106.00	159.00	174.90	318.00	386.00
538	214.50	107.30	160.90	177.00	321.80	389.60
548	217.20	108.60	162.90	179.20	325.80	393.60
556	219.70	109.90	164.80	181.30	329.60	396.80
563	222.00	111.00	166.50	183.20	333.00	399.60
570	224.30	112.20	168.30	185.10	336.60	402.40
577	226.60	113.30	170.00	187.00	340.00	405.20
584	228.90	114.50	171.70	188.90	343.40	408.00
591	231.20	115.60	173.40	190.80	346.80	410.80
598	233.50	116.80	175.20	192.70	350.40	413.60
605	235.80	117.90	176.90	194.60	353.80	416.40
612	238.10	119.10	178.60	196.50	357.20	419.20
620	240.40	120.20	180.30	198.40	360.60	422.40
627	242.70	121.40	182.10	200.30	364.20	425.20
634	245.00	122.50	183.80	202.20	367.60	428.00
641	247.30	123.70	185.50	204.10	371.00	430.80
648	249.60	124.80	187.20	206.00	374.40	433.60
650	250.70	125.40	188.10	206.90	376.20	434.40

* Amounts shown are those payable beginning at age 65. To determine benefits beginning between 62 and 65, see Table of Reduction Factors on last page. (There is no reduction in the benefit of a wife under 65 who has an entitled child in her care.)
** Amounts shown payable beginning at age 62.

TABLE C-12

RSFPP COST TABLES FOR SERVICE RETIREMENT¹ (Effective November 1, 1968)

Table 1. Option 1: Wife Only Until Her Remarriage or Death²

Member's Age at Retirement	Years Member is Older than Wife																Years Wife is Older than Member									
	15	14	13	12	11	10	9	8	7	6	5	4	3	2	1	0	1	2	3	4	5	6	7	8	9	10
35	.18	.18	.17	.17	.17	.17	.17	.15	.16	.16	.15	.14	.14	.14	.13	.13	.12	.12	.11	.11	.11	.10	.10	.09	.09	.09
36	.19	.19	.18	.18	.18	.17	.17	.16	.16	.17	.15	.16	.15	.15	.14	.14	.13	.13	.12	.12	.12	.11	.11	.10	.09	.09
37	.20	.20	.20	.20	.19	.19	.18	.17	.17	.17	.17	.16	.16	.16	.15	.15	.14	.13	.13	.13	.12	.12	.12	.11	.10	.09
38	.21	.21	.21	.21	.20	.19	.19	.18	.18	.18	.17	.17	.16	.16	.15	.15	.14	.14	.13	.13	.13	.12	.12	.11	.11	.10
39	.22	.22	.21	.21	.20	.20	.20	.18	.19	.19	.18	.17	.17	.16	.15	.15	.15	.14	.14	.14	.13	.13	.13	.12	.12	.11
40	.23	.22	.22	.21	.21	.21	.20	.19	.20	.20	.19	.18	.18	.17	.16	.16	.15	.15	.14	.14	.14	.13	.13	.12	.12	.11
41	.24	.23	.23	.23	.22	.21	.21	.20	.21	.21	.20	.19	.19	.18	.17	.17	.16	.15	.15	.15	.14	.14	.13	.13	.12	.12
42	.25	.24	.24	.23	.24	.23	.22	.21	.22	.22	.21	.20	.20	.19	.18	.18	.17	.16	.16	.15	.15	.14	.14	.13	.13	.12
43	.26	.26	.26	.24	.25	.24	.24	.23	.25	.24	.23	.21	.21	.20	.19	.19	.18	.17	.17	.16	.16	.15	.14	.14	.14	.13
44	.28	.27	.27	.26	.26	.25	.25	.24	.26	.25	.24	.22	.22	.21	.20	.20	.19	.18	.17	.17	.16	.16	.15	.15	.14	.13
45	.29	.29	.28	.28	.27	.26	.26	.25	.27	.27	.26	.23	.23	.22	.21	.20	.19	.18	.18	.18	.17	.16	.15	.15	.14	.13
46	.31	.30	.30	.29	.28	.27	.27	.26	.28	.28	.27	.24	.24	.23	.22	.21	.20	.19	.19	.19	.18	.17	.16	.16	.15	.14
47	.32	.31	.31	.30	.30	.28	.28	.27	.29	.29	.28	.25	.25	.23	.22	.22	.21	.20	.20	.19	.18	.18	.17	.16	.16	.15
48	.34	.32	.33	.33	.31	.29	.30	.28	.30	.30	.29	.27	.26	.25	.24	.23	.22	.21	.21	.20	.19	.18	.18	.17	.17	.16
49	.35	.35	.34	.33	.33	.32	.31	.29	.32	.32	.31	.28	.27	.26	.25	.24	.23	.22	.23	.22	.22	.19	.19	.18	.18	.17
50	.37	.36	.36	.35	.34	.32	.32	.30	.32	.32	.31	.28	.28	.27	.26	.24	.24	.23	.24	.20	.20	.19	.18	.18	.17	.16
51	.39	.38	.39	.36	.36	.33	.33	.32	.35	.34	.33	.30	.29	.28	.27	.25	.24	.23	.25	.20	.20	.20	.19	.19	.18	.17
52	.40	.39	.38	.38	.36	.34	.34	.32	.37	.35	.34	.30	.30	.29	.28	.26	.25	.24	.26	.21	.21	.20	.19	.19	.18	.17
53	.42	.41	.40	.39	.39	.38	.36	.35	.40	.38	.37	.32	.31	.30	.29	.28	.26	.25	.27	.22	.22	.21	.20	.20	.19	.18
54	.44	.42	.41	.41	.39	.39	.38	.35	.41	.39	.38	.33	.32	.31	.30	.28	.27	.26	.28	.23	.23	.22	.21	.20	.20	.18
55	.46	.45	.44	.43	.42	.40	.39	.38	.40	.40	.41	.34	.34	.33	.32	.30	.27	.26	.26	.26	.25	.24	.23	.20	.19	.16
56	.49	.47	.47	.45	.45	.43	.42	.40	.43	.42	.43	.34	.35	.33	.32	.30	.28	.27	.27	.27	.24	.24	.24	.21	.20	.17
57	.50	.49	.47	.47	.46	.44	.43	.41	.45	.43	.44	.36	.36	.35	.33	.31	.29	.28	.28	.27	.25	.25	.24	.22	.21	.17
58	.53	.52	.50	.49	.48	.46	.45	.42	.47	.45	.46	.38	.38	.36	.35	.33	.30	.29	.29	.28	.26	.25	.25	.23	.22	.18
59	.55	.55	.53	.51	.50	.48	.47	.44	.49	.47	.48	.39	.39	.38	.36	.34	.33	.32	.31	.29	.27	.26	.25	.24	.22	.21
60	.58	.56	.55	.53	.52	.49	.49	.45	.50	.50	.52	.41	.39	.39	.38	.35	.33	.32	.32	.30	.27	.27	.25	.24	.22	.21

Table 2. Option 2: Children Only²

Member's Age at Retirement	Age of Youngest Child																						
	0	1	2	3	4	5	6	7	8	9	10	11	12	13	14	15	16	17	18	19	20	21	22
35	.03	.03	.03	.02	.02	.02	.02	.02	.01	.01	.01	.01	.01	.01	.01	.01	.01	.01	.01	.01	.01	.01	.01
36	.03	.03	.03	.02	.02	.02	.02	.02	.01	.01	.01	.01	.01	.01	.01	.01	.01	.01	.01	.01	.01	.01	.01
37	.04	.03	.03	.03	.03	.02	.02	.02	.01	.01	.01	.01	.01	.01	.01	.01	.01	.01	.01	.01	.01	.01	.01
38	.04	.04	.03	.03	.03	.03	.02	.02	.01	.01	.01	.01	.01	.01	.01	.01	.01	.01	.01	.01	.01	.01	.01
39	.04	.04	.04	.03	.03	.03	.02	.02	.02	.02	.02	.01	.01	.01	.01	.01	.01	.01	.01	.01	.01	.01	.01
40	.05	.04	.04	.03	.03	.03	.03	.03	.02	.02	.01	.01	.01	.01	.02	.02	.01	.01	.01	.01	.01	.01	.01
41	.05	.04	.04	.04	.04	.03	.03	.03	.02	.02	.02	.02	.02	.02	.02	.02	.02	.01	.01	.01	.01	.01	.01
42	.05	.05	.05	.04	.04	.04	.03	.03	.03	.03	.02	.02	.02	.02	.02	.02	.02	.02	.01	.01	.01	.01	.01
43	.06	.05	.05	.05	.05	.04	.04	.04	.04	.04	.03	.03	.03	.03	.03	.03	.02	.02	.02	.01	.01	.01	.01
44	.06	.06	.06	.05	.05	.05	.04	.04	.05	.05	.04	.03	.03	.03	.03	.03	.03	.02	.02	.01	.01	.01	.01
45	.08	.07	.07	.06	.06	.05	.05	.04	.04	.04	.03	.03	.03	.03	.02	.02	.01	.01	.01	.01	.01	.01	.01
46	.08	.08	.07	.07	.07	.06	.05	.05	.05	.04	.04	.03	.03	.03	.02	.02	.02	.01	.01	.01	.01	.01	.01
47	.09	.08	.08	.08	.07	.06	.06	.06	.05	.05	.04	.04	.03	.03	.03	.03	.02	.02	.01	.01	.01	.01	.01
48	.10	.09	.09	.08	.08	.08	.07	.06	.06	.06	.05	.04	.04	.04	.03	.03	.02	.02	.02	.01	.01	.01	.01
49	.11	.10	.10	.10	.08	.08	.07	.06	.06	.06	.05	.05	.04	.04	.04	.03	.03	.02	.02	.01	.01	.01	.01
50	.12	.11	.11	.10	.09	.08	.08	.07	.06	.06	.05	.05	.05	.04	.04	.03	.03	.02	.02	.01	.01	.01	.01
51	.13	.12	.12	.11	.10	.09	.08	.08	.08	.07	.06	.05	.05	.04	.04	.03	.03	.03	.02	.01	.01	.01	.01
52	.14	.13	.12	.12	.11	.11	.10	.09	.08	.08	.07	.06	.06	.05	.05	.04	.04	.03	.03	.02	.02	.01	.01
53	.16	.15	.14	.14	.13	.12	.11	.10	.09	.08	.08	.07	.07	.06	.05	.04	.04	.04	.03	.02	.02	.01	.01
54	.17	.16	.15	.15	.14	.13	.12	.11	.10	.09	.08	.07	.07	.06	.06	.05	.04	.04	.03	.02	.02	.01	.01
55	.19	.17	.16	.15	.14	.13	.12	.11	.10	.09	.08	.07	.06	.06	.05	.05	.04	.03	.03	.02	.02	.01	.01
56	.20	.19	.17	.17	.15	.14	.13	.12	.11	.10	.09	.08	.07	.06	.06	.05	.04	.04	.03	.03	.02	.01	.01
57	.22	.20	.19	.18	.16	.15	.14	.13	.12	.11	.10	.09	.08	.07	.06	.05	.05	.04	.03	.03	.02	.02	.01
58	.24	.22	.21	.20	.18	.17	.15	.14	.13	.12	.11	.10	.08	.08	.07	.06	.05	.04	.04	.03	.02	.02	.01
59	.26	.24	.22	.21	.20	.18	.16	.15	.14	.13	.11	.10	.09	.08	.07	.06	.05	.04	.04	.03	.03	.02	.01
60	.28	.26	.24	.22	.21	.19	.17	.16	.15	.13	.12	.11	.09	.08	.07	.06	.05	.05	.04	.03	.03	.02	.01

¹ These tables are correct to within one-half of one percent. They may be used by a member to estimate for himself the approximate monthly costs of the survivor protection he desires. They may also be used for counseling purposes. Exact costs will be computed by the finance center at the time the member's retired pay account is established.

² Cost factors are shown in dollars. They are not applicable to disability retirement with less than 19 years of service. In these cases personnel officials should be consulted.

TABLE C-13

MORTALITY TABLES

Age	Commissioners 1958 Standard Ordinary (1950-1954) Deaths Per 1,000	Expectation of Life (Years)	United States Total Population (1959-1961) Deaths Per 1,000	Expectation of Life (Years)	Age	Commissioners 1958 Standard Ordinary (1950-1954) Deaths Per 1,000	Expectation of Life (Years)	United States Total Population (1959-1961) Deaths Per 1,000	Expectation of Life (Years)
0	7.08	68.30	25.93	69.89	51	9.11	22.82	8.52	24.49
1	1.76	67.78	1.70	70.75	52	9.96	22.03	9.29	23.69
2	1.52	66.90	1.04	69.87	53	10.89	21.25	10.05	22.91
3	1.46	66.00	.80	68.94	54	11.90	20.47	10.82	22.14
4	1.40	65.10	.67	67.99	55	13.00	19.71	11.61	21.37
5	1.35	64.19	.59	67.04	56	14.21	18.97	12.49	20.62
6	1.30	63.27	.52	66.08	57	15.54	18.23	13.52	19.87
7	1.26	62.35	.47	65.11	58	17.00	17.51	14.73	19.14
8	1.23	61.43	.43	64.14	59	18.59	16.81	16.11	18.42
9	1.21	60.51	.39	63.17	60	20.34	16.12	17.61	17.71
10	1.21	59.58	.37	62.19	61	22.24	15.44	19.17	17.02
11	1.23	58.65	.37	61.22	62	24.31	14.78	20.82	16.34
12	1.26	57.72	.40	60.24	63	26.57	14.14	22.52	15.68
13	1.32	56.80	.48	59.26	64	29.04	13.51	24.31	15.03
14	1.39	55.87	.59	58.29	65	31.75	12.90	26.22	14.39
15	1.46	54.95	.71	57.33	66	34.74	12.31	28.28	13.76
16	1.54	54.03	.82	56.37	67	38.04	11.73	30.53	13.15
17	1.62	53.11	.93	55.41	68	41.68	11.17	33.01	12.55
18	1.69	52.19	1.02	54.46	69	45.61	10.64	35.73	11.96
19	1.74	51.28	1.08	53.52	70	49.79	10.12	38.66	11.38
20	1.79	50.37	1.15	52.58	71	54.15	9.63	41.82	10.82
21	1.83	49.46	1.22	51.64	72	58.65	9.15	45.30	10.27
22	1.86	48.55	1.27	50.70	73	63.26	8.69	49.15	9.74
23	1.89	47.64	1.28	49.76	74	68.12	8.24	53.42	9.21
24	1.91	46.73	1.27	48.83	75	73.37	7.81	57.99	8.71
25	1.93	45.82	1.26	47.89	76	79.18	7.39	62.96	8.21
26	1.96	44.90	1.25	46.95	77	85.70	6.98	68.67	7.73
27	1.99	43.99	1.26	46.00	78	93.06	6.59	75.35	7.26
28	2.03	43.08	1.30	45.06	79	101.19	6.21	83.02	6.81
29	2.08	42.16	1.36	44.12	80	109.98	5.85	92.08	6.39
30	2.13	41.25	1.43	43.18	81	119.35	5.51	102.19	5.98
31	2.19	40.34	1.51	42.24	82	129.17	5.19	112.44	5.61
32	2.25	39.43	1.60	41.30	83	139.38	4.89	121.95	5.25
33	2.32	38.51	1.70	40.37	84	150.01	4.60	130.67	4.91
34	2.40	37.60	1.81	39.44	85	161.14	4.32	143.80	4.58
35	2.51	36.69	1.94	38.51	86	172.82	4.06	158.16	4.26
36	2.64	35.78	2.09	37.58	87	185.13	3.80	173.55	3.97
37	2.80	34.88	2.28	36.66	88	198.25	3.55	190.32	3.70
38	3.01	33.97	2.49	35.74	89	212.46	3.31	208.35	3.45
39	3.25	33.07	2.73	34.83	90	228.14	3.06	227.09	3.22
40	3.53	32.18	3.00	33.92	91	245.77	2.82	245.98	3.02
41	3.84	31.29	3.30	33.02	92	265.93	2.58	264.77	2.85
42	4.17	30.41	3.62	32.13	93	289.30	2.33	282.84	2.69
43	4.53	29.54	3.97	31.25	94	316.66	2.07	299.52	2.55
44	4.92	28.67	4.35	30.37	95	351.24	1.80	314.16	2.43
45	5.35	27.81	4.76	29.50	96	400.56	1.51	329.15	2.32
46	5.83	26.95	5.21	28.64	97	488.42	1.18	344.50	2.21
47	6.36	26.11	5.73	27.79	98	668.15	.83	360.18	2.10
48	6.95	25.27	6.33	26.94	99	1,000.00	.50	376.16	2.01
49	7.60	24.45	7.00	26.11	100			392.42	1.91
50	8.32	23.63	7.74	25.29	101			408.91	1.83
					102			425.62	1.75
					103			442.50	1.67
					104			459.51	1.60
					105			476.62	1.53
					106			493.78	1.46
					107			510.95	1.40
					108			528.10	1.35
					109			545.19	1.29

TABLE C-14

APPENDIX D —
PERSONAL AFFAIRS RECORD

PERSONAL AFFAIRS RECORD
OF

_____ _____ _____ _____
(Name)   (Grade)   (Service No.)   (Component)

I. PERSONAL DATA

Religious Preference_____
Birthdate_____Place of Birth_____
Permanent Legal Address_____
Local (or emergency) Address_____
   Telephone No._____
Father's Name & Address_____
   Father's Date & Place of Birth_____
Mother's Name & Address_____
   Mother's Date & Place of Birth_____
Names, Addresses, & Ages of Brothers & Sisters:
_____
_____
_____
_____

Date & Place of Marriage_____
Location of Marriage Certificate_____
Name of Spouse_____Social Security No._____
Permanent Legal Address_____
Birthdate_____Place of Birth_____
Children's Names, Date, and Place of Birth_____
_____
_____
_____
_____

Birth Certificates Located as Follows:
   Myself_____Wife_____
   Children_____

Social Security Cards are Located at_____
Pay Status
   Base Pay   _____
   Quarters Allowance   _____
   Subsistence   _____
   Hazardous Duty Pay   _____
   Other Pay   _____
        Total   _____
Former Service Numbers_____
Entered Military Service on_____At_____
Military Service (List here or separately all military service to include
units, grades, and periods of service)_____
_____
_____
_____
_____
_____

II. WILL

Date & Location of Will_____
Where Made_____
Executor's Name & Address_____
Spouse or Joint Will?_____
Date & Location of Spouse's Will_____
Where Made_____
Executor's Name & Address_____

III. POWER OF ATTORNEY

Does a Power of Attorney exist?_____
Type (General, Limited). If limited, for what purpose?_____

Date of Execution_____Date of Expiration_____
Name & Address of Grantee_____

IV. TAXES

Federal Income Taxes paid through calendar year_____
State   "   "   "   "   "
Real Estate Taxes Paid until_____
Personal Property Taxes Paid until_____
Location of Tax Return Records_____

V. PROPERTY OWNERSHIP

(1) Real Estate
Description of real estate owned_____
_____
Names in which held_____
Date acquired_____
Purchase price_____Estimated Present Value_____
Mortgage amount_____Held by_____
Name & Address of Insurance Company_____
Policy No._____Expiration Date_____
in the Amount of $_____
against_____
                    (fire, damage, liability, etc,)
Lease on rented property expiration date_____
Pertinent documents located at_____

(2) Automobile Record
Make_____Model_____Year_____
Serial Number_____Motor No._____Color_____
License Plate No._____Year_____State_____
Title no._____Title state_____Date_____
Insurance Co._____Address_____
Insurance Policy no._____Expiration Date_____
Insured Against: YES   NO   LIMITS
   Bodily Injury   ____   ____   _____
   Property Damage   ____   ____   _____
   Public Liability   ____   ____   _____
   Collision   ____   ____   _____
   Comprehensive   ____   ____   _____
   Other (explain)   ____   ____   _____
Name & Address of Finance Co._____
Balance due_____Monthly payments_____
Automobile papers located at_____

(3) Other Personal Property
(Jewelry, Boats, Trailers, etc.)

List Property of Great Value	Value	Am't of Lien & Monthly Payment	Lien Held By	Insurance (Company, Limits, Policy no., exp. date)
_____	_____	_____	____	_____
_____	_____	_____	____	_____
_____	_____	_____	____	_____
_____	_____	_____	____	_____
_____	_____	_____	____	_____

VI. CREDIT CARDS

Company	Card No.	No. of Cards	Expiration Date

Credit Card Insurance?_____ Amount_____
Name of Insurance Co._____ Policy No._____

VII. BANK ACCOUNTS & SAVINGS DEPOSITS

Name and Address of Bank	Type Account	Account Number

VIII. U.S. BONDS

Denomination	Number	In Name Of

Bonds are located at_____

IX. STOCKS, MUTUAL FUNDS & OTHER SECURITIES

Company	Date Purchased	Purchase Price	Certificate Number

Carried in Account Number_____maintained with_____
                     (Name & Address of Broker)

X. INSURANCE

(1) I (do) (do not) have Government life insurance.
    This insurance is (U.S. Government Life Insurance)
                      (National Service Life Insurance)
                      (Servicemen's Group Life Insurance)
    The policy number is_____Type of Insurance_____
    Amount of Government Insurance_____
    The policy is located at_____

(2) I have in effect the following commercial life insurance:

Company	Address	Policy Number	Amount

These policies are located at_____
The following loans are outstanding against these policies:
_____
_____

(4) I have accomplished an insurance program which outlines the manner
    in which the proceeds of each are to be paid. It is located at_____
_____

(4) Primary beneficiary_____
Contingent beneficiaries_____

(5) Life insurance in effect upon the lives of my wife and children:

Name& Relationship	Company	Policy No.	Amount	Premium Due
_____	_____	_____	_____	_____
_____	_____	_____	_____	_____
_____	_____	_____	_____	_____
_____	_____	_____	_____	_____

(6) The property and casualty insurance policies presently in effect are:

	Company	Address	Policy No.
Personal Property	_____	_____	_____
Personal Liability	_____	_____	_____
Hospitalization and Health	_____	_____	_____

XI. MONEYS OWED TO ME

Amount	Debtor

XII. LIABILITIES - (Loans, Notes not previously listed)

Amount	Lender	Date Made	Date Due

XIII. SAFE-DEPOSIT BOX

Location of box_____
Safe-Deposit box key located at _____

XIV. BURIAL

I desire to be interred at_____
I desire (that the Government grave marker be utilized) (that a monument
be erected at the place of my interment at a cost not to exceed $_____).

XV. OTHER PERTINENT INFORMATION & INSTRUCTIONS:

_____
_____
_____

XVI. THIS RECORD WAS LAST CHECKED ON_____

NOTES

BIRTH AND MARRIAGE CERTIFICATES should be obtained in advance. At least
fifteen (15) copies of each should be on hand, as they are generally required for pensions, Social Security, and sometimes by commercial insurance
companies.

BURIAL may be at a Post or National Cemetery. A Government grave marker is
furnished gratuitously.

SOME RIGHTS OF WIDOWS:

(a) Entitled to purchase at Commissary and Post Exchanges.
(b) Entitled to medical care and hospitalization when facilities are
available.
(c) May be entitled to State bonus.
(d) Eligible, if unremarried, for G.I. home or business loans to same
extent as veteran.
(e) Entitled to preference in Federal Civil Service examination.
(f) Entitled to transportation for self, children, and household goods
to new home.
(g) Entitled to G.I. educational benefits.

INDEX